NIST Special Publica

Revision 2

Guide to Industrial Control Systems (ICS) Security

Supervisory Control and Data Acquisition (SCADA) systems, Distributed Control Systems (DCS), and other control system configurations such as Programmable Logic Controllers (PLC)

Keith Stouffer
Intelligent Systems Division
Engineering Laboratory

Victoria Pillitteri
Suzanne Lightman
Computer Security Division
Information Technology Laboratory

Marshall Abrams
The MITRE Corporation

Adam Hahn
Washington State University

May 2015

U.S. Department of Commerce
Penny Pritzker, Secretary

National Institute of Standards and Technology
Willie May, Under Secretary of Commerce for Standards and Technology and Director

Authority

This publication has been developed by NIST to further its statutory responsibilities under the Federal Information Security Modernization Act (FISMA) of 2014, 44 U.S.C. § 3541 *et seq.*, Public Law (P.L.) 113-283. NIST is responsible for developing information security standards and guidelines, including minimum requirements for federal information systems, but such standards and guidelines shall not apply to national security systems without the express approval of appropriate federal officials exercising policy authority over such systems. This guideline is consistent with the requirements of the Office of Management and Budget (OMB) Circular A-130, Section 8b(3), *Securing Agency Information Systems*, as analyzed in Circular A-130, Appendix IV: *Analysis of Key Sections.* Supplemental information is provided in Circular A-130, Appendix III, *Security of Federal Automated Information Resources.*

Nothing in this publication should be taken to contradict the standards and guidelines made mandatory and binding on federal agencies by the Secretary of Commerce under statutory authority. Nor should these guidelines be interpreted as altering or superseding the existing authorities of the Secretary of Commerce, Director of the OMB, or any other federal official. This publication may be used by nongovernmental organizations on a voluntary basis and is not subject to copyright in the United States. Attribution would, however, be appreciated by NIST.

National Institute of Standards and Technology Special Publication 800-82, Revision 2 Natl. Inst. Stand. Technol. Spec. Publ. 800-82, Rev. 2, 247 pages (May 2015)

CODEN: NSPUE2

Certain commercial entities, equipment, or materials may be identified in this document in order to describe an experimental procedure or concept adequately. Such identification is not intended to imply recommendation or endorsement by NIST, nor is it intended to imply that the entities, materials, or equipment are necessarily the best available for the purpose.

There may be references in this publication to other publications currently under development by NIST in accordance with its assigned statutory responsibilities. The information in this publication, including concepts and methodologies, may be used by federal agencies even before the completion of such companion publications. Thus, until each publication is completed, current requirements, guidelines, and procedures, where they exist, remain operative. For planning and transition purposes, federal agencies may wish to closely follow the development of these new publications by NIST.

Organizations are encouraged to review all draft publications during public comment periods and provide feedback to NIST. All NIST Computer Security Division publications, other than the ones noted above, are available at http://csrc.nist.gov/publications.

Comments on this publication may be submitted to:

National Institute of Standards and Technology
Attn: Computer Security Division, Information Technology Laboratory
100 Bureau Drive (Mail Stop 8930) Gaithersburg, MD 20899-8930
Electronic Mail: nist800-82rev2comments@nist.gov

Reports on Computer Systems Technology

The Information Technology Laboratory (ITL) at the National Institute of Standards and Technology (NIST) promotes the U.S. economy and public welfare by providing technical leadership for the Nation's measurement and standards infrastructure. ITL develops tests, test methods, reference data, proof of concept implementations, and technical analyses to advance the development and productive use of information technology. ITL's responsibilities include the development of management, administrative, technical, and physical standards and guidelines for the cost-effective security and privacy of other than national security-related information in federal information systems. The Special Publication 800-series reports on ITL's research, guidelines, and outreach efforts in information system security, and its collaborative activities with industry, government, and academic organizations.

Abstract

This document provides guidance on how to secure Industrial Control Systems (ICS), including Supervisory Control and Data Acquisition (SCADA) systems, Distributed Control Systems (DCS), and other control system configurations such as Programmable Logic Controllers (PLC), while addressing their unique performance, reliability, and safety requirements. The document provides an overview of ICS and typical system topologies, identifies typical threats and vulnerabilities to these systems, and provides recommended security countermeasures to mitigate the associated risks.

Keywords

Computer security; distributed control systems (DCS); industrial control systems (ICS); information security; network security; programmable logic controllers (PLC); risk management; security controls; supervisory control and data acquisition (SCADA) systems

Acknowledgments for Revision 2

The authors gratefully acknowledge and appreciate the significant contributions from individuals and organizations in the public and private sectors, whose thoughtful and constructive comments improved the overall quality, thoroughness, and usefulness of this publication. A special acknowledgement to Lisa Kaiser, Department of Homeland Security, the Department of Homeland Security Industrial Control System Joint Working Group (ICSJWG), and Office of the Deputy Undersecretary of Defense for Installations and Environment, Business Enterprise Integration Directorate staff, Daryl Haegley and Michael Chipley, for their exceptional contributions to this publication.

Acknowledgments for Previous Versions

The original authors, Keith Stouffer, Joe Falco, and Karen Scarfone of NIST, wish to thank their colleagues who reviewed drafts of the original version of the document and contributed to its technical content. The authors would particularly like to acknowledge Tim Grance, Ron Ross, Stu Katzke, and Freemon Johnson of NIST for their keen and insightful assistance throughout the development of the document. The authors also gratefully acknowledge and appreciate the many contributions from the public and private sectors whose thoughtful and constructive comments improved the quality and usefulness of the publication. The authors would particularly like to thank the members of ISA99. The authors would also like to thank the UK National Centre for the Protection of National Infrastructure (CPNI)) for allowing portions of the *Good Practice Guide on Firewall Deployment for SCADA and Process Control Network* to be used in the document as well as ISA for allowing portions of the ISA-62443 Standards to be used in the document.

Note to Readers

This document is the second revision to NIST SP 800-82, Guide to Industrial Control Systems (ICS) Security. Updates in this revision include:

Updates to ICS threats and vulnerabilities.

Updates to ICS risk management, recommended practices, and architectures.

Updates to current activities in ICS security.

Updates to security capabilities and tools for ICS.

Additional alignment with other ICS security standards and guidelines.

New tailoring guidance for NIST SP 800-53, Revision 4 security controls including the introduction of overlays.

An ICS overlay for NIST SP 800-53, Revision 4 security controls that provides tailored security control baselines for Low, Moderate, and High impact ICS.

Table of Contents

List of Appendices

List of Figures

List of Tables

Executive Summary

This document provides guidance for establishing secure industrial control systems (ICS). These ICS, which include supervisory control and data acquisition (SCADA) systems, distributed control systems (DCS), and other control system configurations such as Programmable Logic Controllers (PLC) are often found in the industrial control sectors. ICS are typically used in industries such as electric, water and wastewater, oil and natural gas, transportation, chemical, pharmaceutical, pulp and paper, food and beverage, and discrete manufacturing (e.g., automotive, aerospace, and durable goods.) SCADA systems are generally used to control dispersed assets using centralized data acquisition and supervisory control. DCS are generally used to control production systems within a local area such as a factory using supervisory and regulatory control. PLCs are generally used for discrete control for specific applications and generally provide regulatory control. These control systems are vital to the operation of the U.S. critical infrastructures that are often highly interconnected and mutually dependent systems. It is important to note that approximately 90 percent of the nation's critical infrastructures are privately owned and operated. Federal agencies also operate many of the ICS mentioned above; other examples include air traffic control and materials handling (e.g., Postal Service mail handling.) This document provides an overview of these ICS and typical system topologies, identifies typical threats and vulnerabilities to these systems, and provides recommended security countermeasures to mitigate the associated risks.

Initially, ICS had little resemblance to traditional information technology (IT) systems in that ICS were isolated systems running proprietary control protocols using specialized hardware and software. Many ICS components were in physically secured areas and the components were not connected to IT networks or systems. Widely available, low-cost Internet Protocol (IP) devices are now replacing proprietary solutions, which increases the possibility of cybersecurity vulnerabilities and incidents. As ICS are adopting IT solutions to promote corporate business systems connectivity and remote access capabilities, and are being designed and implemented using industry standard computers, operating systems (OS) and network protocols, they are starting to resemble IT systems. This integration supports new IT capabilities, but it provides significantly less isolation for ICS from the outside world than predecessor systems, creating a greater need to secure these systems. The increasing use of wireless networking places ICS implementations at greater risk from adversaries who are in relatively close physical proximity but do not have direct physical access to the equipment. While security solutions have been designed to deal with these security issues in typical IT systems, special precautions must be taken when introducing these same solutions to ICS environments. In some cases, new security solutions are needed that are tailored to the ICS environment.

Although some characteristics are similar, ICS also have characteristics that differ from traditional information processing systems. Many of these differences stem from the fact that logic executing in ICS has a direct effect on the physical world. Some of these characteristics include significant risk to the health and safety of human lives and serious damage to the environment, as well as serious financial issues such as production losses, negative impact to a nation's economy, and compromise of proprietary information. ICS have unique performance and reliability requirements and often use operating systems and applications that may be considered unconventional to typical IT personnel. Furthermore, the goals of safety and efficiency sometimes conflict with security in the design and operation of control systems.

ICS cybersecurity programs should always be part of broader ICS safety and reliability programs at both industrial sites and enterprise cybersecurity programs, because cybersecurity is essential to the safe and reliable operation of modern industrial processes. Threats to control systems can come from numerous sources, including hostile governments, terrorist groups, disgruntled employees, malicious intruders, complexities, accidents, and natural disasters as well as malicious or accidental actions by insiders. ICS security objectives typically follow the priority of availability and integrity, followed by confidentiality.

Possible incidents an ICS may face include the following:

- Blocked or delayed flow of information through ICS networks, which could disrupt ICS operation.

- Unauthorized changes to instructions, commands, or alarm thresholds, which could damage, disable, or shut down equipment, create environmental impacts, and/or endanger human life.

- Inaccurate information sent to system operators, either to disguise unauthorized changes, or to cause the operators to initiate inappropriate actions, which could have various negative effects.

- ICS software or configuration settings modified, or ICS software infected with malware, which could have various negative effects.

- Interference with the operation of equipment protection systems, which could endanger costly and difficult-to-replace equipment.

- Interference with the operation of safety systems, which could endanger human life.

Major security objectives for an ICS implementation should include the following:

- **Restricting logical access to the ICS network and network activity.** This may include using unidirectional gateways, a demilitarized zone (DMZ) network architecture with firewalls to prevent network traffic from passing directly between the corporate and ICS networks, and having separate authentication mechanisms and credentials for users of the corporate and ICS networks. The ICS should also use a network topology that has multiple layers, with the most critical communications occurring in the most secure and reliable layer.

- **Restricting physical access to the ICS network and devices.** Unauthorized physical access to components could cause serious disruption of the ICS's functionality. A combination of physical access controls should be used, such as locks, card readers, and/or guards.

- **Protecting individual ICS components from exploitation.** This includes deploying security patches in as expeditious a manner as possible, after testing them under field conditions; disabling all unused ports and services and assuring that they remain disabled; restricting ICS user privileges to only those that are required for each person's role; tracking and monitoring audit trails; and using security controls such as antivirus software and file integrity checking software where technically feasible to prevent, deter, detect, and mitigate malware.

- **Restricting unauthorized modification of data.** This includes data that is in transit (at least across the network boundaries) and at rest.

- **Detecting security events and incidents.** Detecting security events, which have not yet escalated into incidents, can help defenders break the attack chain before attackers attain their objectives. This includes the capability to detect failed ICS components, unavailable services, and exhausted resources that are important to provide proper and safe functioning of the ICS.

- **Maintaining functionality during adverse conditions.** This involves designing the ICS so that each critical component has a redundant counterpart. Additionally, if a component fails, it should fail in a manner that does not generate unnecessary traffic on the ICS or other networks, or does not cause another problem elsewhere, such as a cascading event. The ICS should also allow for graceful degradation such as moving from "normal operation" with full automation to "emergency operation" with operators more involved and less automation to "manual operation" with no automation.

■ **Restoring the system after an incident.** Incidents are inevitable and an incident response plan is essential. A major characteristic of a good security program is how quickly the system can be recovered after an incident has occurred.

To properly address security in an ICS, it is essential for a cross-functional cybersecurity team to share their varied domain knowledge and experience to evaluate and mitigate risk to the ICS. The cybersecurity team should consist of a member of the organization's IT staff, control engineer, control system operator, network and system security expert, a member of the management staff, and a member of the physical security department at a minimum. For continuity and completeness, the cybersecurity team should consult with the control system vendor and/or system integrator as well. The cybersecurity team should coordinate closely with site management (e.g., facility superintendent) and the company's Chief Information Officer (CIO) or Chief Security Officer (CSO), who in turn, accepts complete responsibility and accountability for the cybersecurity of the ICS, and for any safety incidents, reliability incidents, or equipment damage caused directly or indirectly by cyber incidents. An effective cybersecurity program for an ICS should apply a strategy known as "defense-in-depth," layering security mechanisms such that the impact of a failure in any one mechanism is minimized. Organizations should not rely on "security by obscurity."

In a typical ICS this means a defense-in-depth strategy that includes:

■ Developing security policies, procedures, training and educational material that applies specifically to the ICS.

■ Considering ICS security policies and procedures based on the Homeland Security Advisory System Threat Level, deploying increasingly heightened security postures as the Threat Level increases.

■ Addressing security throughout the lifecycle of the ICS from architecture design to procurement to installation to maintenance to decommissioning.

■ Implementing a network topology for the ICS that has multiple layers, with the most critical communications occurring in the most secure and reliable layer.

■ Providing logical separation between the corporate and ICS networks (e.g., stateful inspection firewall(s) between the networks, unidirectional gateways).

■ Employing a DMZ network architecture (i.e., prevent direct traffic between the corporate and ICS networks).

■ Ensuring that critical components are redundant and are on redundant networks.

■ Designing critical systems for graceful degradation (fault tolerant) to prevent catastrophic cascading events.

■ Disabling unused ports and services on ICS devices after testing to assure this will not impact ICS operation.

■ Restricting physical access to the ICS network and devices.

■ Restricting ICS user privileges to only those that are required to perform each person's job (i.e., establishing role-based access control and configuring each role based on the principle of least privilege).

■ Using separate authentication mechanisms and credentials for users of the ICS network and the corporate network (i.e., ICS network accounts do not use corporate network user accounts).

■ Using modern technology, such as smart cards for Personal Identity Verification (PIV).

■ Implementing security controls such as intrusion detection software, antivirus software and file integrity checking software, where technically feasible, to prevent, deter, detect, and mitigate the introduction, exposure, and propagation of malicious software to, within, and from the ICS.

■ Applying security techniques such as encryption and/or cryptographic hashes to ICS data storage and communications where determined appropriate.

■ Expeditiously deploying security patches after testing all patches under field conditions on a test system if possible, before installation on the ICS.

■ Tracking and monitoring audit trails on critical areas of the ICS.

■ Employing reliable and secure network protocols and services where feasible.

The National Institute of Standards and Technology (NIST), in cooperation with the public and private sector ICS community, has developed specific guidance on the application of the security controls in NIST Special Publication (SP) 800-53 Revision 4, *Security and Privacy Controls for Federal Information Systems and Organizations* [22], to ICS.

While many controls in Appendix F of NIST SP 800-53 are applicable to ICS as written, many controls require ICS-specific interpretation and/or augmentation by adding one or more of the following to the control:

- ICS Supplemental Guidance provides organizations with additional information on the application of the security controls and control enhancements in Appendix F of NIST SP 800-53 to ICS and the environments in which these specialized systems operate. The Supplemental Guidance also provides information as to why a particular security control or control enhancement may not be applicable in some ICS environments and may be a candidate for tailoring (i.e., the application of scoping guidance and/or compensating controls). ICS Supplemental Guidance does not replace the original Supplemental Guidance in Appendix F of NIST SP 800-53.
- ICS Enhancements (one or more) that provide enhancement augmentations to the original control that may be required for some ICS.
- ICS Enhancement Supplemental Guidance that provides guidance on how the control enhancement applies, or does not apply, in ICS environments.

The most successful method for securing an ICS is to gather industry recommended practices and engage in a proactive, collaborative effort between management, the controls engineer and operator, the IT organization, and a trusted automation advisor. This team should draw upon the wealth of information available from ongoing federal government, industry groups, vendor and standards organizational activities listed in Appendix D—.

1. Introduction

1.1 Purpose and Scope

The purpose of this document is to provide guidance for securing industrial control systems (ICS), including supervisory control and data acquisition (SCADA) systems, distributed control systems (DCS), and other systems performing control functions. The document provides a notional overview of ICS, reviews typical system topologies and architectures, identifies known threats and vulnerabilities to these systems, and provides recommended security countermeasures to mitigate the associated risks. Additionally, it presents an ICS-tailored security control overlay, based on NIST SP 800-53 Rev. 4 [22], to provide a customization of controls as they apply to the unique characteristics of the ICS domain. The body of the document provides context for the overlay, but the overlay is intended to stand alone.

ICS are found in many industries such as electric, water and wastewater, oil and natural gas, chemical, pharmaceutical, pulp and paper, food and beverage, and discrete manufacturing (e.g., automotive, aerospace, and durable goods). Because there are many different types of ICS with varying levels of potential risk and impact, the document provides a list of many different methods and techniques for securing ICS. The document should not be used purely as a checklist to secure a specific system. Readers are encouraged to perform a risk-based assessment on their systems and to tailor the recommended guidelines and solutions to meet their specific security, business and operational requirements. The range of applicability of the basic concepts for securing control systems presented in this document continues to expand.

1.2 Audience

This document covers details specific to ICS. Readers of this document should be acquainted with general computer security concepts, and communication protocols such as those used in networking. The document is technical in nature; however, it provides the necessary background to understand the topics that are discussed.

Relationship to Executive Order 13636 "Improving Critical Infrastructure Cybersecurity"

Recognizing that the national and economic security of the United States depends on the reliable functionality of critical infrastructure, the President under the Executive Order "Improving Critical Infrastructure Cybersecurity" [82] directed NIST to work with stakeholders to develop a voluntary framework for reducing cyber risks to critical infrastructure. The Cybersecurity Framework (CSF) [83] consists of standards, guidelines, and best practices to promote the protection of critical infrastructure. The prioritized, flexible, repeatable, performance-based, and cost-effective approach of the Framework will help owners and operators of critical infrastructure to manage cybersecurity-related risk while protecting business confidentiality, individual privacy and civil liberties. The initial CSF, published in February 2014, resulted in a national-level framework that is flexible enough to apply across multiple sectors and for different operational environments. The CSF was developed based on stakeholder input to help ensure that existing work within the various sectors can be utilized within the Framework. Industrial control system cybersecurity standards, guidelines, and practices can be leveraged to address the CSF functions in the context of an organization's risk management program.

The intended audience is varied and includes the following:

- Control engineers, integrators, and architects who design or implement secure ICS.

- System administrators, engineers, and other information technology (IT) professionals who administer, patch, or secure ICS.

- Security consultants who perform security assessments and penetration testing of ICS.

- Managers who are responsible for ICS.

- Senior management who are trying to understand implications and consequences as they justify and apply an ICS cybersecurity program to help mitigate impacts to business functionality.

- Researchers and analysts who are trying to understand the unique security needs of ICS.

- Vendors that are developing products that will be deployed as part of an ICS.

1.3   Document Structure

The remainder of this guide is divided into the following major sections:

- Section 2 provides an overview of ICS including a comparison between ICS and IT systems.

- Section 3 provides a discussion of ICS risk management and assessment.

- Section 4 provides an overview of the development and deployment of an ICS security program to mitigate the risk of the vulnerabilities identified in Appendix C.

- Section 5 provides recommendations for integrating security into network architectures typically found in ICS, with an emphasis on network segregation practices.

- Section 6 provides a summary of the management, operational, and technical controls identified in NIST Special Publication 800-53, *Security and Privacy Controls for Federal Information Systems and Organizations*, and provides initial guidance on how these security controls apply to ICS.

The guide also contains several appendices with supporting material, as follows:

- Appendix A— provides a list of acronyms and abbreviations used in this document.

- Appendix B— provides a glossary of terms used in this document.

- Appendix C— provides a list of ICS threats, vulnerabilities and incidents.

- Appendix D— provides a list of ICS security activities.

- Appendix E— provides a list of ICS security capabilities and tools

- Appendix F— provides a list of references used in the development of this document.

- Appendix G— provides an ICS overlay, listing security controls, enhancements, and supplemental guidance that apply specifically to ICS.

2. Overview of Industrial Control Systems

Industrial control system (ICS) is a general term that encompasses several types of control systems, including supervisory control and data acquisition (SCADA) systems, distributed control systems (DCS), and other control system configurations such as Programmable Logic Controllers (PLC) often found in the industrial sectors and critical infrastructures. An ICS consists of combinations of control components (e.g., electrical, mechanical, hydraulic, pneumatic) that act together to achieve an industrial objective (e.g., manufacturing, transportation of matter or energy). The part of the system primarily concerned with producing the output is referred to as the process. The control part of the system includes the specification of the desired output or performance. Control can be fully automated or may include a human in the loop. Systems can be configured to operate open-loop, closed-loop, and manual mode. In open-loop control systems the output is controlled by established settings. In closed-loop control systems, the output has an effect on the input in such a way as to maintain the desired objective. In manual mode the system is controlled completely by humans. The part of the system primarily concerned with maintaining conformance with specifications is referred to as the controller (or control). A typical ICS may contain numerous control loops, Human Machine Interfaces (HMIs), and remote diagnostics and maintenance tools built using an array of network protocols. ICS control industrial processes are typically used in electrical, water and wastewater, oil and natural gas, chemical, transportation, pharmaceutical, pulp and paper, food and beverage, and discrete manufacturing (e.g., automotive, aerospace, and durable goods) industries.

ICS are critical to the operation of the U.S. critical infrastructures that are often highly interconnected and mutually dependent systems. It is important to note that approximately 85 percent of the nation's critical infrastructures are privately owned and operated[1]. Federal agencies also operate many of the industrial processes mentioned above as well as air traffic control. This section provides an overview of SCADA, DCS, and PLC systems, including typical topologies and components. Several diagrams are presented to depict the network topology, connections, components, and protocols typically found on each system to facilitate the understanding of these systems. These examples only attempt to identify notional topology concepts. Actual implementations of ICS may be hybrids that blur the line between DCS and SCADA systems. Note that the diagrams in this section do not focus on securing ICS. Security architecture and security controls are discussed in Section 5 and Section 6 of this document respectively.

2.1 Evolution of Industrial Control Systems

Many of today's ICS evolved from the insertion of IT capabilities into existing physical systems, often replacing or supplementing physical control mechanisms. For example, embedded digital controls replaced analog mechanical controls in rotating machines and engines. Improvements in cost-and performance have encouraged this evolution, resulting in many of today's "smart" technologies such as the smart electric grid, smart transportation, smart buildings, and smart manufacturing. While this increases the connectivity and criticality of these systems, it also creates a greater need for their adaptability, resilience, safety, and security.

Engineering of ICS continues to evolve to provide new capabilities while maintaining the typical long lifecycles of these systems. The introduction of IT capabilities into physical systems presents emergent behavior that has security implications. Engineering models and analysis are evolving to address these emergent properties including safety, security, privacy, and environmental impact interdependencies.

---

[1] http://www.dhs.gov/critical-infrastructure-sector-partnerships (last updated April 2014)

2.2   ICS Industrial Sectors and Their Interdependencies

Control systems are used in many different industrial sectors and critical infrastructures, including manufacturing, distribution, and transportation.

2.2.1   Manufacturing Industries

Manufacturing presents a large and diverse industrial sector with many different processes, which can be categorized into *process-based* and *discrete-based* manufacturing.

The *process-based* manufacturing industries typically utilize two main processes [1]:

- **Continuous Manufacturing Processes.** These processes run continuously, often with transitions to make different grades of a product. Typical continuous manufacturing processes include fuel or steam flow in a power plant, petroleum in a refinery, and distillation in a chemical plant.

- **Batch Manufacturing Processes.** These processes have distinct processing steps, conducted on a quantity of material. There is a distinct start and end step to a batch process with the possibility of brief steady state operations during intermediate steps. Typical batch manufacturing processes include food manufacturing.

The *discrete-based* manufacturing industries typically conduct a series of steps on a single device to create the end product. Electronic and mechanical parts assembly and parts machining are typical examples of this type of industry.

Both process-based and discrete-based industries utilize the same types of control systems, sensors, and networks. Some facilities are a hybrid of discrete and process-based manufacturing.

2.2.2   Distribution Industries

ICS are used to control geographically dispersed assets, often scattered over thousands of square kilometers, including distribution systems such as water distribution and wastewater collection systems, agricultural irrigation systems, oil and natural gas pipelines, electrical power grids, and railway transportation systems.

2.2.3   Differences between Manufacturing and Distribution ICS

While control systems used in manufacturing and distribution industries are very similar in operation, they are different in some aspects. Manufacturing industries are usually located within a confined factory or plant-centric area, when compared to geographically dispersed distribution industries. Communications in manufacturing industries are usually performed using local area network (LAN) technologies that are typically more reliable and high speed as compared to the long-distance communication wide-area networks (WAN) and wireless/RF (radio frequency) technologies used by distribution industries. The ICS used in distribution industries are designed to handle long-distance communication challenges such as delays and data loss posed by the various communication media used. The security controls may differ among network types.

2.2.4   ICS and Critical Infrastructure Interdependencies

The U.S. critical infrastructure is often referred to as a "system of systems" because of the interdependencies that exist between its various industrial sectors as well as interconnections between business partners [8] [9]. Critical infrastructures are highly interconnected and mutually dependent in complex ways, both physically and through a host of information and communications technologies. An incident in one infrastructure can directly and indirectly affect other infrastructures through cascading and escalating failures.

Both the electrical power transmission and distribution grid industries use geographically distributed SCADA control technology to operate highly interconnected and dynamic systems consisting of thousands of public and private utilities and rural cooperatives for supplying electricity to end users. Some SCADA systems monitor and control electricity distribution by collecting data from and issuing commands to geographically remote field control stations from a centralized location. SCADA systems are also used to monitor and control water, oil and natural gas distribution, including pipelines, ships, trucks, and rail systems, as well as wastewater collection systems.

SCADA systems and DCS are often networked together. This is the case for electric power control centers and electric power generation facilities. Although the electric power generation facility operation is controlled by a DCS, the DCS must communicate with the SCADA system to coordinate production output with transmission and distribution demands.

Electric power is often thought to be one of the most prevalent sources of disruptions of interdependent critical infrastructures. As an example, a cascading failure can be initiated by a disruption of the microwave communications network used for an electric power transmission SCADA system. The lack of monitoring and control capabilities could cause a large generating unit to be taken offline, an event that would lead to loss of power at a transmission substation. This loss could cause a major imbalance, triggering a cascading failure across the power grid. This could result in large area blackouts that could potentially affect oil and natural gas production, refinery operations, water treatment systems, wastewater collection systems, and pipeline transport systems that rely on the grid for electric power.

2.3   ICS Operation and Components

The basic operation of an ICS is shown in Figure 2-1 [2]. Some critical processes may also include safety systems. Key components include the following:

A typical ICS contains numerous control loops, human interfaces, and remote diagnostics and maintenance tools built using an array of network protocols on layered network architectures. A control loop utilizes sensors, actuators, and controllers (e.g., PLCs) to manipulate some controlled process. A sensor is a device that produces a measurement of some physical property and then sends this information as controlled variables to the controller. The controller interprets the signals and generates corresponding manipulated variables, based on a control algorithm and target set points, which it transmits to the actuators. Actuators such as control valves, breakers, switches, and motors are used to directly manipulate the controlled process based on commands from the controller.

Operators and engineers use human interfaces to monitor and configure set points, control algorithms, and to adjust and establish parameters in the controller. The human interface also displays process status information and historical information. Diagnostics and maintenance utilities are used to prevent, identify, and recover from abnormal operation or failures.

Sometimes these control loops are nested and/or cascading –whereby the set point for one loop is based on the process variable determined by another loop. Supervisory-level loops and lower-level loops operate continuously over the duration of a process with cycle times ranging on the order of milliseconds to minutes.

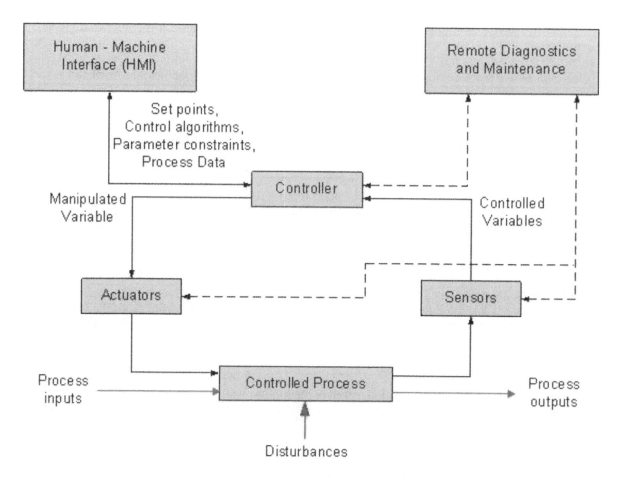

Figure 2-1. ICS Operation

To support subsequent discussions, this section defines key ICS components that are used in control and networking. Some of these components can be described generically for use in SCADA systems, DCS and PLCs, while others are unique to one. The Glossary of Terms in Appendix B— contains a more detailed listing of control and networking components. Additionally, Figure 2-5 and Figure 2-6 show SCADA implementation examples; Figure 2-7 shows a DCS implementation example and Figure 2-8 shows a PLC implementation example that incorporates these components.

2.3.1 ICS System Design Considerations

While Section 2.3 introduced the basic components of an ICS, the design of an ICS, including whether a SCADA, DCS, or PLC-based topologies are used depends on many factors. This section identifies key factors that drive design decisions regarding the control, communication, reliability, and redundancy properties of the ICS. Because these factors heavily influence the design of the ICS, they will also help determine the security needs of the system.

■ **Control Timing Requirements.** ICS processes have a wide range of time-related requirements, including very high speed, consistency, regularity, and synchronization. Humans may not be able to reliably and consistently meet these requirements; automated controllers may be necessary. Some systems may require the computation to be performed as close to the sensor and actuators as possible to reduce communication latency and perform necessary control actions on time.

- **Geographic Distribution.** Systems have varying degrees of distribution, ranging from a small system (e.g., local PLC-controlled process) to large, distributed systems (e.g., oil pipelines, electric power grid). Greater distribution typically implies a need for wide area (e.g., leased lines, circuit switching, and packet switching) and mobile communication.

- **Hierarchy.** Supervisory control is used to provide a central location that can aggregate data from multiple locations to support control decisions based on the current state of the system. Often a hierarchical/centralized control is used to provide human operators with a comprehensive view of the entire system.

- **Control Complexity.** Often control functions can be performed by simple controllers and preset algorithms. However, more complex systems (e.g., air traffic control) require human operators to ensure that all control actions are appropriate to meet the larger objectives of the system.

- **Availability.** The system's availability (i.e., reliability) requirements are also an important factor in design. Systems with strong availability/up-time requirements may require more redundancy or alternate implementations across all communication and control.

- **Impact of Failures.** The failure of a control function could incur substantially different impacts across domains. Systems with greater impacts often require the ability to continue operations through redundant controls, or the ability to operate in a degraded state. The design needs to address these requirements.

- **Safety.** The system's safety requirements area also an important factor in design. Systems must be able to detect unsafe conditions and trigger actions to reduce unsafe conditions to safe ones. In most safety-critical operations, human oversight and control of a potentially dangerous process is an essential part of the safety system.

2.3.2 SCADA Systems

SCADA systems are used to control dispersed assets where centralized data acquisition is as important as control [3] [4]. These systems are used in distribution systems such as water distribution and wastewater collection systems, oil and natural gas pipelines, electrical utility transmission and distribution systems, and rail and other public transportation systems. SCADA systems integrate data acquisition systems with data transmission systems and HMI software to provide a centralized monitoring and control system for numerous process inputs and outputs. SCADA systems are designed to collect field information, transfer it to a central computer facility, and display the information to the operator graphically or textually, thereby allowing the operator to monitor or control an entire system from a central location in near real time. Based on the sophistication and setup of the individual system, control of any individual system, operation, or task can be automatic, or it can be performed by operator commands.

Typical hardware includes a control server placed at a control center, communications equipment (e.g., radio, telephone line, cable, or satellite), and one or more geographically distributed field sites consisting of Remote Terminal Units (RTUs) and/or PLCs, which controls actuators and/or monitors sensors. The control server stores and processes the information from RTU inputs and outputs, while the RTU or PLC controls the local process. The communications hardware allows the transfer of information and data back and forth between the control server and the RTUs or PLCs. The software is programmed to tell the system what and when to monitor, what parameter ranges are acceptable, and what response to initiate when parameters change outside acceptable values. An Intelligent Electronic Device (IED), such as a protective relay, may communicate directly to the control server, or a local RTU may poll the IEDs to collect the data and pass it to the control server. IEDs provide a direct interface to control and monitor equipment and sensors. IEDs may be directly polled and controlled by the control server and in most cases have local programming that allows for the IED to act without direct instructions from the control center. SCADA systems are usually designed to be fault-tolerant systems with significant redundancy built into the system. Redundancy may not be a sufficient countermeasure in the face of malicious attack.

Figure 2-2 shows the components and general configuration of a SCADA system. The control center houses a control server and the communications routers. Other control center components include the HMI, engineering workstations, and the data historian, which are all connected by a LAN. The control center collects and logs information gathered by the field sites, displays information to the HMI, and may generate actions based upon detected events. The control center is also responsible for centralized alarming, trend analyses, and reporting. The field site performs local control of actuators and monitors sensors (Note that sensors and actuators are only shown in Figure 2-5). Field sites are often equipped with a remote access capability to allow operators to perform remote diagnostics and repairs usually over a separate dial up modem or WAN connection. Standard and proprietary communication protocols running over serial and network communications are used to transport information between the control center and field sites using telemetry techniques such as telephone line, cable, fiber, and radio frequency such as broadcast, microwave and satellite.

SCADA communication topologies vary among implementations. The various topologies used, including point-to-point, series, series-star, and multi-drop [5], are shown in Figure 2-3.

Point-to-point is functionally the simplest type; however, it is expensive because of the individual channels needed for each connection. In a series configuration, the number of channels used is reduced; however, channel sharing has an impact on the efficiency and complexity of SCADA operations. Similarly, the series-star and multi-drop configurations' use of one channel per device results in decreased efficiency and increased system complexity.

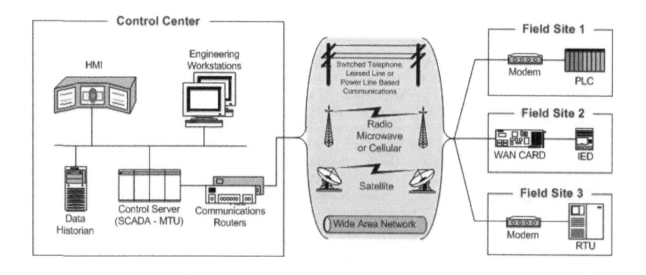

Figure 2-2. SCADA System General Layout

The four basic topologies Figure 2-3 can be further augmented using dedicated devices to manage communication exchanges as well as message switching and buffering. Large SCADA systems containing hundreds of RTUs often employee a sub-control server to alleviate the burden on the primary server. This type of topology is shown in Figure 2-4.

Figure 2-5 shows an example of a SCADA system implementation. This particular SCADA system consists of a primary control center and three field sites. A second backup control center provides redundancy in the event of a primary control center malfunction. Point-to-point connections are used for all control center to field site communications, with two connections using radio telemetry. The third field site is local to the control center and uses the WAN for communications. A regional control center resides above the primary control center for a higher level of supervisory control. The corporate network has access to all control centers through the WAN, and field sites can be accessed remotely for troubleshooting and maintenance operations. The primary control center polls field devices for data at defined intervals (e.g., 5 seconds, 60 seconds) and can send new set points to a field device as required. In addition to polling and issuing high-level commands, the control server also watches for priority interrupts coming from field site alarm systems.

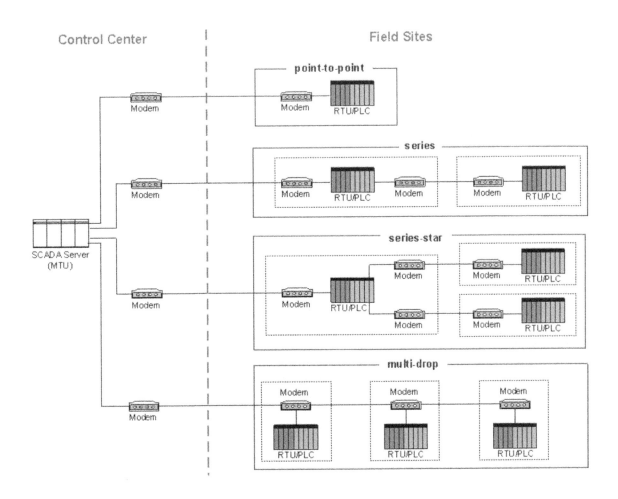

Figure 2-3. Basic SCADA Communication Topologies

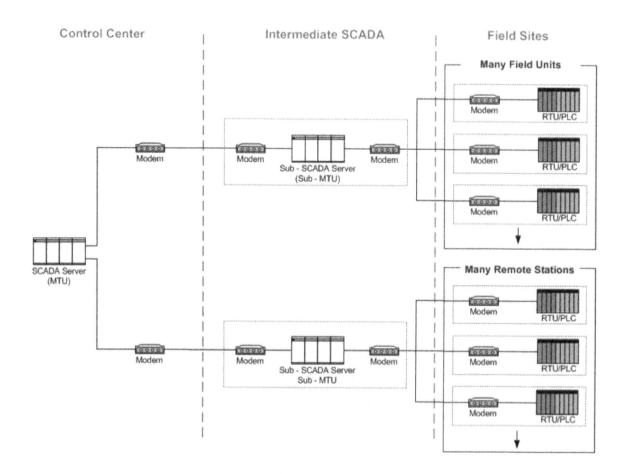

Figure 2-4. Large SCADA Communication Topology

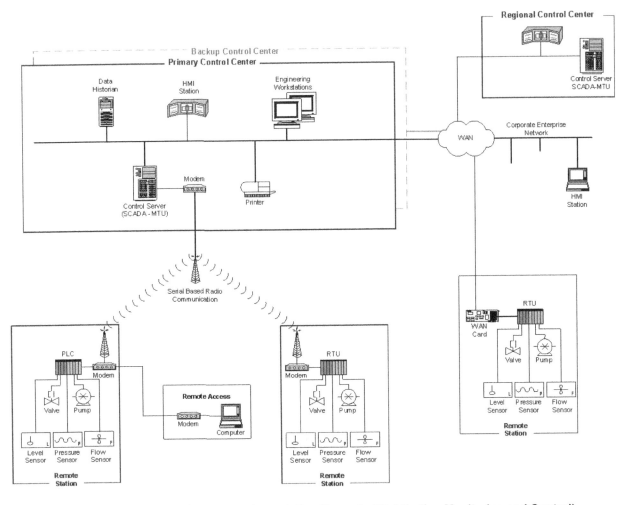

Figure 2-5. SCADA System Implementation Example (Distribution Monitoring and Control)

Figure 2-6 shows an example implementation for rail monitoring and control. This example includes a rail control center that houses the SCADA system and three sections of a rail system. The SCADA system polls the rail sections for information such as the status of the trains, signal systems, traction electrification systems, and ticket vending machines. This information is also fed to operator consoles at the HMI station within the rail control center. The SCADA system also monitors operator inputs at the rail control center and disperses high-level operator commands to the rail section components. In addition, the SCADA system monitors conditions at the individual rail sections and issues commands based on these conditions (e.g., stopping a train to prevent it from entering an area that has been determined to be flooded or occupied by another train based on condition monitoring).

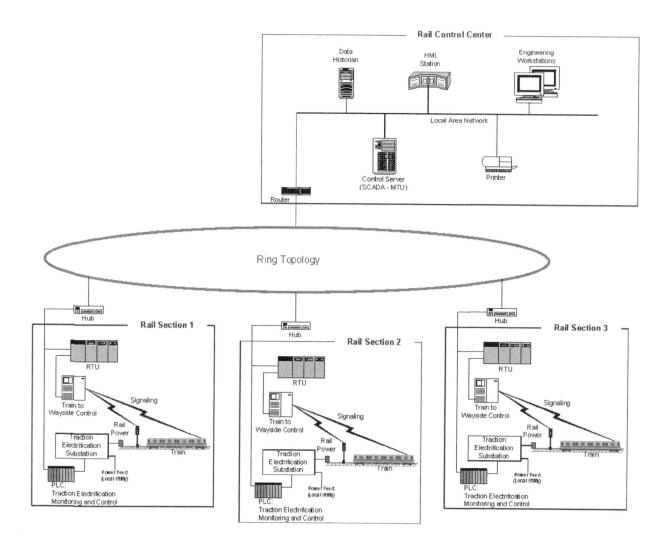

Figure 2-6. SCADA System Implementation Example (Rail Monitoring and Control)

2.3.3   Distributed Control Systems

DCS are used to control production systems within the same geographic location for industries such as oil refineries, water and wastewater treatment, electric power generation plants, chemical manufacturing plants, automotive production, and pharmaceutical processing facilities. These systems are usually process control or discrete part control systems.

DCS are integrated as a control architecture containing a supervisory level of control overseeing multiple, integrated sub-systems that are responsible for controlling the details of a localized process. A DCS uses a centralized supervisory control loop to mediate a group of localized controllers that share the overall tasks of carrying out an entire production process [6]. Product and process control are usually achieved by deploying feedback or feedforward control loops whereby key product and/or process conditions are automatically maintained around a desired set point. To accomplish the desired product and/or process tolerance around a specified set point, specific process controllers, or more capable PLCs, are employed in the field and are tuned to provide the desired tolerance as well as the rate of self-correction during process upsets. By modularizing the production system, a DCS reduces the impact of a single fault on the overall system. In many modern systems, the DCS is interfaced with the corporate network to give business operations a view of production.

An example implementation showing the components and general configuration of a DCS is depicted in Figure 2-7. This DCS encompasses an entire facility from the bottom-level production processes up to the corporate or enterprise layer. In this example, a supervisory controller (control server) communicates to its subordinates via a control network. The supervisor sends set points to and requests data from the distributed field controllers. The distributed controllers control their process actuators based on control server commands and sensor feedback from process sensors.

Figure 2-7 gives examples of low-level controllers found on a DCS system. The field control devices shown include a PLC, a process controller, a single loop controller, and a machine controller. The single loop controller interfaces sensors and actuators using point-to-point wiring, while the other three field devices incorporate fieldbus networks to interface with process sensors and actuators. Fieldbus networks eliminate the need for point-to-point wiring between a controller and individual field sensors and actuators. Additionally, a fieldbus allows greater functionality beyond control, including field device diagnostics, and can accomplish control algorithms within the fieldbus, thereby avoiding signal routing back to the PLC for every control operation. Standard industrial communication protocols designed by industry groups such as Modbus and Fieldbus [7] are often used on control networks and fieldbus networks.

In addition to the supervisory-level and field-level control loops, intermediate levels of control may also exist. For example, in the case of a DCS controlling a discrete part manufacturing facility, there could be an intermediate level supervisor for each cell within the plant. This supervisor would encompass a manufacturing cell containing a machine controller that processes a part and a robot controller that handles raw stock and final products. There could be several of these cells that manage field-level controllers under the main DCS supervisory control loop.

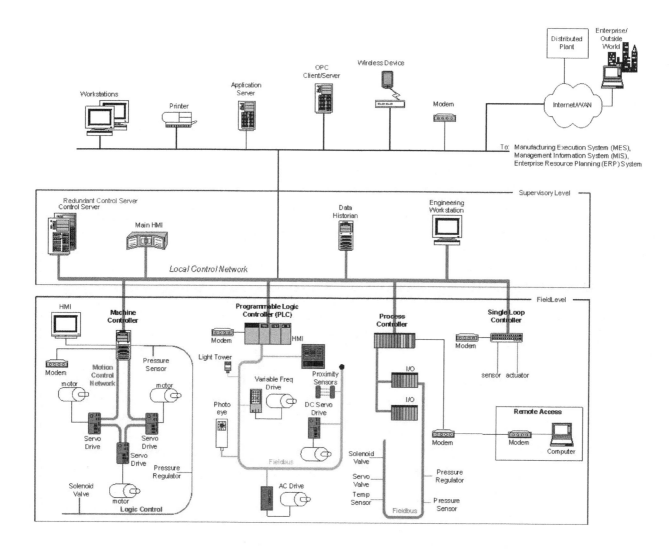

Figure 2-7. DCS Implementation Example

2.3.4 Programmable Logic Controller Based Topologies

PLCs are used in both SCADA and DCS systems as the control components of an overall hierarchical system to provide local management of processes through feedback control as described in the sections above. In the case of SCADA systems, they may provide the same functionality of RTUs. When used in DCS, PLCs are implemented as local controllers within a supervisory control scheme.

In addition to PLC usage in SCADA and DCS, PLCs are also implemented as the primary controller in smaller control system configurations to provide operational control of discrete processes such as automobile assembly lines and power plant soot blower controls These topologies differ from SCADA and DCS in that they generally lack a central control server and HMI and, therefore, primarily provide closed-loop control without direct human involvement. PLCs have a user-programmable memory for storing instructions for the purpose of implementing specific functions such as I/O control, logic, timing, counting, three mode proportional-integral-derivative (PID) control, communication, arithmetic, and data and file processing.

Figure 2-8 shows control of a manufacturing process being performed by a PLC over a fieldbus network. The PLC is accessible via a programming interface located on an engineering workstation, and data is stored in a data historian, all connected on a LAN.

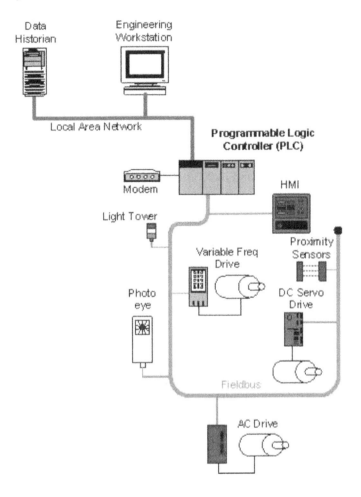

Figure 2-8. PLC Control System Implementation Example

2.4   Comparing ICS and IT Systems Security

ICS control the physical world and IT systems manage data. ICS have many characteristics that differ from traditional IT systems, including different risks and priorities. Some of these include significant risk to the health and safety of human lives, serious damage to the environment, and financial issues such as production losses, and negative impact to a nation's economy. ICS have different performance and reliability requirements, and also use operating systems and applications that may be considered unconventional in a typical IT network environment. Security protections must be implemented in a way that maintains system integrity during normal operations as well as during times of cyber attack [17].

Initially, ICS had little resemblance to IT systems in that ICS were isolated systems running proprietary control protocols using specialized hardware and software. Widely available, low-cost Ethernet and Internet Protocol (IP) devices are now replacing the older proprietary technologies, which increases the possibility of cybersecurity vulnerabilities and incidents. As ICS are adopting IT solutions to promote corporate connectivity and remote access capabilities, and are being designed and implemented using industry standard computers, operating systems (OS) and network protocols, they are starting to resemble IT systems. This integration supports new IT capabilities, but it provides significantly less isolation for ICS from the outside world than predecessor systems, creating a greater need to secure these systems. While security solutions have been designed to deal with these security issues in typical IT systems, special precautions must be taken when introducing these same solutions to ICS environments. In some cases, new security solutions are needed that are tailored to the ICS environment.

The environments in which ICS and IT systems operate are constantly changing. The environments of operation include, but are not limited to: the threat space; vulnerabilities; missions/business functions; mission/business processes; enterprise and information security architectures; information technologies; personnel; facilities; supply chain relationships; organizational governance/culture; procurement/acquisition processes; organizational policies/procedures; organizational assumptions, constraints, risk tolerance, and priorities/trade-offs).

The following lists some special considerations when considering security for ICS:

- **Timeliness and Performance Requirements.** ICS are generally time-critical, with the criterion for acceptable levels of delay and jitter dictated by the individual installation. Some systems require reliable, deterministic responses. High throughput is typically not essential to ICS. In contrast, IT systems typically require high throughput, and they can typically withstand some level of delay and jitter. For some ICS, automated response time or system response to human interaction is very critical. Some ICS are built on real-time operating systems (RTOS), where real-time refers to timeliness requirements. The units of real-time are very application dependent and must be explicitly stated.

- **Availability Requirements.** Many ICS processes are continuous in nature. Unexpected outages of systems that control industrial processes are not acceptable. Outages often must be planned and scheduled days or weeks in advance. Exhaustive pre-deployment testing is essential to ensure high availability (i.e., reliability) for the ICS. Control systems often cannot be easily stopped and started without affecting production. In some cases, the products being produced or equipment being used is more important than the information being relayed. Therefore, the use of typical IT strategies such as rebooting a component, are usually not acceptable solutions due to the adverse impact on the requirements for high availability, reliability and maintainability of the ICS. Some ICS employ redundant components, often running in parallel, to provide continuity when primary components are unavailable.

■ **Risk Management Requirements.** In a typical IT system, data confidentiality and integrity are typically the primary concerns. For an ICS, human safety and fault tolerance to prevent loss of life or endangerment of public health or confidence, regulatory compliance, loss of equipment, loss of intellectual property, or lost or damaged products are the primary concerns. The personnel responsible for operating, securing, and maintaining ICS must understand the important link between safety and security. Any security measure that impairs safety is unacceptable.

■ **Physical Effects.** ICS field devices (e.g., PLC, operator station, DCS controller) are directly responsible for controlling physical processes. ICS can have very complex interactions with physical processes and consequences in the ICS domain that can manifest in physical events. Understanding these potential physical effects often requires communication between experts in control systems and in the particular physical domain.

■ **System Operation.** ICS operating systems (OS) and control networks are often quite different from IT counterparts, requiring different skill sets, experience, and levels of expertise. Control networks are typically managed by control engineers, not IT personnel. Assumptions that differences are not significant can have disastrous consequences on system operations.

■ **Resource Constraints.** ICS and their real time OSs are often resource-constrained systems that do not include typical contemporary IT security capabilities. Legacy systems are often lacking resources common on modern IT systems. Many systems may not have desired features including encryption capabilities, error logging, and password protection. Indiscriminate use of IT security practices in ICS may cause availability and timing disruptions. There may not be computing resources available on ICS components to retrofit these systems with current security capabilities. Adding resources or features may not be possible.

■ **Communications.** Communication protocols and media used by ICS environments for field device control and intra-processor communication are typically different from most IT environments, and may be proprietary.

■ **Change Management.** Change management is paramount to maintaining the integrity of both IT and control systems. Unpatched software represents one of the greatest vulnerabilities to a system. Software updates on IT systems, including security patches, are typically applied in a timely fashion based on appropriate security policy and procedures. In addition, these procedures are often automated using server-based tools. Software updates on ICS cannot always be implemented on a timely basis. These updates need to be thoroughly tested by both the vendor of the industrial control application and the end user of the application before being implemented. Additionally, the ICS owner must plan and schedule ICS outages days/weeks in advance. The ICS may also require revalidation as part of the update process. Another issue is that many ICS utilize older versions of operating systems that are no longer supported by the vendor. Consequently, available patches may not be applicable. Change management is also applicable to hardware and firmware. The change management process, when applied to ICS, requires careful assessment by ICS experts (e.g., control engineers) working in conjunction with security and IT personnel.

■ **Managed Support.** Typical IT systems allow for diversified support styles, perhaps supporting disparate but interconnected technology architectures. For ICS, service support is sometimes via a single vendor, which may not have a diversified and interoperable support solution from another vendor. In some instances, third-party security solutions are not allowed due to ICS vendor license and service agreements, and loss of service support can occur if third party applications are installed without vendor acknowledgement or approval.

- **Component Lifetime.** Typical IT components have a lifetime on the order of 3 to 5 years, with brevity due to the quick evolution of technology. For ICS where technology has been developed in many cases for very specific use and implementation, the lifetime of the deployed technology is often in the order of 10 to 15 years and sometimes longer.

- **Component Location.** Most IT components and some ICS are located in business and commercial facilities physically accessible by local transportation. Remote locations may be utilized for backup facilities. Distributed ICS components may be isolated, remote, and require extensive transportation effort to reach. Component location also needs to consider necessary physical and environmental security measures.

Table 2-1 summarizes some of the typical differences between IT systems and ICS.

Table 2-1. Summary of IT System and ICS Differences

Category	Information Technology System	Industrial Control System
Performance Requirements	Non-real-time Response must be consistent High throughput is demanded High delay and jitter may be acceptable Less critical emergency interaction Tightly restricted access control can be implemented to the degree necessary for security	Real-time Response is time-critical Modest throughput is acceptable High delay and/or jitter is not acceptable Response to human and other emergency interaction is critical Access to ICS should be strictly controlled, but should not hamper or interfere with human-machine interaction
Availability (Reliability) Requirements	Responses such as rebooting are acceptable Availability deficiencies can often be tolerated, depending on the system's operational requirements	Responses such as rebooting may not be acceptable because of process availability requirements Availability requirements may necessitate redundant systems Outages must be planned and scheduled days/weeks in advance High availability requires exhaustive pre-deployment testing
Risk Management Requirements	Manage data Data confidentiality and integrity is paramount Fault tolerance is less important – momentary downtime is not a major risk Major risk impact is delay of business operations	Control physical world Human safety is paramount, followed by protection of the process Fault tolerance is essential, even momentary downtime may not be acceptable Major risk impacts are regulatory non-compliance, environmental impacts, loss of life, equipment, or production
System Operation	Systems are designed for use with typical operating systems Upgrades are straightforward with the availability of automated deployment tools	Differing and possibly proprietary operating systems, often without security capabilities built in Software changes must be carefully made, usually by software vendors, because of the specialized control algorithms and perhaps modified hardware and software involved
Resource Constraints	Systems are specified with enough resources to support the addition of third-party applications such as security solutions	Systems are designed to support the intended industrial process and may not have enough memory and computing resources to support the addition of security capabilities

Category	Information Technology System	Industrial Control System
Communications	Standard communications protocols Primarily wired networks with some localized wireless capabilities Typical IT networking practices	Many proprietary and standard communication protocols Several types of communications media used including dedicated wire and wireless (radio and satellite) Networks are complex and sometimes require the expertise of control engineers
Change Management	Software changes are applied in a timely fashion in the presence of good security policy and procedures. The procedures are often automated.	Software changes must be thoroughly tested and deployed incrementally throughout a system to ensure that the integrity of the control system is maintained. ICS outages often must be planned and scheduled days/weeks in advance. ICS may use OSs that are no longer supported
Managed Support	Allow for diversified support styles	Service support is usually via a single vendor
Component Lifetime	Lifetime on the order of 3 to 5 years	Lifetime on the order of 10 to 15 years
Components Location	Components are usually local and easy to access	Components can be isolated, remote, and require extensive physical effort to gain access to them

In summary, the operational and risk differences between ICS and IT systems create the need for increased sophistication in applying cybersecurity and operational strategies. A cross-functional team of control engineers, control system operators and IT security professionals needs to work closely to understand the possible implications of the installation, operation, and maintenance of security solutions in conjunction with control system operation. IT professionals working with ICS need to understand the reliability impacts of information security technologies before deployment. Some of the OSs and applications running on ICS may not operate correctly with commercial-off-the-shelf (COTS) IT cybersecurity solutions because of specialized ICS environment architectures.

2.5   Other Types of Control Systems

Although this guide provides guidance for securing ICS, other types of control systems share similar characteristics and many of the recommendations from this guide are applicable and could be used as a reference to protect such systems against cybersecurity threats. For example, although many building, transportation, medical, security and logistics systems use different protocols, ports and services, and are configured and operate in different modes than ICS, they share similar characteristics to traditional ICS [18]. Examples of some of these systems and protocols include:

Other Types of Control Systems

- Advanced Metering Infrastructure.
- Building Automation Systems.
- Building Management Control Systems.
- Closed-Circuit Television (CCTV) Surveillance Systems.
- CO_2 Monitoring.
- Digital Signage Systems.
- Digital Video Management Systems.
- Electronic Security Systems.
- Emergency Management Systems.

- Energy Management Systems.
- Exterior Lighting Control Systems.
- Fire Alarm Systems.
- Fire Sprinkler Systems.
- Interior Lighting Control Systems.
- Intrusion Detection Systems.
- Physical Access Control Systems.
- Public Safety/Land Mobile Radios.
- Renewable Energy Geothermal Systems.
- Renewable Energy Photo Voltaic Systems.
- Shade Control Systems.
- Smoke and Purge Systems.
- Vertical Transport System (Elevators and Escalators).
- Laboratory Instrument Control Systems.
- Laboratory Information Management Systems (LIMS).

Protocols/Ports and Services

- Modbus: Master/Slave - Port 502.
- BACnet[2]: Master/Slave - Port 47808.
- LonWorks/LonTalk[3]: Peer to Peer - Port 1679.
- DNP3: Master/Slave – Port 19999 when using Transport Layer Security (TLS), Port 20000 when not using TLS.
- IEEE 802.x - Peer to Peer.
- ZigBee - Peer to Peer.
- Bluetooth – Master/Slave.

The security controls provided in Appendix G— of this guide are general and flexible enough be used to evaluate other types of control systems, but subject matter experts should review the controls and tailor them as appropriate to address the uniqueness of other types of control systems. There is no "one size fits all," and the risks may not be the same, even within a particular group. For example, a building has many different sub-systems such as building automation, fire alarm, physical access control, digital signage, CCTV, etc. Critical life safety systems such as the fire alarm and physical access control systems may drive the impact level to be a "High," while the other systems will usually be "Low." An organization might decide to evaluate each sub-system individually, or decide to use an aggregated approach. The control systems evaluation should be coupled to the Business Impact, Contingency Plan, and Incident Response Plan to ensure organizational critical functions and operations can be recovered and restored as defined by the organizations Recovery Time Objectives.

---

[2] http://www.bacnet.org/
[3] http://en.wikipedia.org/wiki/LonWorks

3. ICS Risk Management and Assessment

3.1 Risk Management

Organizations manage risk every day in meeting their business objectives. These risks may include financial risk, risk of equipment failure, and personnel safety risk, to name just a few. Organizations must develop processes to evaluate the risks associated with their business and to decide how to deal with those risks based on organizational priorities and both internal and external constraints. This management of risk is conducted as an interactive, ongoing process as part of normal operations. Organizations that use ICS have historically managed risk through good practices in safety and engineering. Safety assessments are well established in most sectors and are often incorporated into regulatory requirements. Information security risk management is an added dimension that can be complementary. The risk management process and framework outlined in this section can be applied to any risk assessment including both safety and information security.

A risk management process should be employed throughout an organization, using a three-tiered approach to address risk at the (i) organization level; (ii) mission/business process level; and (iii) information system level (IT and ICS). The risk management process is carried out seamlessly across the three tiers with the overall objective of continuous improvement in the organization's risk-related activities and effective inter-tier and intra-tier communication among all stakeholders having a shared interest in the mission/business success of the organization.

This section focuses primarily on ICS considerations at the information system level, however, it is important to note that the risk management activities, information, and artifacts at each tier impact and inform the other tiers. Section 6 extends the concepts presented here to the control family level and provides ICS-specific recommendations to augment security control families. Throughout the following discussion of risk management, ICS considerations will be highlighted and the impact that these considerations have on the risk management process will be discussed.

For more information on multi-tiered risk management and the risk management process, refer to NIST Special Publication 800-39, *Managing Information Security Risk: Organization, Mission and Information System View* [20]. NIST Special Publication 800-37 Revision 1, *Guide for Applying the Risk Management Framework to Federal Information Systems: A Security Life Cycle Approach* [21], provides guidelines for applying the Risk Management Framework to federal information systems to include conducting the activities of security categorization,[4] security control selection and implementation, security control assessment, information system authorization,[5] and security control monitoring. NIST Special Publication 800-30, *Guide for Conducting Risk Assessments*, provides a step-by-step process for organizations on: (i) how to prepare for risk assessments; (ii) how to conduct risk assessments; (iii) how to communicate risk assessment results to key organizational personnel; and (iv) how to maintain the risk assessments over time [79].

---

[4] FIPS 199 provides security categorization guidance for non-national security systems [15]. CNSS Instruction 1253 provides similar guidance for national security systems.

[5] Security authorization is the official management decision given by a senior organizational official to authorize operation of an information system and to explicitly accept the risk to organizational operations and assets, individuals, other organizations, and the Nation based on the implementation of an agreed-upon set of security controls.

3.2   Introduction to the Risk Management Process

As shown in Figure 3-1, the risk management process has four components: *framing, assessing, responding* and *monitoring*. These activities are interdependent and often occur simultaneously within an organization. For example, the results of the monitoring component will feed into the framing component. As the environment in which organizations operate is always changing, risk management must be a continuous process where all components have on-going activities. It is important to remember that these components apply to the management of any risk whether information security, physical security, safety or financial.

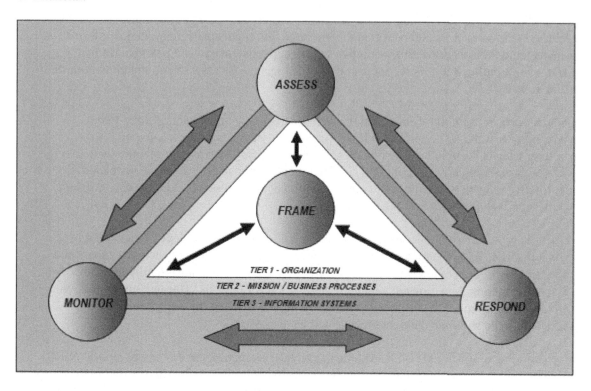

Figure 3-1. Risk Management Process Applied Across the Tiers

The *framing component* in the risk management process consists of developing a framework for the risk management decisions to be made. The level of risk that an organization is willing to accept is its *risk tolerance* [21, p.6].

The framing component should include review of existing documentation, such as prior risk assessments. There may be related activities; such as community wide disaster management planning that also should be considered since they impact the requirements that a risk assessment must consider.

ICS-specific Recommendations and Guidance

For operators of ICS, safety is the major consideration that directly affects decisions on how systems are engineered and operated. Safety can be defined as "freedom from conditions that can cause death, injury, occupational illness, damage to or loss of equipment or property, or damage to the environment."[6] Part of the framing component for an ICS organization is determining how these requirements interact with information security. For example, if safety requirements conflict with good security practice, how will the organization decide between the two priorities? Most ICS operators would answer that safety is the main consideration – the framing component makes such assumptions explicit so that there is agreement throughout the process and the organization.

Another major concern for ICS operators is the availability of services provided by the ICS. The ICS may be part of critical infrastructure (for example, water or power systems), where there is a significant need for continuous and reliable operations. As a result, ICS may have strict requirements for availability or for recovery. Such assumptions should be developed and stated in the framing component. Otherwise, the organization may make risk decisions that result in unintended consequences on those who depend on the services provided.

The physical operating environment is another aspect of risk framing that organizations should consider when working with ICS. ICS often have specific environmental requirements (e.g., a manufacturing process may require precise temperature), or they may be tied to their physical environment for operations. Such requirements and constraints should be explicitly stated in the framing component so that the risks arising from these constraints can be identified and considered.

Assessing risk requires that organizations identify their threats and vulnerabilities, the harm that such threats and vulnerabilities may cause the organization and the likelihood that adverse events arising from those threats and vulnerabilities may actually occur.

ICS-specific Recommendations and Guidance

The DHS National Cybersecurity & Communications Integration Center (NCCIC)[7] serves as a centralized location where operational elements involved in cybersecurity and communications reliance are coordinated and integrated. The Industrial Control Systems Cyber Emergency Response Team (ICS-CERT)[8] collaborates with international and private sector Computer Emergency Response Teams (CERTs) to share control systems-related security incidents and mitigation measures. ICS-CERT works to reduce risks within and across all critical infrastructure sectors by partnering with law enforcement agencies and the intelligence community and coordinating efforts among Federal, state, local, and tribal governments and control systems owners, operators, and vendors.

When assessing the potential impact to an organization's mission from a potential ICS incident, it is important to incorporate the effect on the physical process/system, impact on dependent systems/processes, and impact on the physical environment among other possibilities. In addition, the potential impact on safety should always be considered.

---

[6] MIL-STD-882E, *Standard Practice – System Safety*, Department of Defense (DoD), May 11, 2012,
   https://acc.dau.mil/CommunityBrowser.aspx?id=683694
[7] http://www.dhs.gov/about-national-cybersecurity-communications-integration-center
[8] https://ics-cert.us-cert.gov/

The *responding component* is based on the concept of a consistent organization-wide response to the *identification* of risk. Response to identification of risk (as opposed to the response to an incident) requires that organizations first identify possible courses of actions to address risk, evaluate those possibilities in light of the organization's risk tolerance and other considerations determined during the framing step, and choose the best alternative for the organization. The response component includes the implementation of the chosen course of action to address the identified risk: *acceptance, avoidance, mitigation, sharing, transfer,* or any combination of those options[9].

ICS-specific Recommendations and Guidance

For ICS, available risk responses may be constrained by system requirements, potential adverse impact on operations, or even regulatory compliance regimes. An example of risk sharing is when utilities enter into agreements to "loan" line workers in an emergency, which reduces the duration of the effect of an incident to acceptable levels.

Monitoring is the fourth component of the risk management activities. Organizations must monitor risk on an on-going basis including: the implementation of chosen risk management strategies; the changes in the environment that may affect the risk calculation; and, the effectiveness and efficiency of risk reduction activities. The activities in the monitoring component impact all the other components.

3.3   Special Considerations for Doing an ICS Risk Assessment

The nature of ICS means that when an organization does a risk assessment, there may be additional considerations that do not exist when doing a risk assessment of a traditional IT system. Because the impact of a cyber incident in an ICS may include both physical and digital effects, risk assessments need to incorporate those potential effects. This section will provide a more in-depth examination of the following:

- Impacts on safety and use of safety assessments.
- Physical impact of a cyber incident on an ICS, including the larger physical environment; effect on the process controlled, and the physical effect on the ICS itself.
- The consequences for risk assessments of non-digital control components within an ICS.

3.3.1   Safety within an ICS Information Security Risk Assessment

The culture of safety and safety assessments is well established within the majority of the ICS user community. Information security risk assessments should be seen as complementary to such assessments though the assessments may use different approaches and cover different areas. Safety assessments are concerned primarily with the physical world. Information security risk assessments primarily look at the digital world. However, in an ICS environment, the physical and the digital are intertwined and significant overlap may occur.

It is important that organizations consider all aspects of risk management for safety (e.g., risk framing, risk tolerances), as well as the safety assessment results, when carrying out risk assessments for information security. The personnel responsible for the information security risk assessment must be able

---

[9] For additional information on accepting, avoiding, mitigating, sharing, or transferring risk, refer to NIST Special Publication 800-39 [20].

to identify and communicate identified risks that could have safety implications. Conversely, the personnel charged with safety assessments must be familiar with the potential physical impacts and their likelihood developed by the information security risk assessment process.

3.3.2   Potential Physical Impacts of an ICS Incident

Evaluating the potential physical damage from a cyber incident should incorporate: i) how an incident could manipulate the operation of sensors and actuators to impact the physical environment; ii) what redundant controls exist in the ICS to prevent an impact; and iii) how a physical incident could emerge based on these conditions. A physical impact could negatively impact the surrounding world through multiple means, including the release of hazardous materials (e.g., pollution, crude oil), damaging kinetic forces (e.g., explosions), and exposure to energy sources (e.g., electricity, steam). The physical incident could negatively impact the ICS and supporting infrastructure, the various processes performed by the ICS, or the larger physical environment. An evaluation of the potential physical impacts should include all parts of an ICS, beginning with evaluating the potential impacts on the set of sensor and actuators. Each of these domains will be further explored below.

Evaluating the impact of a cyber incident on the physical environment should focus on potential damage to human safety, the natural environment, and other critical infrastructures. Human safety impacts should be evaluated based on whether injury, disease, or death is possible from a malfunction of the ICS. This should incorporate any previously performed safety impact assessments performed by the organization regarding both employees and the general public. Environmental impacts also may need to be addressed. This analysis should incorporate any available environmental impact assessments performed by the organization to determine how an incident could impact natural resources and wildlife over the short or long term. In addition, it should be noted that ICS may not be located within a single, controlled location and can be distributed over a wide physical area and exposed to uncontrolled environments. Finally, the impact on the physical environment should explore the extent to which an incident could damage infrastructures external to the ICS (e.g., electric generation/delivery, transportation infrastructures, and water services).

3.3.3   Impact of Physical Disruption of an ICS Process

In addition to the impact on the physical environment, the risk assessment should also evaluate potential effects to the physical process performed by the ICS under consideration, as well as other systems. An incident that impacts the ICS and disrupts the dependent process may cause cascading impacts into other related ICS processes and the general public's dependence on the resulting products and services. Impact to related ICS processes could include both systems and processes within the organization (e.g., a manufacturing process that depends on the process controlled by the system under consideration) or systems and processes external to the organization (e.g., a utility selling generated energy to a nearby plant).

A cyber incident can also negatively impact the physical ICS under consideration. This type of impact primarily includes the physical infrastructure of the plant (e.g., tanks, valves, motors), along with both the digital and non-digital control mechanisms (e.g., cables, PLCs, pressure gauge). Damage to the ICS or physical plant may cause either short or long term outages depending on the degree of the incident. An example of a cyber incident impacting the ICS is the Stuxnet malware, which caused physical damage to the centrifuges as well as disrupting dependent processes.

3.3.4   Incorporating Non-digital Aspects of ICS into Impact Evaluations

The impacts on the ICS cannot be adequately determined by focusing only on the digital aspects of the system, as there are often non-digital mechanisms available that provide fault tolerance and prevent the ICS from acting outside of acceptable parameters. Therefore, these mechanisms may help reduce any negative impact that a digital incident on the ICS might have and must be incorporated into the risk assessment process. For example, ICS often have non-digital control mechanisms that can prevent the ICS from operating outside of a safe boundary, and thereby limit the impact of an attack (e.g., a mechanical relief pressure valve). In addition, analog mechanisms (e.g., meters, alarms) can be used to observe the physical system state to provide operators with reliable data if digital readings are unavailable or corrupted. Table 3-1 provides a categorization of non-digital control mechanisms that could be available to reduce the impact of an ICS incident.

Table 3-1. Categories of Non-Digital ICS Control Components

System Type	Description
Analog Displays or Alarms	Non-digital mechanisms that measure and display the state of the physical system (e.g., temperature, pressure, voltage, current) and can provide the operator with accurate information in situations when digital displays are unavailable or corrupted. The information may be provided to the operator on some non-digital display (e.g., thermometers, pressure gauges) and through audible alarms.
Manual Control Mechanisms	Manual control mechanisms (e.g., manual valve controls, physical breaker switches) provide operators with the ability to manually control an actuator without relying on the digital control system. This ensures that an actuator can be controlled even if the control system is unavailable or compromised.
Analog Control Systems	Analog control systems use non-digital sensors and actuators to monitor and control a physical process. These may be able to prevent the physical process from entering an undesired state in situations when the digital control system is unavailable or corrupted. Analog controls include devices such as regulators, governors, and electromechanical relays.

Determination of the potential impact that a cyber incident may have on the ICS should incorporate analysis of all non-digital control mechanisms and the extent to which they can mitigate potential negative impacts to the ICS. There are multiple considerations when considering the possible mitigation effects of non-digital control mechanisms, such as:

- Non-digital control mechanisms may require additional time and human involvement to perform necessary monitoring or control functions and these efforts may be substantial. For example, such mechanisms may require operators to travel to a remote site to perform certain control functions. Such mechanisms may also depend on human response times, which may be slower than automated controls.

- Manual and analog systems may not provide monitoring or control capabilities with the same degree of accuracy and reliability as the digital control system. This may present risk if the primary control system is unavailable or corrupted due to reduced quality, safety, or efficiency of the system. For example, a digital/numeric protection relay provides more accuracy and reliable detection of faults than analog/static relays, therefore, the system maybe more likely to exhibit a spurious relay tripping if the digital relays are not available.

3.3.5   Incorporating the Impact of Safety Systems

Safety systems may also reduce the impact of a cyber incident to the ICS. Safety systems are often deployed to perform specific monitoring and control functions to ensure the safety of people, the environment, process, and ICS. While these systems are traditionally implemented to be fully redundant with respect to the primary ICS, they may not provide complete redundancy from cyber incidents, specifically from a sophisticated attacker. The impact of the implemented security controls on the safety system should be evaluated to determine that they do not negatively impact the system.

3.3.6   Considering the Propagation of Impact to Connected Systems

Evaluating the impact of an incident must also incorporate how the impact from the ICS could *propagate* to a connected ICS or physical system. An ICS may be interconnected with other systems, such that failures in one system or process can easily cascade to other systems either within or external to the organization. Impact propagation could occur due to both physical and logical dependencies. Proper communication of the results of risk assessments to the operators of connected or interdependent systems and processes is one way to mitigate such impacts.

Logical damage to an interconnected ICS could occur if the cyber incident propagated to the connected control systems. An example could be if a virus or worm propagated to a connected ICS and then impacted that system. Physical damage could also propagate to other interconnected ICS. If an incident impacts the physical environment of an ICS, it may also impact other related physical domains. For example, the impact could result in a physical hazard which degrades nearby physical environments. Additionally, the impact could also degrade the common shared dependencies (e.g., power supply), or result in a shortage of material needed for a later stage in an industrial process.

4.   ICS Security Program Development and Deployment

Section 2 addresses critical operational differences between ICS and IT systems, and Section 3 addresses risk management. This section combines these two concerns by addressing how organizations should develop and deploy an ICS security program. ICS security plans and programs should be consistent and integrated with existing IT security experience, programs, and practices, but must account for the specific requirements and characteristics of ICS technologies and environments. Organizations should review and update their ICS security plans and programs regularly to reflect changes in technologies, operations, standards, and regulations, as well as the security needs of specific facilities.

This section provides an overview of the development and deployment of an ICS security program. Section 4.1 describes how to establish a business case for an ICS security program, including suggested content for the business case. Sections 4.2 through 4.5 discuss the development of a comprehensive ICS security program and provide information on several major steps in deploying the program. Information on specific security controls that might be implemented as part of the security program is provided in Section 6.

Effectively integrating security into an ICS requires defining and executing a comprehensive program that addresses all aspects of security, ranging from identifying objectives to day-to-day operation and ongoing auditing for compliance and improvement. An ICS information security manager with appropriate scope, responsibility, and authority must be identified. This section describes the basic process for developing a security program, including the following:

■ Develop a business case for security.

■ Build and train a cross-functional team.

■ Define charter and scope.

■ Define specific ICS policies and procedures.

■ Implement an ICS Security Risk Management Framework.

    o   Define and inventory ICS assets.

    o   Develop security plan for ICS Systems.

    o   Perform a risk assessment.

    o   Define the mitigation controls.

■ Provide training and raise security awareness for ICS staff.

More detailed information on the various steps is provided in ISA-62443-2-1 *Security for Industrial Automation and Control Systems: Establishing an Industrial Automation and Control Systems Security Program* [34].

The commitment to a security program begins at the top. Senior management must demonstrate a clear commitment to information security. Information security is a business responsibility shared by all members of the enterprise and especially by leading members of the business, process, and management teams. Information security programs with adequate funding and visible, top-level support from organization leaders are more likely to achieve compliance, function more smoothly, and have greater success than programs that lack that support.

Whenever a new system is being designed and installed, it is imperative to take the time to address security throughout the lifecycle, from architecture to procurement to installation to maintenance to decommissioning. There are serious risks in deploying systems to production based on the assumption that they will be secured later. If there is insufficient time and resources to secure the system properly before deployment, it is unlikely that there will be sufficient time and resources later to address security.

Designing and implementing a new system is quite rare. It is much more common to improve, expand, or update an existing system. Everything in this section, indeed in this document, applies to managing the risk of existing ICS. Building an ICS Security Program and applying it to existing systems is much more complex and challenging.

4.1 Business Case for Security

The first step in implementing an information security program for ICS is to develop a compelling business case for the unique needs of the organization. The business case should capture the business concerns of senior management while being founded in the experience of those who are already dealing with many of the same risks. The business case provides the business impact and financial justification for creating an integrated information security program. It should include detailed information about the following:

■ Benefits, including improved control system reliability and availability, of creating an integrated security program.

■ Prioritized potential costs and damage scenarios if an information security program for the ICS is not implemented.

■ High-level overview of the process required to implement, operate, monitor, review, maintain, and improve the information security program.

■ Costs and resources required to develop, implement and maintain the security program.

Before presenting the business case to management, there should be a well-thought-out and developed security implementation and cost plan. For example, simply requesting a firewall is insufficient.

4.1.1 Benefits

Responsible risk management policy mandates that the threat to the ICS should be measured and monitored to protect the interests of employees, the public, shareholders, customers, vendors, society, and the nation. Risk analysis enables costs and benefits to be weighed so that informed decisions can be made on protective actions. In addition to reducing risks, exercising due-diligence and displaying responsibility also helps organizations by:

■ Improving control system safety, reliability and availability.
■ Improving employee morale, loyalty, and retention.
■ Reducing community concerns.
■ Increasing investor confidence.
■ Reducing legal liabilities.
■ Meeting regulatory requirements.
■ Enhancing the corporate image and reputation.
■ Helping with insurance coverage and cost.
■ Improving investor and banking relations.

A strong safety and information security management program is fundamental to a sustainable business model.

Improved control systems security and control system specific security policies can potentially enhance control system reliability and availability. This also includes minimizing unintentional control system information security impacts from inappropriate testing, policies, and misconfigured systems.

4.1.2 Potential Consequences

The importance of secure systems should be further emphasized as business reliance on interconnectivity increases. Denial of Service (DoS) attacks and malware (e.g., worms, viruses) have become all too common and have already impacted ICS. Cyber attacks can have significant physical and consequential impacts. Risk management is addressed in Section 3. The major categories of impacts are as follows:

- **Physical Impacts.** Physical impacts encompass the set of direct consequences of ICS failure. The potential effects of paramount importance include personal injury and loss of life. Other effects include the loss of property (including data) and potential damage to the environment.

- **Economic Impacts.** Economic impacts are a second-order effect from physical impacts ensuing from an ICS incident. Physical impacts could result in repercussions to system operations, which in turn inflict a greater economic loss on the facility, organization, or others dependent on the ICS. Unavailability of critical infrastructure (e.g., electrical power, transportation) can have economic impact far beyond the systems sustaining direct and physical damage These effects could negatively impact the local, regional, national, or possibly global economy.

- **Social Impacts.** Another second-order effect, the consequence from the loss of national or public confidence in an organization, is many times overlooked. It is, however, a very real consequence that could result from an ICS incident.

The program to control such risks is addressed in Section 3. Note that items in this list are not independent. In fact, one can lead to another. For example, release of hazardous material can lead to injury or death. Examples of potential consequences of an ICS incident are listed below:

- Impact on national security—facilitate an act of terrorism.
- Reduction or loss of production at one site or multiple sites simultaneously.
- Injury or death of employees.
- Injury or death of persons in the community.
- Damage to equipment.
- Release, diversion, or theft of hazardous materials.
- Environmental damage.
- Violation of regulatory requirements.
- Product contamination.
- Criminal or civil legal liabilities.
- Loss of proprietary or confidential information.
- Loss of brand image or customer confidence.

Undesirable incidents of any sort detract from the value of an organization, but safety and security incidents can have longer-term negative impacts than other types of incidents on all stakeholders—employees, shareholders, customers, and the communities in which an organization operates.

The list of potential business consequences needs to be prioritized to focus on the particular business consequences that senior management will find the most compelling. The highest priority items shown in the list of prioritized business consequences should be evaluated to obtain an estimate of the annual business impact, preferably but not necessarily in financial terms.

The Sarbanes-Oxley Act requires corporate leaders to sign off on compliance with information accuracy and protection of corporate information.[10] Also, the demonstration of due diligence is required by most internal and external audit firms to satisfy shareholders and other organization stakeholders. By implementing a comprehensive information security program, management is exercising due diligence.

4.1.3   Resources for Building Business Case

Significant resources for information to help form a business case can be found in external resources in other organizations in similar lines of business–either individually or in information sharing exchanges, trade and standards organizations, consulting firms–and internal resources in related risk management programs or engineering and operations. External organizations can often provide useful tips as to what factors most strongly influenced management to support their efforts and what resources within their organizations proved most helpful. For different industries, these factors may be different, but there may be similarities in the roles that other risk management specialists can play. Appendix D— provides a list and short description of some of the current activities in ICS security.

Internal resources in related risk management efforts (e.g., information security, health, safety and environmental risk, physical security, business continuity) can provide tremendous assistance based on their experience with related incidents in the organization. This information is helpful from the standpoint of prioritizing threats and estimating business impact. These resources can also provide insight into which managers are focused on dealing with which risks and, thus, which managers might be the most appropriate or receptive to serving as a champion. Internal resources in control systems engineering and operations can provide insight into the details of how control systems are deployed within the organization, such as the following:

- How networks are typically partitioned and segregated.
- What remote access connections are generally employed.
- How high-risk control systems or safety instrumented systems are typically designed.
- What security countermeasures are commonly used.

4.1.4   Presenting the Business Case to Leadership

Section 3 describes a three-tiered approach that addresses risk at the: (i) *organization* level; (ii) *mission/business process* level; and (iii) *information system* level. The risk management process is carried out seamlessly across the three tiers with the overall objective of continuous improvement in the organization's risk-related activities and effective inter-tier and intra-tier communication among all stakeholders having a shared interest in the mission/business success of the organization.

It is critical for the success of the ICS security program that organization level management buy into and participate in the ICS security program. Tier 1 organization level management that encompasses both IT and ICS operations has the perspective and authority to understand and take responsibility for the risks.

The Tier 1 business leadership will be responsible for approving and driving information security policies, assigning security roles and responsibilities, and implementing the information security program across the organization. Funding for the entire program can usually be done in phases. While some

---

[10] More information on the Sarbanes-Oxley Act, and a copy of the act itself, can be found at
    http://www.sec.gov/about/laws.shtml.

funding may be required to start the information security activity, additional funding can be obtained later as the security vulnerabilities and needs of the program are better understood and additional strategies are developed. Additionally, the costs (both direct and indirect) should be considered for retrofitting the ICS for security vs. addressing security to begin with.

Often, a good approach to obtain management buy-in to address the problem is to ground the business case in a successful actual third-party example. The business case should present to management that the other organization had the same problem and then present that they found a solution and how they solved it. This will often prompt management to ask what the solution is and how it might be applicable to their organization.

4.2   Build and Train a Cross-Functional Team

It is essential for a cross-functional information security team to share their varied domain knowledge and experience to evaluate and mitigate risk in the ICS. At a minimum, the information security team should consist of a member of the organization's IT staff, a control engineer, a control system operator, security subject matter experts, and a member of the enterprise risk management staff. Security knowledge and skills should include network architecture and design, security processes and practices, and secure infrastructure design and operation. Contemporary thinking that both safety and security are emergent properties of connected systems with digital control suggests including a safety expert. For continuity and completeness, the information security team should also include the control system vendor and/or system integrator.

The information security team should report directly to the information security manager at the mission/business process or organization tier, who in turn reports to the mission/business process manager (e.g., facility superintendent) or enterprise information security manager (e.g., the company's CIO/CSO), respectively. Ultimate authority and responsibility rests in the Tier 1 risk executive function that provides a comprehensive, organization-wide approach to risk management. The risk executive function works with the top management to accept a level of residual risk and accountability for the information security of the ICS. Management level accountability will help ensure an ongoing commitment to information security efforts.

While the control engineers will play a large role in securing the ICS, they will not be able to do so without collaboration and support from both the IT department and management. IT often has years of security experience, much of which is applicable to ICS. As the cultures of control engineering and IT are often significantly different, their integration will be essential for the development of a collaborative security design and operation.

4.3   Define Charter and Scope

The information security manager should establish policy that defines the guiding charter of the information security organization and the roles, responsibilities, and accountabilities of system owners, mission/business process managers, and users. The information security manager should decide upon and document the objective of the security program, the business organizations affected, all the computer systems and networks involved, the budget and resources required, and the division of responsibilities. The scope can also address business, training, audit, legal, and regulatory requirements, as well as timetables and responsibilities. The guiding charter of the information security organization is a constituent of the information security architecture which is part of the enterprise architecture, as discussed in Section 3.

There may already be an information security program in place or being developed for the organization's IT business systems. The ICS information security manager should identify which existing practices to leverage and which practices are specific to the control system. In the long run, it will be easier to get positive results if the team can share resources with others in the organization that have similar objectives.

4.4 Define ICS-specific Security Policies and Procedures

Policies and procedures are at the root of every successful security program. Wherever possible, ICS-specific security policies and procedures should be integrated with existing operational/management policies and procedures. Policies and procedures help to ensure that security protection is both consistent and current to protect against evolving threats. Appendix C cites a lack of security policy as an important vulnerability. Appendix G—, the ICS overlay, contains many ICS information security policy recommendations. After an information security risk analysis has been performed, the information security manager should examine existing security policies to see if they adequately address the risks to the ICS. If needed, existing policies should be revised or new policies created.

As discussed in Section 3, Tier 1 management is responsible for developing and communicating the risk tolerance of the organization–the level of risk the organization is willing to accept–which allows the information security manager to determine the level of risk mitigation that should be taken to reduce residual risk to acceptable levels. The development of the security policies should be based on a risk assessment that will set the security priorities and goals for the organization so that the risks posed by the threats are mitigated sufficiently. Procedures that support the policies need to be developed so that the policies are implemented fully and properly for the ICS. Security procedures should be documented, tested, and updated periodically in response to policy, technology, and threat changes.

4.5 Implement an ICS Security Risk Management Framework

From an abstract viewpoint, the management of ICS risks is another risk added to the list of risks confronting an organization (e.g., financial, safety, IT, environmental). In each case, managers with responsibility for the mission or business process establish and conduct a risk management program in coordination with top management's risk executive function. NIST Special Publication 800-39, *Managing Information Security Risk–Organization, Mission, and Information System View* [20], is the foundation of such a risk management program. Just like the other mission/business process areas, the personnel concerned with ICS apply their specialized subject matter knowledge to establishing and conducting ICS security risk management and to communicating with enterprise management to support effective risk management across all the enterprise. NIST Special Publication 800-37, *Guide for Applying the Risk Management Framework to Federal Information Systems* [21], introduces the risk management framework which addresses the process of implementing the framework. The following sections summarize this process and apply the RMF to an ICS environment.

The RMF process includes a set of well-defined risk-related tasks that are to be carried out by selected individuals or groups within well-defined organizational roles (e.g., risk executive [function], authorizing official, authorizing official designated representative, chief information officer, senior information security officer, enterprise architect, information security architect, information owner/steward, information system owner, common control provider, information system security officer, and security control assessor). Many risk management roles have counterpart roles defined in the routine system development life cycle processes. RMF tasks are executed concurrently with or as part of system development life cycle processes, taking into account appropriate dependencies.

Organizations may also wish to consult ISA-62443-2-1, *Security for Industrial Automation and Control Systems: Establishing an Industrial Automation and Control Systems Security Program*, which describes another view of the elements contained in a cybersecurity management system for use in the industrial automation and control systems environment [34]. It provides guidance on how to meet the requirements described for each element. Sections 4 through 6 correspond most closely to NIST SP 800-39; other sections correspond to other NIST Special Publications and to the ICS overlay in Appendix G— of this document. All of these guidance documents recognize that one size does not fit all; rather, domain knowledge should be applied in tailoring or adapting the guidance to the specific organization.

4.5.1   Categorize ICS Systems and Networks Assets

The information security team should define, inventory, and categorize the applications and computer systems within the ICS, as well as the networks within and interfacing to the ICS. The focus should be on systems rather than just devices, and should include PLCs, DCS, SCADA, and instrument-based systems that use a monitoring device such as an HMI. Assets that use a routable protocol or are dial-up accessible should be documented. The team should review and update the ICS asset list annually and after each asset addition or removal.

There are several commercial enterprise IT inventory tools that can identify and document all hardware and software resident on a network. Care must be taken before using these tools to identify ICS assets; teams should first conduct an assessment of how these tools work and what impact they might have on the connected control equipment. Tool evaluation may include testing in similar, non-production control system environments to ensure that the tools do not adversely impact the production systems. Impact could be due to the nature of the information or the volume of network traffic. While this impact may be acceptable in IT systems, it may not be acceptable in an ICS.

An automated management system for inventory (e.g., Computerized Maintenance Management System (CMMS), Computer Aided Facility Management System (CAFM), Building Information Model (BIM), Geospatial Information System (GIS), Construction-Operations Building information exchange data (COBie, Building Automation Management information exchange (BAMie), Sustainment Management Systems (SMS) Builder) allows an organization to keep an accurate account of what is on the system for security reasons and budgetary reasons as well.

4.5.2   Select ICS Security Controls

The security controls selected based on the security categorization of the ICS are documented in the security plan to provide an overview of the security requirements for the ICS information security program and describes the security controls in place or planned for meeting those requirements. The development of security plans is addressed in NIST Special Publication 800-18 Revision 1, *Guide for Developing Security Plans for Federal Information Systems* [19]. The security plan can be one document, or it can be the set of all documents addressing the security concerns for a system and the plans for countering these concerns. In addition to security controls, NIST Special Publication 800-53 Revision 4, *Security and Privacy Controls for Federal Information Systems and Organizations* [20], provides a set of information security program management (PM) controls that are typically implemented at the organization level and not directed at individual organizational information systems. This section addresses how an organization establishes and carries out these program management controls.

The successful implementation of security controls for organizational information systems depends on the successful implementation of organization-wide program management controls. The manner in which organizations implement the program management controls depends on specific organizational characteristics including, for example, the size, complexity, and mission/business requirements of the respective organizations. The program management controls complement the security controls and focus on the programmatic, organization-wide information security requirements that are independent of any particular information system and are essential for managing information security programs. Organizations document program management controls in the *information security program plan*. The organization-wide information security program plan supplements the individual security plans developed for each organizational information system. Together, the security plans for the individual information systems and the information security program cover the totality of security controls employed by the organization.

4.5.3 Perform Risk Assessment

Because every organization has a limited set of resources, organizations should assess the impacts to organizational operations (i.e., mission, functions, image, and reputation), organizational assets, individuals, other organizations, and the Nation (e.g., using FIPS 199 [15] or a more granular approach). As discussed in Section 3, organizations can experience the consequences/impact of adverse events at the individual ICS system level (e.g., failing to perform as required), at the mission/business process level (e.g., failing to fully meet mission/business objectives), and at the organizational level (e.g., failing to comply with legal or regulatory requirements, damaging reputation or relationships, or undermining long-term viability). An adverse event can have multiple consequences and different types of impact, at different levels, and in different time frames. NIST SP 800-53 [22] and the ICS overlay in Appendix G— incorporate baseline security controls that derive from this determination of impact.

The organization may perform a detailed risk assessment for the highest impact systems and assessments for lower impact systems as deemed prudent and as resources allow. The risk assessment will help identify any weaknesses that contribute to information security risks and mitigation approaches to reduce the risks. Risk assessments are conducted multiple times during a system's life cycle. The focus and level of detail varies according to the system's maturity.

4.5.4 Implement the Security Controls

Organizations should analyze the detailed risk assessment and the impacts to organizational operations (i.e., mission, functions, image, and reputation), organizational assets, individuals, other organizations, and the Nation, and prioritize selection of mitigation controls. Organizations should focus on mitigating risk with the greatest potential impact. Security control implementation is consistent with the organization's enterprise architecture and information security architecture.

The controls to mitigate a specific risk may vary among types of systems. For example, user authentication controls might be different for ICS than for corporate payroll systems and e-commerce systems. The ICS information security manager should document and communicate the selected controls, along with the procedures for using the controls. Some risks may be identified that can be mitigated by "quick fix" solutions—low-cost, high-value practices that can significantly reduce risk. Examples of these solutions are restricting Internet access and eliminating email access on operator control stations or consoles. Organizations should identify, evaluate, and implement suitable quick fix solutions as soon as possible to reduce security risks and achieve rapid benefits. The Department of Energy (DOE) has a "21 Steps to Improve Cyber Security of SCADA Networks" [33] document that could be used as a starting point to outline specific actions to increase the security of SCADA systems and other ICS.

5.   ICS Security Architecture

When designing a network architecture for an ICS deployment, it is usually recommended to separate the ICS network from the corporate network. The nature of network traffic on these two networks is different: Internet access, FTP, email, and remote access will typically be permitted on the corporate network but should not be allowed on the ICS network. Rigorous change control procedures for network equipment, configuration, and software changes may not be in place on the corporate network. If ICS network traffic is carried on the corporate network, it could be intercepted or be subjected to DoS or Man-in-the-Middle attacks [5.14]. By having separate networks, security and performance problems on the corporate network should not be able to affect the ICS network.

Practical considerations, such as cost of ICS installation or maintaining a homogenous network infrastructure, often mean that a connection is required between the ICS and corporate networks. This connection is a significant security risk and should be protected by boundary protection devices. If the networks must be connected, it is strongly recommended that only minimal (single if possible) connections be allowed and that the connection is through a firewall and a DMZ. A DMZ is a separate network segment that connects directly to the firewall. Servers containing the data from the ICS that needs to be accessed from the corporate network are put on this network segment. Only these systems should be accessible from the corporate network. With any external connections, the minimum access should be permitted through the firewall, including opening only the ports required for specific communication. The following sections elaborate on these architectural considerations. The ICS-CERT recommended practices working group provides additional guidance as recommended practices[11].

5.1   Network Segmentation and Segregation

This section addresses partitioning the ICS into security domains and separating the ICS from other networks, such as the corporate network, and presents illustrative security architecture. Operational risk analysis should be performed to determine critical parts of each ICS network and operation and help define what parts of the ICS need to be segmented. Network segmentation involves partitioning the network into smaller networks. For example, one large ICS network is partitioned into multiple ICS networks, where the partitioning is based on factors such as management authority, uniform policy and level of trust, functional criticality, and amount of communications traffic that crosses the domain boundary. Network segmentation and segregation is one of the most effective architectural concepts that an organization can implement to protect its ICS. Segmentation establishes security domains, or enclaves, that are typically defined as being managed by the same authority, enforcing the same policy, and having a uniform level of trust. Segmentation can minimize the method and level of access to sensitive information, ICS communication and equipment configuration, and can make it significantly more difficult for a malicious cyber adversary and can contain the effects of non-malicious errors and accidents. A practical consideration in defining a security domain is the amount of communications traffic that crosses the domain boundary, because domain protection typically involves examining boundary traffic and determining whether it is permitted.

The aim of network segmentation and segregation is to minimize access to sensitive information for those systems and people who don't need it, while ensuring that the organization can continue to operate effectively. This can be achieved using a number of techniques and technologies depending on the network's architecture and configuration.

---

[11] ICS-CERT recommended practices may be found at http://ics-cert.us-cert.gov/Recommended-Practices.

Traditionally, network segmentation and segregation is implemented at the gateway between domains. ICS environments often have multiple well-defined domains, such as operational LANs, control LANs, and operational DMZs, as well as gateways to non-ICS and less trustworthy domains such as the Internet and the corporate LANs. When insider attacks, social engineering, mobile devices, and other vulnerabilities and predisposing conditions discussed in Appendix C— are considered, protecting domain gateways is prudent and worth considering.

Network segregation involves developing and enforcing a ruleset controlling which communications are permitted through the boundary. Rules typically are based on source and destination identity and the type or content of the data being transferred.

When implementing network segmentation and segregation correctly you are minimizing the method and level of access to sensitive information. This can be achieved using a variety of technologies and methods. Depending on the architecture and configuration of your network, some of the common technologies and methods used include:

- Logical network separation enforced by encryption or network device-enforced partitioning.
    - o Virtual Local Area Networks (VLANS).
    - o Encrypted Virtual Private Networks (VPNs) use cryptographic mechanisms to separate traffic combined on one network.
    - o Unidirectional gateways restrict communications between connections to a single direction, therefore, segmenting the network.

- Physical network separation to completely prevent any interconnectivity of traffic between domains.

- Network traffic filtering which can utilize a variety of technologies at various network layers to enforce security requirements and domains.
    - o Network layer filtering that restricts which systems are able to communicate with others on the network based on IP and route information.
    - o State-based filtering that restricts which systems are able to communicate with others on the network based on their intended function or current state of operation.
    - o Port and/or protocol level filtering that restricts the number and type of services that each system can use to communicate with others on the network.
    - o Application filtering that commonly filters the content of communications between systems at the application layer. This includes application-level firewalls, proxies, and content-based filter.

Some vendors are making products to filter ICS protocols at the application level which they market as ICS firewalls.

Regardless of the technology chosen to implement network segmentation and segregation, there are four common themes that implement the concept of defense-in-depth by providing for good network segmentation and segregation:

- Apply technologies at more than just the network layer. Each system and network should be segmented and segregated, where possible, from the data link layer up to and including the application layer.

- Use the principles of least privilege and need-to-know. If a system doesn't need to communicate with another system, it should not be allowed to. If a system needs to talk only to another system on a specific port or protocol and nothing else–or it needs to transfer a limited set of labeled or fixed-format data, it should be restricted as such.

- Separate information and infrastructure based on security requirements. This may include using different hardware or platforms based on different threat and risk environments in which each system or network segment operates. The most critical components require more strict isolation from other components. In addition to network separation, the use of virtualization could be employed to accomplish the required isolation.

- Implement whitelisting[12] instead of blacklisting; that is, grant access to the known good, rather than denying access to the known bad. The set of applications that run in ICS is essentially static, making whitelisting more practical. This will also improve an organization's capacity to analyze log files.

5.2 Boundary Protection

Boundary protection devices control the flow of information between interconnected security domains to protect the ICS against malicious cyber adversaries and non-malicious errors and accidents. Transferring information between systems representing different security domains with different security policies introduces risk that such transfers violate one or more domain security policies. Boundary protection devices are key components of specific architectural solutions that enforce specific security policies. Organizations can isolate ICS and business system components performing different missions and/or business functions. Such isolation limits unauthorized information flows among system components and also provides the opportunity to deploy greater levels of protection for selected components. Separating system components with boundary protection mechanisms provides the capability for increased protection of individual components and more effective control of information flows between those components.

Boundary protection controls include gateways, routers, firewalls, guards, network-based malicious code analysis and virtualization systems, intrusion detection systems (networked and host-based), encrypted tunnels, managed interfaces, mail gateways, and unidirectional gateways (e.g., data diodes). Boundary protection devices determine whether data transfer is permitted, often by examining the data or associated metadata.

Network and ICS security architects must decide which domains are to be permitted direct communication, the policies governing permitted communication, the devices to be used to enforce the policy, and the topology for provisioning and implementing these decisions, which are typically based on the trust relationship between domains. Trust involves the degree of control that the organization has over the external domain (e.g., another domain in the same organization, a contracted service provider, the Internet).

Boundary protection devices are arranged in accordance with organizational security architecture. A common architectural construct is the demilitarized zones (DMZ), a host or network segment inserted as a "neutral zone" between security domains. Its purpose is to enforce the ICS domain's information security policy for external information exchange and to provide external domains with restricted access while shielding the ICS domain from outside threats.

Additional architectural considerations and functions that can be performed by boundary protection devices for inter-domain communications include:

---

[12] A **whitelist** is a list or register of those that are being provided a particular privilege, service, mobility, access or recognition. Only those on the list will be accepted, approved or recognized (i.e., permitted). Whitelisting is the reverse of blacklisting, the practice of identifying those that are denied, unrecognized, or ostracized (i.e., prohibited).

- Denying communications traffic by default and allowing communications traffic by exception (i.e., deny all, permit by exception). A deny-all, permit-by-exception communications traffic policy ensures that only those connections which are approved are allowed. This is known as a white-listing policy.

- Implementing proxy servers that act as an intermediary for external domains' requesting information system resources (e.g., files, connections, or services) from the ICS domain. External requests established through an initial connection to the proxy server are evaluated to manage complexity and to provide additional protection by limiting direct connectivity.

- Preventing the unauthorized exfiltration of information. Techniques include, for example, deep packet inspection firewalls and XML gateways. These devices verify adherence to protocol formats and specification at the application layer and serve to identify vulnerabilities that cannot be detected by devices operating at the network or transport layers. The limited number of formats, especially the prohibition of free form text in email, eases the use of such techniques at ICS boundaries.

- Only allowing communication between authorized and authenticated source and destinations address pairs by one or more of the organization, system, application, and individual.

- Extending the DMZ concept to other separate subnetworks is useful, for example, in isolating ICS to prevent adversaries from discovering the analysis and forensics techniques of organizations.

- Enforcing physical access control to limit authorized access to ICS components.

- Concealing network addresses of ICS components from discovery (e.g., network address not published or entered in domain name systems), requiring prior knowledge for access.

- Disabling control and troubleshooting services and protocols, especially those employing broadcast messaging, which can facilitate network exploration.

- Configuring boundary protection devices to fail in a predetermined state. Preferred failure states for ICS involve balancing multiple factors including safety and security.

- Configuring security domains with separate network addresses (i.e., as disjoint subnets).

- Disabling feedback (e.g., non-verbose mode) to senders when there is a failure in protocol validation format to prevent adversaries from obtaining information.

- Implementing one-way data flow, especially between different security domains.

- Establishing passive monitoring of ICS networks to actively detect anomalous communications and provide alerts.

5.3　Firewalls

Network firewalls are devices or systems that control the flow of network traffic between networks employing differing security postures. In most modern applications, firewalls and firewall environments are discussed in the context of Internet connectivity and the UDP/IP protocol suite. However, firewalls have applicability in network environments that do not include or require Internet connectivity. For example, many corporate networks employ firewalls to restrict connectivity to and from internal networks servicing more sensitive functions, such as the accounting or human resource departments. Firewalls can further restrict ICS inter-subnetwork communications between functional security subnets and devices. By employing firewalls to control connectivity to these areas, an organization can prevent unauthorized access to the respective systems and resources within the more sensitive areas. There are three general classes of firewalls:

■ **Packet Filtering Firewalls.** The most basic type of firewall is called a packet filter. Packet filter firewalls are essentially routing devices that include access control functionality for system addresses and communication sessions. The access control is governed by a set of directives collectively referred to as a rule set. In their most basic form, packet filters operate at layer 3 (network) of the Open Systems Interconnection (OSI), ISO/IEC 7498 model. This type of firewall checks basic information in each packet, such as IP addresses, against a set of criteria before forwarding the packet. Depending on the packet and the criteria, the firewall can drop the packet, forward it, or send a message to the originator. This type of firewall can offer a high level of security, but could result in overhead and delay impacts on network performance.

■ **Stateful Inspection Firewalls.** Stateful inspection firewalls are packet filters that incorporate added awareness of the OSI model data at layer 4 (transport). Stateful inspection firewalls filter packets at the network layer, determine whether session packets are legitimate, and evaluate the contents of packets at the transport layer (e.g., TCP, UDP) as well. Stateful inspection keeps track of active sessions and uses that information to determine if packets should be forwarded or blocked. It offers a high level of security and good performance, but it may be more expensive and complex to administer. Additional rule sets for ICS applications may be required.

■ **Application-Proxy Gateway Firewalls.** This class of firewalls examines packets at the application layer and filters traffic based on specific application rules, such as specified applications (e.g., browsers) or protocols (e.g., FTP). Firewalls of this type can be very effective in preventing attacks on the remote access and configuration services provided by ICS components. They offer a high level of security, but could have overhead and delay impacts on network performance, which can be unacceptable in an ICS environment. NIST SP 800-41 Revision 1, *Guidelines on Firewalls and Firewall Policy* [85], provides general guidance for the selection of firewalls and the firewall policies.

In an ICS environment, firewalls are most often deployed between the ICS network and the corporate network [34]. Properly configured, they can greatly restrict undesired access to and from control system host computers and controllers, thereby improving security. They can also potentially improve a control network's responsiveness by removing non-essential traffic from the network. When properly designed, configured, and maintained, dedicated hardware firewalls can contribute significantly to increasing the security of today's ICS environments.

Firewalls provide several tools to enforce a security policy that cannot be accomplished locally on the current set of process control devices available in the market, including the ability to:

■ Block all communications with the exception of specifically enabled communications between devices on the unprotected LAN and protected ICS networks. Blocking can be based on, for example, source and destination IP address pairs, services, ports, state of the connection, and specified applications or protocols supported by the firewall. Blocking can occur on both inbound and outbound packets, which is helpful in limiting high-risk communications such as email.

■ Enforce secure authentication of all users seeking to gain access to the ICS network. There is flexibility to employ varying protection levels of authentication methods including simple passwords, complex passwords, multi-factor authentication technologies, tokens, biometrics and smart cards. Select the particular method based upon the vulnerability of the ICS network to be protected, rather than using the method that is available at the device level.

■ Enforce destination authorization. Users can be restricted and allowed to reach only the nodes on the control network necessary for their job function. This reduces the potential of users intentionally or accidentally gaining access to and control of devices for which they are not authorized, but adds to the complexity for on-the-job-training or cross-training employees.

■ Record information flow for traffic monitoring, analysis, and intrusion detection.

■ Permit the ICS to implement operational policies appropriate to the ICS but that might not be appropriate in an IT network, such as prohibition of less secure communications like email, and permitted use of easy-to-remember usernames and group passwords.

■ Be designed with documented and minimal (single if possible) connections that permit the ICS network to be severed from the corporate network, should that decision be made, in times of serious cyber incidents.

Other possible deployments include using either host-based firewalls or small standalone hardware firewalls in front of, or running on, individual control devices. Using firewalls on an individual device basis can create significant management overhead, especially in change management of firewall configurations, however this practice will also simplify individual configuration rulesets.

There are several issues that must be addressed when deploying firewalls in ICS environments, particularly the following:

■ The possible addition of delay to control system communications.

■ The lack of experience in the design of rule sets suitable for industrial applications. Firewalls used to protect control systems should be configured so they do not permit either incoming or outgoing traffic by default. The default configuration should be modified only when it is necessary to permit connections to or from trusted systems to perform authorized ICS functions.

Firewalls require ongoing support, maintenance, and backup. Rule sets need to be reviewed to make sure that they are providing adequate protection in light of ever-changing security threats. System capabilities (e.g., storage space for firewall logs) should be monitored to make sure that the firewall is performing its data collection tasks and can be depended upon in the event of a security violation. Real-time monitoring of firewalls and other security sensors is required to rapidly detect and initiate response to cyber incidents.

5.4   Logically Separated Control Network

The ICS network should, at a minimum, be logically separated from the corporate network on physically separate network devices. Based on the ICS network configuration, additional separation needs to be considered for Safety Instrumented Systems and Security Systems (e.g., physical monitoring and access controls, doors, gates, cameras, VoIP, access card readers) that are often either part of the ICS network or utilize the same communications infrastructure for remote sites. When enterprise connectivity is required:

■ There should be documented and minimal (single if possible) access points between the ICS network and the corporate network. Redundant (i.e., backup) access points, if present, must be documented.

■ A stateful firewall between the ICS network and corporate network should be configured to deny all traffic except that which is explicitly authorized.

■ The firewall rules should at a minimum provide source and destination filtering (i.e., filter on media access control [MAC] address), in addition to TCP and User Datagram Protocol (UDP) port filtering and Internet Control Message Protocol (ICMP) type and code filtering.

An acceptable approach to enabling communication between an ICS network and a corporate network is to implement an intermediate DMZ network. The DMZ should be connected to the firewall such that specific (restricted) communication may occur between only the corporate network and the DMZ, and the ICS network and the DMZ. The corporate network and the ICS network should not communicate directly with each other. This approach is described in Sections 5.5.4 and 5.5.5. Additional security may be obtained by implementing a Virtual Private Network (VPN) between the ICS and external networks.

5.5 Network Segregation

ICS networks and corporate networks can be segregated to enhance cybersecurity using different architectures. This section describes several possible architectures and explains the advantages and disadvantages of each. Please note that the intent of the diagrams in Section 5.5 is to show the placement of firewalls to segregate the network. Not all devices that would be typically found on the control network or corporate network are shown. Section 5.6 provides guidance on a recommended defense-in-depth architecture.

5.5.1 Dual-Homed Computer/Dual Network Interface Cards (NIC)

Dual-homed computers can pass network traffic from one network to another. A computer without proper security controls could pose additional threats. To prevent this, no systems other than firewalls should be configured as dual-homed to span both the control and corporate networks. All connections between the control network and the corporate network should be through a firewall. This configuration provides no security improvement and should not be used to bridge networks (e.g., ICS and corporate networks).

5.5.2 Firewall between Corporate Network and Control Network

By introducing a simple two-port firewall between the corporate and control networks, as shown in Figure 5-1, a significant security improvement can be achieved. Properly configured, a firewall significantly reduces the chance of a successful external attack on the control network.

Unfortunately, two issues still remain with this design. First, if the data historian resides on the corporate network, the firewall must allow the data historian to communicate with the control devices on the control network. A packet originating from a malicious or incorrectly configured host on the corporate network (appearing to be the data historian) would be forwarded to individual PLCs/DCS.

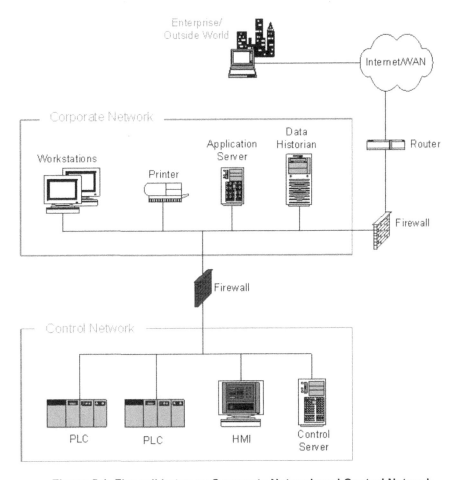

Figure 5-1. Firewall between Corporate Network and Control Network

If the data historian resides on the control network, a firewall rule must exist that allows all hosts from the enterprise to communicate with the historian. Typically, this communication occurs at the application layer as Structured Query Language (SQL) or Hypertext Transfer Protocol (HTTP) requests. Flaws in the historian's application layer code could result in a compromised historian. Once the historian is compromised, the remaining nodes on the control network are vulnerable to a worm propagating or an interactive attack.

Another issue with having a simple firewall between the networks is that spoofed packets can be constructed that can affect the control network, potentially permitting covert data to be tunneled in allowed protocols. For example, if HTTP packets are allowed through the firewall, then Trojan horse software accidentally introduced on an HMI or control network laptop could be controlled by a remote entity and send data (such as captured passwords) to that entity, disguised as legitimate traffic.

In summary, while this architecture is a significant improvement over a non-segregated network, it requires the use of firewall rules that allow direct communications between the corporate network and control network devices. This can result in possible security breaches if not very carefully designed and monitored [35].

5.5.3   Firewall and Router between Corporate Network and Control Network

A slightly more sophisticated design, shown in Figure 5-2, is the use of a router/firewall combination. The router sits in front of the firewall and offers basic packet filtering services, while the firewall handles the more complex issues using either stateful inspection or proxy techniques. This type of design is very popular in Internet-facing firewalls because it allows the faster router to handle the bulk of the incoming packets, especially in the case of DoS attacks, and reduces the load on the firewall. It also offers improved defense-in-depth because there are two different devices an adversary must bypass [35].

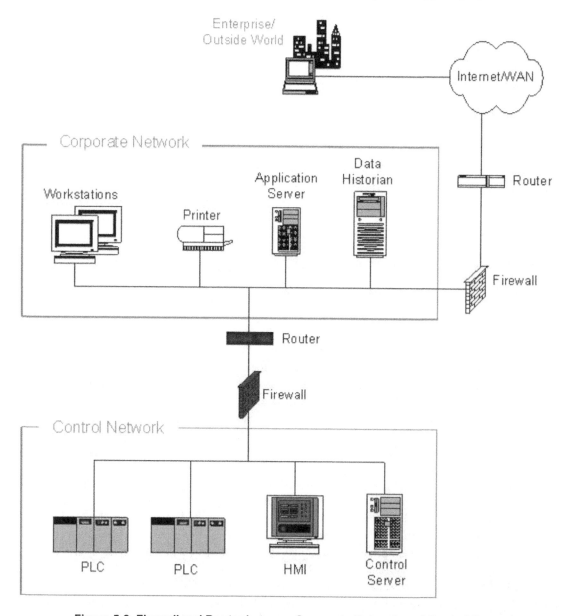

Figure 5-2. Firewall and Router between Corporate Network and Control Network

5.5.4 Firewall with DMZ between Corporate Network and Control Network

A significant improvement is the use of firewalls with the ability to establish a DMZ between the corporate and control networks. Each DMZ holds one or more critical components, such as the data historian, the wireless access point, or remote and third party access systems. In effect, the use of a DMZ-capable firewall allows the creation of an intermediate network.

Creating a DMZ requires that the firewall offer three or more interfaces, rather than the typical public and private interfaces. One of the interfaces is connected to the corporate network, the second to the control network, and the remaining interfaces to the shared or insecure devices such as the data historian server or wireless access points on the DMZ network. Implementing continuous ingress and egress traffic monitoring on the DMZ is recommended. Additionally, firewall rulesets that only permit connections between the control network and DMZ that are initiated by control network devices are recommended. Figure 5-3 provides an example of this architecture.

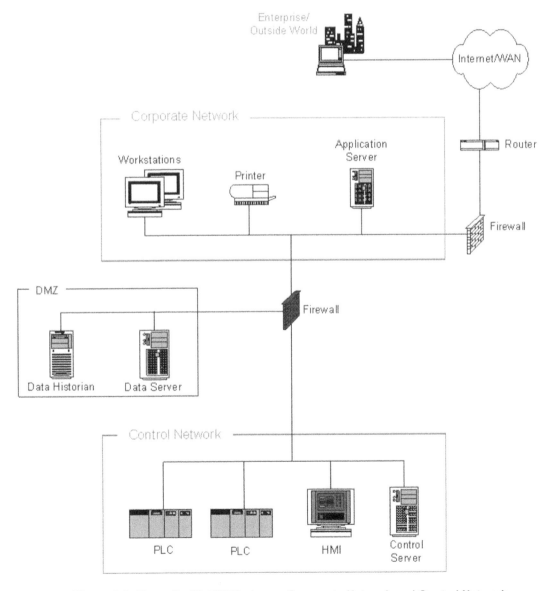

Figure 5-3. Firewall with DMZ between Corporate Network and Control Network

By placing corporate-accessible components in the DMZ, no direct communication paths are required from the corporate network to the control network; each path effectively ends in the DMZ. Most firewalls can allow for multiple DMZs, and can specify what type of traffic may be forwarded between zones. As Figure 5-3 shows, the firewall can block arbitrary packets from the corporate network from entering the control network, and can also regulate traffic from the other network zones including the control network. With well-planned rule sets, a clear separation can be maintained between the control network and other networks, with little or no traffic passing directly between the corporate and control networks.

If a patch management server, an antivirus server, or other security server is to be used for the control network, it should be located directly on the DMZ. Both functions could reside on a single server. Having patch management and antivirus management dedicated to the control network allows for controlled and secure updates that can be tailored for the unique needs of the ICS environment. It may also be helpful if the antivirus product chosen for ICS protection is not the same as the antivirus product used for the corporate network. For example, if a malware incident occurs and one antivirus product cannot detect or stop the malware, it is somewhat likely that another product may have that capability.

The primary security risk in this type of architecture is that if a computer in the DMZ is compromised, then it can be used to launch an attack against the control network via application traffic permitted from the DMZ to the control network. This risk can be greatly reduced if a concerted effort is made to harden and actively patch the servers in the DMZ and if the firewall ruleset permits only connections between the control network and DMZ that are initiated by control network devices. Other concerns with this architecture are the added complexity and the potential increased cost of firewalls with several ports. For more critical systems, however, the improved security should more than offset these disadvantages [35].

5.5.5 Paired Firewalls between Corporate Network and Control Network

A variation on the firewall with a DMZ solution is to use a pair of firewalls positioned between the corporate and ICS networks, as shown in Figure 5-4. Common servers such as the data historian are situated between the firewalls in a DMZ-like network zone sometimes referred to as a Manufacturing Execution System (MES) layer. As in the architectures described previously, the first firewall blocks arbitrary packets from proceeding to the control network or the shared historians. The second firewall can prevent unwanted traffic from a compromised server from entering the control network, and prevent control network traffic from impacting the shared servers.

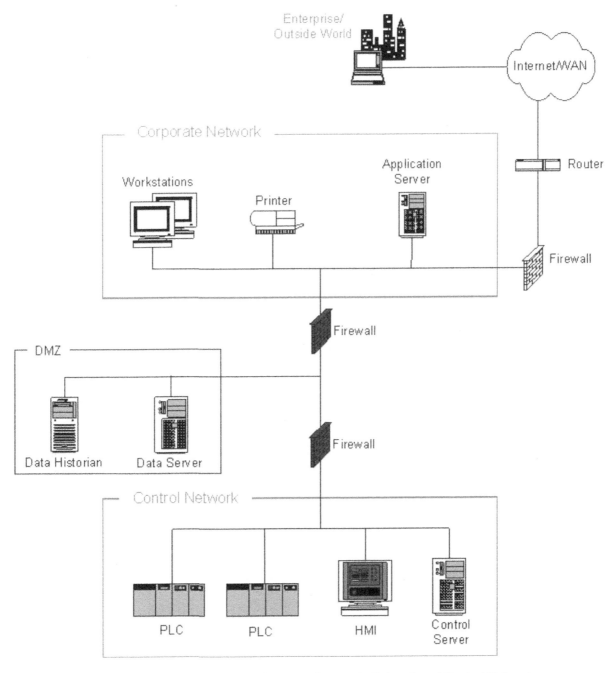

Figure 5-4. Paired Firewalls between Corporate Network and Control Network

If firewalls from two different manufacturers are used, then this solution may offer an advantage. It also allows the control group and the IT group to have clearly separated device responsibility because each can manage a firewall on its own, if the decision is made within the organization to do so. The primary disadvantage with two-firewall architectures is the increased cost and management complexity. For environments with stringent security requirements or the need for clear management separation, this architecture has some strong advantages.

5.5.6 Network Segregation Summary

In summary, dual-homed computers generally not provide suitable isolation between control networks and corporate networks. The two-zone solutions (no DMZ) are not recommended because they provide only weak protection. If used, they should only be deployed with extreme care. The most secure, manageable, and scalable control network and corporate network segregation architectures are typically based on a system with at least three zones, incorporating one or more DMZs.

5.6 Recommended Defense-in-Depth Architecture

A single security product, technology or solution cannot adequately protect an ICS by itself. A multiple layer strategy involving two (or more) different overlapping security mechanisms, a technique also known as defense-in-depth, is desired so that the impact of a failure in any one mechanism is minimized. A defense-in-depth architecture strategy includes the use of firewalls, the creation of demilitarized zones, intrusion detection capabilities along with effective security policies, training programs, incident response mechanisms and physical security. In addition, an effective defense-in-depth strategy requires a thorough understanding of possible attack vectors on an ICS. These include:

- Backdoors and holes in network perimeter.
- Vulnerabilities in common protocols.
- Attacks on field devices.
- Database attacks.
- Communications hijacking and 'man-in-the-middle' attacks.
- Spoofing attacks.
- Attacks on privileged and/or shared accounts.

Figure 5-5 shows an ICS defense-in-depth architecture strategy that has been developed by the DHS Control Systems Security Program (CSSP) NCCIC/ICS-CERT Recommended Practices committee[13] as described in the *Control Systems Cyber Security: Defense in Depth Strategies* [36] document. Additional supporting documents that cover specific issues and associated mitigations are also included on the site.

The *Control Systems Cyber Security: Defense in Depth Strategies* document provides guidance and direction for developing defense-in-depth architecture strategies for organizations that use control system networks while maintaining a multi-tiered information architecture that requires:

- Maintenance of various field devices, telemetry collection, and/or industrial-level process systems.
- Access to facilities via remote data link or modem.
- Public facing services for customer or corporate operations.

---

[13] Information on the CSSP Recommended Practices is located at http://ics-cert.us-cert.gov/Recommended-Practices

This strategy includes firewalls, the use of demilitarized zones and intrusion detection capabilities throughout the ICS architecture. The use of several demilitarized zones in Figure 5-5 provides the added capability to separate functionalities and access privileges and has proved to be very effective in protecting large architectures comprised of networks with different operational mandates. Intrusion detection deployments apply different rule-sets and signatures unique to each domain being monitored.

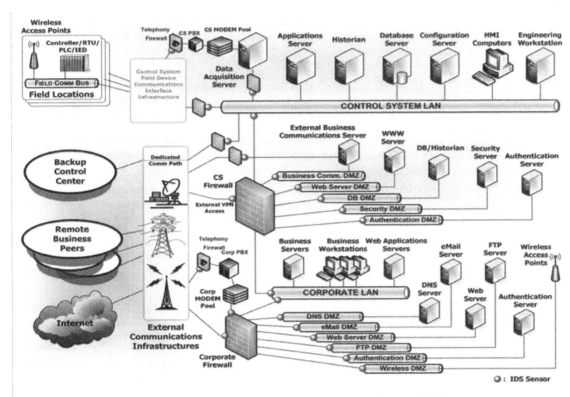

Figure 5-5. CSSP Recommended Defense-In-Depth Architecture

5.7 General Firewall Policies for ICS

Once the defense-in-depth architecture is in place, the work of determining exactly what traffic should be allowed through the firewalls begins. Configuring the firewalls to deny all except for the traffic absolutely required for business needs is every organization's basic premise, but the reality is much more difficult. Exactly what does "absolutely required for business" mean and what are the security impacts of allowing that traffic through? For example, many organizations considered allowing SQL traffic through the firewall as required for business for many data historian servers. Unfortunately, the SQL vulnerability was also the target for the Slammer worm [Table C-8. Example Adversarial Incidents]. Many important protocols used in the industrial world, such as HTTP, FTP, OPC/DCOM, EtherNet/IP, and Modbus/TCP, have significant security vulnerabilities.

The remaining material in this section summarizes some of the key points from the Centre for the Protection of National Infrastructure's (CPNI) *Firewall Deployment for SCADA and Process Control Networks: Good Practice Guide* [35].

When installing a single two-port firewall without a DMZ for shared servers (i.e., the architecture described in Section 5.5.2), particular care needs to be taken with the rule design. At a minimum, all rules should be stateful rules that are both IP address and port (application) specific. The address portion of the rules should restrict incoming traffic to a very small set of shared devices (e.g., the data historian) on the control network from a controlled set of addresses on the corporate network. Allowing any IP addresses on the corporate network to access servers inside the control network is not recommended. In addition, the allowed ports should be carefully restricted to relatively secure protocols such as Hypertext Transfer Protocol Secure (HTTPS). Allowing HTTP, FTP, or other unsecured protocols to cross the firewall is a security risk due to the potential for traffic sniffing and modification. Rules should be added to deny hosts outside the control network from initiating connections with hosts on the control network. Rules should only allow devices internal to the control network the ability to establish connections outside the control network.

On the other hand, if the DMZ architecture is being used, then it is possible to configure the system so that no traffic will go directly between the corporate network and the control network. With a few special exceptions (noted below), all traffic from either side can terminate at the servers in the DMZ. This allows more flexibility in the protocols allowed through the firewall. For example, Modbus/TCP might be used to communicate from the PLCs to the data historian, while HTTP might be used for communication between the historian and enterprise clients. Both protocols are inherently insecure, yet in this case they can be used safely because neither actually crosses between the two networks. An extension to this concept is the idea of using "disjoint" protocols in all control network to corporate network communications. That is, if a protocol is allowed between the control network and DMZ, then it is explicitly **not** allowed between the DMZ and corporate network. This design greatly reduces the chance of a worm such as Slammer actually making its way into the control network, because the worm would have to use two different exploits over two different protocols.

One area of considerable variation in practice is the control of outbound traffic from the control network, which could represent a significant risk if unmanaged. One example is Trojan horse software that uses HTTP tunneling to exploit poorly defined outbound rules. Thus, it is important that outbound rules be as stringent as inbound rules.

Example outbound rules include:

- Outbound traffic through the control network firewall should be limited to essential communications only and should be limited to authorized traffic originating from DMZ servers.

- All outbound traffic from the control network to the corporate network should be source and destination-restricted by service and port.

In addition to these rules, the firewall should be configured with outbound filtering to stop forged IP packets from leaving the control network or the DMZ. In practice this is achieved by checking the source IP addresses of outgoing packets against the firewall's respective network interface address. The intent is to prevent the control network from being the source of spoofed (i.e., forged) communications, which are often used in DoS attacks. Thus, the firewalls should be configured to forward IP packets only if those packets have a correct source IP address for the control network or DMZ networks. Finally, Internet access by devices on the control network should be strongly discouraged.

In summary, the following should be considered as recommended practice for general firewall rule sets:

- The base rule set should be deny all, permit none.

- Ports and services between the control network environment and the corporate network should be enabled and permissions granted on a specific case-by-case basis. There should be a documented business justification with risk analysis and a responsible person for each permitted incoming or outgoing data flow.

- All "permit" rules should be both IP address and TCP/UDP port specific, and stateful if appropriate.

- All rules should restrict traffic to a specific IP address or range of addresses.

- Traffic should be prevented from transiting directly from the control network to the corporate network. All traffic should terminate in the DMZ.

- Any protocol allowed between the control network and DMZ should explicitly NOT be allowed between the DMZ and corporate networks (and vice-versa).

- All outbound traffic from the control network to the corporate network should be source and destination-restricted by service and port.

- Outbound packets from the control network or DMZ should be allowed only if those packets have a correct source IP address that is assigned to the control network or DMZ devices.

- Control network devices should not be allowed to access the Internet.

- Control networks should not be directly connected to the Internet, even if protected via a firewall.

- All firewall management traffic should be carried on either a separate, secured management network (e.g., out of band) or over an encrypted network with multi-factor authentication. Traffic should also be restricted by IP address to specific management stations.

- All firewall policies should be tested periodically.

- All firewalls should be backed up immediately prior to commissioning.

These should be considered only as guidelines. A careful assessment of each control environment is required before implementing any firewall rule sets.

5.8 Recommended Firewall Rules for Specific Services

Beside the general rules described above, it is difficult to outline all-purpose rules for specific protocols. The needs and recommended practices vary significantly between industries for any given protocol and should be analyzed on an organization-by-organization basis. The Industrial Automation Open Networking Association (IAONA) offers a template for conducting such an analysis [37], assessing each of the protocols commonly found in industrial environments in terms of function, security risk, worst case impact, and suggested measures. Some of the key points from the IAONA document are summarized in this section. The reader is advised to consult this document directly when developing rule sets.

5.8.1 Domain Name System (DNS)

Domain Name System (DNS) is primarily used to translate between domain names and IP addresses. For example, a DNS could map a domain name such as *control.com* to an IP address such as *192.168.1.1*. Most Internet services rely heavily on DNS, but its use on the control network is relatively rare at this time. In most cases there is little reason to allow DNS requests out of the control network to the corporate network and no reason to allow DNS requests into the control network. DNS requests from the control network to DMZ should be addressed on a case-by-case basis. Local DNS or the use of host files is recommended.

5.8.2 Hypertext Transfer Protocol (HTTP)

HTTP is the protocol underlying Web browsing services on the Internet. Like DNS, it is critical to most Internet services. It is seeing increasing use on the plant floor as well as an all-purpose query tool. Unfortunately, it has little inherent security, and many HTTP applications have vulnerabilities that can be exploited. HTTP can be a transport mechanism for many manually performed attacks and automated worms.

In general, HTTP should not be allowed to cross from the public/corporate to the control network. If web-based technologies are absolutely required, the following best practices should be applied:

- Control access to web-based services on the physical or network layer using white-listing;
- Apply access control to both source and destination;
- Implement authorization to access the service on the application layer (instead of physical or network-layer checks);
- Implement service using only the necessary technologies (e.g., scripts are used only if they are required);
- Check service according to known application security practices;
- Log all attempts of service usage ; and
- Use HTTPS rather than HTTP, and only for specific authorized devices.

5.8.3 FTP and Trivial File Transfer Protocol (TFTP)

FTP and Trivial File Transfer Protocol (TFTP) are used for transferring files between devices. They are implemented on almost every platform including many SCADA systems, DCS, PLCs, and RTUs, because they are very well known and use minimum processing power. Unfortunately, neither protocol was created with security in mind; for FTP, the login password is not encrypted, and for TFTP, no login is required at all. Furthermore, some FTP implementations have a history of buffer overflow vulnerabilities. As a result, all TFTP communications should be blocked, while FTP communications should be allowed for outbound sessions only or if secured with additional token-based multi-factor authentication and an encrypted tunnel. More secure protocols, such as Secure FTP (SFTP) or Secure Copy (SCP), should be employed whenever possible.

5.8.4 Telnet

The telnet protocol defines an interactive, text-based communications session between a client and a host. It is used mainly for remote login and simple control services to systems with limited resources or to systems with limited needs for security. It is a severe security risk because all telnet traffic, including passwords, is unencrypted, and it can allow a remote individual considerable control over a device. It is recommended to use the Secure Shell (SSH) protocol [5.8.6] for remote administration. Inbound telnet sessions from the corporate to the control network should be prohibited unless secured with token-based multi-factor authentication and an encrypted tunnel. Outbound telnet sessions should be allowed only over encrypted tunnels (e.g., VPN) to specific authorized devices.

5.8.5   Dynamic Host Configuration Protocol (DHCP)

DHCP is used on IP networks for dynamically distributing network configuration parameters, such as IP addresses for interfaces and services. The base DHCP includes no mechanism for authenticating servers and clients. Rogue DHCP servers can provide incorrect information to clients. Unauthorized clients can gain access to server and cause exhaustion of available resources (e.g., IP addresses). To prevent this, it is recommended to use static configuration instead of dynamic address allocation, which should be the typical configuration for ICS devices. If dynamic allocation is necessary, it is recommended to enable DHCP snooping to defend against rogue DHCP servers, Address Resolution Protocol (ARP) and IP spoofing. The DHCP servers should be placed in the same network segment as configured equipment (e.g., on the router). DHCP relaying is not recommended.

5.8.6   Secure Shell (SSH)

SSH allows remote access to a device. It provides secure authentication and authorization based on cryptography. If remote access is required to the control network, SSH is recommended as the alternative to telnet, rlogin, rsh, rcp and other insecure remote access tools.

5.8.7   Simple Object Access Protocol (SOAP)

SOAP is an XML-based format syntax to exchange messages. Traffic flows related to SOAP-based services should be controlled at the firewall between corporate and ICS network segments. If these services are necessary, deep-packet inspection and/or application layer firewalls should be used to restrict the contents of messages.

5.8.8   Simple Mail Transfer Protocol (SMTP)

SMTP is the primary email transfer protocol on the Internet. Email messages often contain malware, so inbound email should not be allowed to any control network device. Outbound SMTP mail messages from the control network to the corporate network are acceptable to send alert messages.

5.8.9   Simple Network Management Protocol (SNMP)

SNMP is used to provide network management services between a central management console and network devices such as routers, printers, and PLCs. Although SNMP is an extremely useful service for maintaining a network, it is very weak in security. Versions 1 and 2 of SNMP use unencrypted passwords to both read and configure devices (including devices such as PLCs), and in many cases the passwords are well known and cannot be changed. Version 3 is considerably more secure but is still limited in use. SNMP V1 & V2 commands both to and from the control network should be prohibited unless they are over a separate, secured management network, whereas SNMP V3 commands may be able to be sent to the ICS using the security features inherent to V3.

5.8.10 Distributed Component Object Model (DCOM)

DCOM is the underlying protocol for OLE for Process Control (OPC). It utilizes Microsoft's Remote Procedure Call (RPC) service which, when not patched, has many vulnerabilities. These vulnerabilities were the basis for the Blaster worm[14] exploits. In addition, OPC, which utilizes DCOM, dynamically opens a wide range of ports (1024 to 65535) that can be extremely difficult to filter at the firewall. This protocol should only be allowed between control network and DMZ networks and explicitly blocked between the DMZ and corporate network. Also, users are advised to restrict the port ranges used by making registry modifications on devices using DCOM.

5.8.11 SCADA and Industrial Protocols

SCADA and industrial protocols, such as Modbus/TCP, EtherNet/IP, IEC 61850, ICCP and DNP3[15], are critical for communications to most control devices. Unfortunately, many of these protocols were designed without security built in and do not typically require any authentication to remotely execute commands on a control device. These protocols should only be allowed within the control network and not allowed to cross into the corporate network.

5.9   Network Address Translation (NAT)

Network address translation (NAT) is a service where IP addresses used on one side of a network device can be mapped to a different set on the other side on an as-needed basis. It was originally designed for IP address reduction purposes so that an organization with a large number of devices that occasionally needed Internet access could get by with a smaller set of assigned Internet addresses.

To do this, most NAT implementations rely on the premise that not every internal device is actively communicating with external hosts at a given moment. The firewall is configured to have a limited number of outwardly visible IP addresses. When an internal host seeks to communicate with an external host, the firewall remaps the internal IP address and port to one of the currently unused, more limited, public IP addresses, effectively concentrating outgoing traffic into fewer IP addresses. The firewall must track the state of each connection and how each private internal IP address and source port was remapped onto an outwardly visible IP address/port pair. When returning traffic reaches the firewall, the mapping is reversed and the packets forwarded to the proper internal host.

For example, a control network device may need to establish a connection with an external, non-control network host (for instance, to send a critical alert email). NAT allows the internal IP address of the initiating control network host to be replaced by the firewall; subsequent return traffic packets are remapped back to the internal IP address and sent to the appropriate control network device. More specifically, if the control network is assigned the private subnet 192.168.1.xxx and the Internet network expects the device to use the corporate assigned addresses in the range 192.6.yyy.zzz, then a NAT firewall will substitute (and track) a 192.6.yyy.zzz source address into every outbound IP packet generated by a control network device.

Producer-consumer protocols, such as EtherNet/IP and Foundation Fieldbus, are particularly troublesome because NAT does not support the multicast-based traffic that these protocols need to offer their full services.

---

[14] http://en.wikipedia.org/wiki/Blaster_%28computer_worm%29

[15] IEEE 1815-2012, *IEEE Standard for Electric Power Systems Communications—Distributed Network Protocol (DNP3),* incorporates DNP3 Secure Authentication version 5 (DNP3-SAv5) which provides strong application layer authentication with remote security credential management. See https://standards.ieee.org/findstds/standard/1815-2012.html.

In general, while NAT offers some distinct advantages, its impact on the actual industrial protocols and configuration should be assessed carefully before it is deployed. Furthermore, certain protocols are specifically broken by NAT because of the lack of direct addressing. For example, OPC requires special third-party tunneling software to work with NAT.

5.10 Specific ICS Firewall Issues

In addition to the issues with firewalls and ICS already discussed, there are some additional problems that need to be examined in more detail. The rest of this section discusses three specific areas of concern: the placement of data historians, remote access for ICS support, and multicast traffic.

5.10.1 Data Historians

The existence of shared control network/corporate network servers such as data historians and asset management servers can have a significant impact on firewall design and configuration. In three-zone systems the placement of these servers in a DMZ is relatively straightforward, but in two-zone designs the issues become complex. Placing the historian on the corporate side of the firewall means that a number of insecure protocols, such as Modbus/TCP or DCOM, must be allowed through the firewall and that every control device reporting to the historian is exposed to the corporate side of the network. On the other hand, putting the historian on the control network side means other equally questionable protocols, such as HTTP or SQL, must be allowed through the firewall, and there is now a server accessible to nearly everyone in the organization sitting on the control network.

In general, the best solution is to avoid two-zone systems (no DMZ) and use a three-zone design, placing the data collector in the control network and the historian component in the DMZ.

5.10.2 Remote Support Access

Another issue for ICS firewall design is user and/or vendor remote access into the control network. Any users accessing the control network from remote networks should be required to authenticate using an appropriately strong mechanism such as token-based authentication. While it is possible for the controls group to set up their own remote access system with multi-factor authentication on the DMZ, in most organizations it is typically more efficient to use existing systems set up by the IT department. In this case a connection through the firewall from the IT remote access server is needed.

Remote support personnel connecting over the Internet or via dialup modems should use an encrypted protocol, such as running a corporate VPN connection client, application server, or secure HTTP access, and authenticate using a strong mechanism, such as a token based multi-factor authentication scheme, in order to connect to the general corporate network. Once connected, they should be required to authenticate a second time at the control network firewall using a strong mechanism, such as a token based multi-factor authentication scheme, to gain access to the control network. Proxy servers can also provide additional capabilities for securing remote support access.

5.10.3 Multicast Traffic

Most industrial producer-consumer (or publisher-subscriber) protocols operating over Ethernet, such as EtherNet/IP and Foundation Fieldbus HSE, are IP multicast-based. The first advantage of IP multicasting is network efficiency; by not repeating the data transmission to the multiple destinations, a significant reduction in network load can occur. The second advantage is that the sending host need not be concerned with knowing every IP address of every destination host listening for the broadcast information. The third, and perhaps most important for industrial control purposes, is that a single multicast message offers far better capabilities for time synchronization between multiple control devices than multiple unicast messages.

If the source and destinations of a multicast packet are connected with no intervening routers or firewalls between them, the multicast transmission is relatively seamless. However, if the source and destinations are not on the same LAN, forwarding the multicast messages to a destination becomes more complicated. To solve the problem of multicast message routing, hosts need to join (or leave) a group by informing the multicast router on their network of the relevant group ID through the use of the Internet Group Management Protocol (IGMP). Multicast routers subsequently know of the members of multicast groups on their network and can decide whether or not to forward a received multicast message onto their network. A multicast routing protocol is also required. From a firewall administration perspective, monitoring and filtering IGMP traffic becomes another series of rule sets to manage, adding to the complexity of the firewall.

Another firewall issue related to multicasting is the use of NAT. A firewall performing NAT that receives a multicast packet from an external host has no reverse mapping for which internal group ID should receive the data. If IGMP-aware, it could broadcast it to every group ID it knows about, because one of them will be correct, but this could cause serious issues if an unintended control packet were broadcast to a critical node. The safest action for the firewall to take is to drop the packet. Thus, multicasting is generally considered NAT-unfriendly.

5.11 Unidirectional Gateways

Hardware-enforced unidirectional gateways (e.g., data diodes) are increasingly deployed at the boundary between ICS and IT networks, as well as between Safety Instrumented System networks and control networks. Unidirectional gateways are a combination of hardware and software. The hardware permits data to flow from one network to another, but is physically unable to send any information at all back into the source network. The software replicates databases and emulates protocol servers and devices.

5.12 Single Points of Failure

Single points of failure can exist at any level of the ANSI/ISO stack. An example is PLC control of safety interlocks. Because security is usually being added to the ICS environment, an evaluation should be done to identify potential failure points and a risk assessment done to evaluate each point's exposure. Remediation methods can then be postulated and evaluated and a "risk versus reward" determination made and design and implementation done.

5.13 Redundancy and Fault Tolerance

ICS components or networks that are classified as critical to the organization have high availability requirements. One method of achieving high availability is through the use of redundancy. Additionally, if a component fails, it should fail in a manner that does not generate unnecessary traffic on the ICS, or does not cause another problem elsewhere, such as a cascading event.

The control system should have the ability to execute an appropriate fail-safe process upon the loss of communications with the ICS or the loss of the ICS itself. The organization should define what "loss of communications" means (e.g., 500 milliseconds, 5 seconds, 5 minutes, etc. without communications). The organization should then, based on potential consequences, define the appropriate fail-safe process for their industry.

Backups should be performed using the "backup-in-depth" approach, with layers of backups (e.g., local, facility, disaster) that are time-sequenced such that rapid recent local backups are available for immediate use and secure backups are available to recover from a massive security incident. A mixture of backup/restore approaches and storage methods should be used to ensure that backups are rigorously produced, securely stored, and appropriately accessible for restoration.

5.14 Preventing Man-in-the-Middle Attacks

A man-in-the-middle attack requires knowledge of the protocol being manipulated. The Address Resolution Protocol (ARP) man-in-the-middle attack is a popular method for an adversary to gain access to the network flow of information on a target system. This is performed by attacking the network ARP cache tables of the controller and the workstation machines. Using the compromised computer on the control network, the adversary poisons the ARP tables on each host and informs them that they must route all their traffic through a specific IP and hardware address (i.e., the adversary's machine). By manipulating the ARP tables, the adversary can insert their machine between the two target machines and/or devices.

The ARP man-in-the-middle attack works by initiating gratuitous ARP commands to confuse each host (i.e., ARP poisoning). These ARP commands cause each of the two target hosts to use the MAC address of the adversary as the address for the other target host. When a successful man-in-the-middle attack is performed, the hosts on each side of the attack are unaware that their network data is taking a different route through the adversary's computer.

Once an adversary has successfully inserted their machine into the information stream, they now have full control over the data communications and could carry out several types of attacks. One possible attack method is the replay attack. In its simplest form, captured data from the control/HMI is modified to instantiate activity when received by the device controller. Captured data reflecting normal operations in the ICS could be played back to the operator as required. This would cause the operator's HMI to appear to be normal and the attack will go unobserved. During this replay attack the adversary could continue to send commands to the controller and/or field devices to cause an undesirable event while the operator is unaware of the true state of the system.

Another attack that could be carried out with the man-in-the-middle attack is sending false messages to the operator, and could take the form of a false negative or a false positive. This may cause the operator to take an action, such as flipping a breaker, when it is not required, or it may cause the operator to think everything is fine and not take an action when an action is required. The adversary could send commands to the operator's console indicating a system change, and when the operator follows normal procedures and attempts to correct the problem, the operator's action could cause an undesirable event. There are variations of the modification and replay of control data which could impact the operations of the system.

Protocol manipulation and the man-in-the-middle attack are among the most popular ways to manipulate insecure protocols, such as those found in control systems. However, there are mitigation techniques [38] that can be applied to secure the systems through MAC address locking, static tables, encryption, authentication, and monitoring.

■ **MAC Address Locking** - The ARP man-in-the-middle attack requires the adversary to be connected to the local network or have control of a local computer on the network. Port security, also called MAC address locking, is one method to secure the physical connection at the end of each port on a network switch. High-end corporate class network switches usually have some kind of option for MAC address locking. MAC address locking is very effective against a rogue individual looking to physically plug into the internal network. Without port security, any open network jack on the wall could be used as an avenue onto the corporate network. Port security locks a specific MAC address to a specific port on a managed switch. If the MAC address does not match, the communication link is disabled and the intruder will not be able to achieve their goal. Some of the more advanced switches have an auto resetting option, which will reset the security measure if the original MAC is returned to the port.

Although port security is not attacker proof, it does add a layer of added security to the physical network. It also protects the local network from employees plugging un-patched and out-of-date systems onto the protected network. This reduces the number of target computers a remote adversary can access. These security measures not only protect against attacks from external networks but provide added physical protection as well.

■ **Static Tables** – An ICS network that stays relatively static could attempt to implement statically coded ARP tables. Most operating systems have the capability to statically code all of the MAC addresses into the ARP table on each computer. Statically coding the ARP tables on each computer prevents the adversary from changing them by sending ARP reply packets to the victim computer. While this technique is not feasible on a large and/or dynamic corporate network, the limited number of hosts on an ICS network could be effectively protected this way.

■ **Encryption** - As a longer-term solution, systems should be designed to include encryption between devices in order to make it very difficult to reverse engineer protocols and forge packets on control system networks. Encrypting the communications between devices would make it nearly impossible to perform this attack. Protocols that provide strong authentication also provide resilience to man-in-the-middle attacks. The impact of encryption on network and operational performance needs to be considered.

■ **Authentication** - Protocols with strong authentication provide resilience to man-in-the-middle attacks.

■ **Monitoring** - Monitoring for ARP poisoning provides an added layer of defense. There are several programs available (e.g., ARPwatch) that can monitor for changing MAC addresses through the ARP packets.

5.15 Authentication and Authorization

An ICS may contain a large number of systems, each of which must be accessed by a variety of users. Performing the authentication and authorization of these users presents a challenge to the ICS. Managing these user's accounts can be problematic as employees are added, removed, and as their roles change. As the number of systems and users grow, the process of managing these accounts becomes more complicated.

The authentication of a user or system is the process of verifying the claimed identity. Authorization, the process of granting the user access privileges, is determined by applying policy rules to the authenticated identity and other relevant information[16]. Authorization is enforced by some access control mechanism. The authentication process can be used to control access to both systems (e.g. HMIs, field devices, SCADA servers) and networks (e.g., remote substations LANs).

Authentication and authorization can be performed either in a distributed or centralized approach. With distributed authentication and authorization, every system performs these steps on their own. Each system is responsible for storing its own set of user accounts, credentials, and roles and performing the identification and authentication of the user. This approach typically does not require any additional infrastructure. However, this approach is problematic in that it does not scale well as the size of the system increases. For example, if a user leaves the organization, the corresponding user account must be removed from each system individually.

In contrast to the distributed approach, centralized authentication and authorization systems are commonly used to manage larger number of users and accounts. A centralized approach utilizes some central authentication system (e.g., Microsoft Active Directory, Lightweight Directory Access Protocol (LDAP) to store all accounts and manage the authentication and authorization of all individuals and systems. An authentication protocol (e.g., Kerberos, RADIUS, TACACS+) is then used to communicate data between the authentication server and the system performing authentication.

While a centralized approach provides substantially improved scalability, it also presents numerous additional concerns that may impact its use in ICS environments. The following considerations apply:

- Authentication servers create a single system that is responsible for managing all system accounts and must be highly secured.
- The authentications server system requires high availability because its failure may prevent users from authenticating to a system during an emergency. Redundancy may be required.
- Some clients may cache user credentials locally to ensure that users can still be authenticated in the absence of the server. Caching may only be available for users that have recently authenticated. Caching also introduces complications for revocation.
- Networks used to support the authentication protocol must be reliable and secure to ensure authentication attempts are not hindered.

---

[16] In general, authorization to perform a set of operations is determined by evaluating attributes associated with the subject, object, requested operations, and, in some cases, environment conditions against policy, rules, or relationships that describe the allowable operations for a given set of attributes. For further information see NIST SP 800-162, *Guide to Attribute Based Access Control (ABAC) Definition and Considerations*, at http://nvlpubs.nist.gov/nistpubs/specialpublications/NIST.SP.800-162.pdf.http://nvlpubs.nist.gov/nistpubs/specialpublications/NIST.sp.800-162.pdf

5.15.1 ICS Implementation Considerations

While centralized authentication and authorization servers are commonly used in an IT environment, there are many challenges to integrating them into ICS. While authentication servers and protocols integrate with many commodity IT products (e.g., Microsoft Windows, Linux, Oracle), often ICS may utilize their own application-specific accounts and authentication mechanisms that were not designed to interface with third party servers and protocols. This limits the adoption of such mechanism in an ICS environment. Older network devices and most field devices do not support any mechanisms to integrated with a centralized authentication system.

5.16 Monitoring, Logging, and Auditing

The security architecture of an ICS must also incorporate mechanisms to monitor, log, and audit activities occurring on various systems and networks. Monitoring, logging, and auditing activities are imperative to understanding the current state of the ICS, validating that the system is operating as intended, and that no policy violations or cyber incidents have hindered the operation of the system. Network security monitoring is valuable to characterize the normal state of the ICS, and can provide indications of compromised systems when signature-based technologies fail. Additionally, strong system monitoring, logging, and auditing is necessary to troubleshoot and perform any necessary forensic analysis of the system[17].

5.17 Incident Detection, Response, and System Recovery

Incidents are inevitable and incident detection, response, and system recovery plans are essential. Major characteristics of a good security program are how soon after an incident has occurred that the incident can be detected and how quickly a system can be recovered after an incident has been detected. Incident response in ICS is closely aligned to disaster recovery, specifically to address the stringent uptime requirements of ICS. Incident Responders must be trained for ICS-specific scenarios, as normal methods of recovering IT systems may not apply to ICS.

---

[17] For further information see NIST SP 800-94, *Guide to Intrusion Detection and Prevention Systems (IDPS)* [55].

6. Applying Security Controls to ICS

A single security product or technology cannot adequately protect an ICS. Securing an ICS is based on a combination of effective security policies and a properly configured set of security controls. The selection and implementation of security controls to apply to an ICS can have major implications on the operations, so it is critical to consider:

■ Which security controls are needed to adequately mitigate risk to an acceptable level that supports the organizational missions and business functions?

■ Have the selected security controls been implemented or is there a realistic implementation plan in place?

■ What is the required level of assurance that the selected security controls are implemented correctly, operating as intended, and producing a desired outcome?

As identified in Section 3, the questions should be answered in the context of an effective, organization-wide risk management process and cybersecurity strategy that identifies, mitigates (as necessary), and continuously monitors risks to its ICS. An effective cybersecurity strategy for an ICS should apply defense-in-depth, a technique of layering security mechanisms so that the impact of a failure in any one mechanism is minimized. Use of such a strategy is explored within the security control discussions and their applications to ICS that follow.

6.1 Executing the Risk Management Framework Tasks for Industrial Control Systems

The following describes the process of applying the Risk Management Framework (RMF) to ICS. The process includes a brief description of each activity and identifies supporting NIST documents. The following steps, while shown sequentially, can be implemented in a different order to be consistent with established management and system development life cycle processes [21].

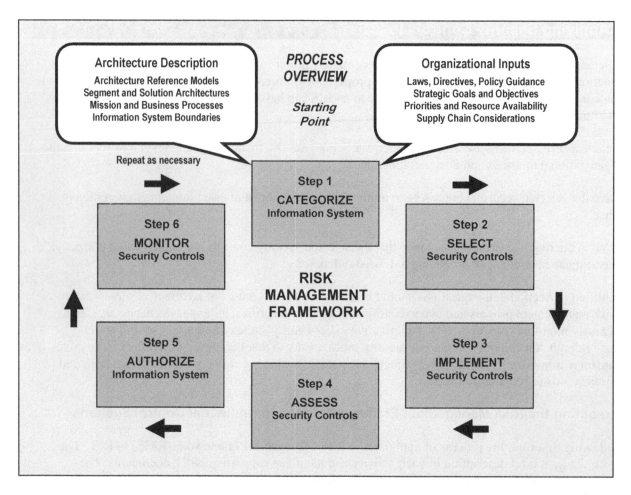

Figure 6-1. Risk Management Framework Tasks

6.1.1 Step 1: Categorize Information System

The first activity in the RMF is to categorize the information and information system according to potential impact of loss. For each information type and information system under consideration, the three FISMA-defined security objectives—confidentiality, integrity, and availability—are associated with one of three levels of potential impact should there be a breach of security. It is important to remember that for an ICS, availability is generally the greatest concern.

The standards and guidance for this categorization process can be found in FIPS 199 [15] and NIST SP 800-60 [25], respectively. NIST is in the process of updating NIST SP 800-60 to provide additional guidance on the categorization of ICS.

The following ICS example is taken from FIPS 199 [15]:

ICS-specific Recommendations and Guidance

A power plant contains a SCADA system controlling the distribution of electric power for a large military installation. The SCADA system contains both real-time sensor data and routine administrative information. The management at the power plant determines that: (i) for the sensor data being acquired by the SCADA system, there is no potential impact from a loss of confidentiality, a high potential impact from a loss of integrity, and a high potential impact from a loss of availability; and (ii) for the administrative information being processed by the system, there is a low potential impact from a loss of confidentiality, a low potential impact from a loss of integrity, and a low potential impact from a loss of availability. The resulting security categories, SC, of these information types are expressed as:

$$SC \text{ sensor data} = \{(\textbf{confidentiality}, NA), (\textbf{integrity}, HIGH), (\textbf{availability}, HIGH)\},$$

and

$$SC \text{ administrative information} = \{(\textbf{confidentiality}, LOW), (\textbf{integrity}, LOW), (\textbf{availability}, LOW)\}.$$

The resulting security category of the information system is initially expressed as:

$$SC \text{ SCADA system} = \{(\textbf{confidentiality}, LOW), (\textbf{integrity}, HIGH), (\textbf{availability}, HIGH)\},$$

representing the high water mark or maximum potential impact values for each security objective from the information types resident on the SCADA system. The management at the power plant chooses to increase the potential impact from a loss of confidentiality from low to moderate, reflecting a more realistic view of the potential impact on the information system should there be a security breach due to the unauthorized disclosure of system-level information or processing functions. The final security category of the information system is expressed as:

$$SC \text{ SCADA system} = \{(\textbf{confidentiality}, MODERATE), (\textbf{integrity}, HIGH), (\textbf{availability}, HIGH)\}.$$

FIPS 199 specifies that information systems be categorized as low-impact, moderate-impact, or high-impact for the security objectives of confidentiality, integrity, and availability. Possible definitions for low, moderate, and high levels of security based on impact for ICS based on ISA99 are provided in Table 6-1. Possible definitions for ICS impact levels based on product produced, industry and security concerns are provided in Table 6-2.

Table 6-1. Possible Definitions for ICS Impact Levels Based on ISA99

Impact Category	Low-Impact	Moderate-Impact	High-Impact
Injury	Cuts, bruises requiring first aid	Requires hospitalization	Loss of life or limb
Financial Loss	$1,000	$100,000	Millions
Environmental Release	Temporary damage	Lasting damage	Permanent damage, off-site damage
Interruption of Production	Minutes	Days	Weeks
Public Image	Temporary damage	Lasting damage	Permanent damage

Table 6-2. Possible Definitions for ICS Impact Levels Based on Product Produced, Industry and Security Concerns

Category	Low-Impact	Moderate-Impact	High-Impact
Product Produced	• Non-hazardous materials or products • Non-ingested consumer products	• Some hazardous products or steps during production • High amount of proprietary information	• Critical infrastructure (e.g., electricity) • Hazardous materials • Ingested products
Industry Examples	• Plastic injection molding • Warehouse applications	• Automotive metal industries • Pulp and paper • Semiconductors	• Utilities • Petrochemical • Food and beverage • Pharmaceutical
Security Concerns	• Protection against minor injuries • Ensuring uptime	• Protection against moderate injuries • Ensuring uptime • Capital investment	• Protection against major injuries/loss of life • Ensuring uptime • Capital investment • Trade secrets • Ensuring basic social services • Regulatory compliance

6.1.2 Step 2: Select Security Controls

This framework activity includes the initial selection of minimum security controls planned or in place to protect the information system based on a set of requirements. FIPS 200 documents a set of minimum-security requirements covering 18 security-related areas with regard to protecting the confidentiality, integrity, and availability of federal information systems and the information processed, stored, and transmitted by those systems [16]. Additional information on each of the 18 security control families is in Section 6.2.

The baseline controls are the starting point for the security control selection process and chosen based on the security category and associate impact level of information systems determined in Step 1.

To address the need for developing community-wide and specialized sets of security controls for information systems and organizations, the concept of *overlays* is introduced. An *overlay* is a fully specified set of security controls, control enhancements, and supplemental guidance derived from the application of tailoring guidance to security control baselines described in NIST SP 800-53.

In general, overlays are intended to reduce the need for ad hoc tailoring of baselines by organizations through the selection of a set of controls and control enhancements that more closely correspond to common circumstances, situations, and/or conditions. However, the use of overlays does not in any way preclude organizations from performing further tailoring (i.e., overlays can also be subject to tailoring) to reflect organization-specific needs, assumptions, or constraints. For further information on creating overlays, refer to SP 800-53, Section 3.3 and Appendix I.

Appendix G— includes an ICS-specific overlay of applicable NIST SP 800-53 controls that provide tailored baselines for low-impact, moderate-impact, and high-impact ICS. These tailored baselines can be utilized as starting specifications and recommendations that can be applied to specific ICS by responsible personnel. As discussed in earlier sections, the use of an overlay does not in any way preclude organizations from performing further tailoring to add or remove controls and control enhancements (i.e., overlays can also be subject to tailoring) to reflect organization-specific needs, assumptions, or constraints.

Additionally, ICS owners can take advantage of the ability to tailor the initial baselines presented in the Appendix G— Overlay when it is not possible or feasible to implement specific security controls contained in the baselines. However, all tailoring activity should, as its primary goal, focus on meeting the intent of the original security controls whenever possible or feasible. For example, in situations where the ICS cannot support, or the organization determines it is not advisable to implement particular security controls or control enhancements in an ICS (e.g., performance, safety, or reliability are adversely impacted), the organization provides a complete and convincing rationale for how the selected compensating controls provide an equivalent security capability or level of protection for the ICS and why the related baseline security controls could not be employed. If the ICS cannot support the use of automated mechanisms, the organization employs non-automated mechanisms or procedures as compensating controls in accordance with the general tailoring guidance in Section 3.3 of NIST SP 800-53. Compensating controls are not exceptions or waivers to the baseline controls; rather, they are alternative safeguards and countermeasures employed within the ICS that accomplish the intent of the original security controls that could not be effectively employed. Organizational decisions on the use of compensating controls are documented in the security plan for the ICS.

6.1.3   Step 3: Implement Security Controls

This activity involves the implementation of security controls in new or legacy information systems. The security control selection process described in this section can be applied to ICS from two different perspectives: (i) new development; and (ii) legacy.

For new development systems, the security control selection process is applied from a requirements definition perspective since the systems do not yet exist and organizations are conducting initial security categorizations. The security controls included in the security plans for the information systems serve as a security specification and are expected to be incorporated into the systems during the development and implementation phases of the system development life cycle.

In contrast, for legacy information systems, the security control selection process is applied from a gap analysis perspective when organizations are anticipating significant changes to the systems (e.g., during major upgrades, modifications, or outsourcing). Since the information systems already exist, organizations in all likelihood have completed the security categorization and security control selection processes resulting in the establishment of previously agreed-upon security controls in the respective security plans and the implementation of those controls within the information systems.

6.1.4   Step 4: Assess Security Controls

This activity determines the extent to which the security controls in the information system are effective in their application. NIST SP 800-53A provides guidance for assessing security controls initially selected from NIST SP 800-53 to ensure that they are implemented correctly, operating as intended, and producing the desired outcome with respect to meeting the security requirements of the system. To accomplish this, NIST SP 800-53A provides expectations based on assurance requirements defined in NIST SP 800-53 for characterizing the expectations of security assessments by FIPS 199 impact level.

6.1.5   Step 5: Authorize Information System

This activity results in a management decision to authorize the operation of an information system and to explicitly accept the risk to agency operations, agency assets, or individuals based on the implementation of an agreed-upon set of security controls.

6.1.6 Step 6: Monitor Security Controls

This activity continuously tracks changes to the information system that may affect security controls and assesses control effectiveness. NIST SP 800-137 provides guidance on information security continuous monitoring [21].

6.2 Guidance on the Application of Security Controls to ICS

Because today's ICS are often a combination of legacy systems, often with a planned life span of twenty to thirty years, or a hybrid of legacy systems augmented with newer hardware and software that are interconnected to other systems, it is often difficult or infeasible to apply some of the security controls contained in NIST SP 800-53. While many controls in Appendix F of NIST SP 800-53 are applicable to ICS as written, several controls did require ICS-specific interpretation and/or augmentation. Appendix I of NIST SP 800-53 provides an example overlay template and additional information on each section of the overlay.

The NIST SP 800-53 controls are organized into 18 families; each family contains security controls related to the general security topic of the family. Security controls may involve aspects of policy, oversight, supervision, manual processes, actions by individuals, or automated mechanisms implemented by information systems/devices. The 18 security-related areas discussed in the following sections are:

- **Access Control (AC):** the process of granting or denying specific requests for obtaining and using information and related information processing services for physical access to areas within the information system environment.

- **Awareness and Training (AT):** policies and procedures to ensure that all information system users are given appropriate security training relative to their usage of the system and that accurate training records are maintained.

- **Audit and Accountability (AU):** independent review and examination of records and activities to assess the adequacy of system controls, to ensure compliance with established policies and operational procedures, and to recommend necessary changes in controls, policies, or procedures.

- **Security Assessment and Authorization (CA):** assurance that the specified controls are implemented correctly, operating as intended, and producing the desired outcome.

- **Contingency Planning (CP):** policies and procedures designed to maintain or restore business operations, including computer operations, possibly at an alternate location, in the event of emergencies, system failures, or disaster.

- **Configuration Management (CM):** policies and procedures for controlling modifications to hardware, firmware, software, and documentation to ensure the information system is protected against improper modifications prior to, during, and after system implementation.

- **Identification and Authentication (IA):** the process of verifying the identity of a user, process, or device, through the use of specific credentials (e.g., passwords, tokens, biometrics), as a prerequisite for granting access to resources in an IT system.

- **Incident Response (IR):** policies and procedures pertaining to incident response training, testing, handling, monitoring, reporting, and support services.

- **Maintenance (MA):** policies and procedures to manage all maintenance aspects of an information system.

- **Media Protection (MP):** policies and procedures to ensure secure handling of media. Controls cover access, labeling, storage, transport, sanitization, destruction, and disposal.

- **Physical and Environmental Protection (PE):** policies and procedures addressing physical, transmission, and display access control as well as environmental controls for conditioning (e.g., temperature, humidity) and emergency provisions (e.g., shutdown, power, lighting, fire protection).

- **Planning (PL):** development and maintenance of a plan to address information system security by performing assessments, specifying and implementing security controls, assigning security levels, and responding to incidents.

- **Personnel Security (PS):** policies and procedures for personnel position categorization, screening, transfer, penalty, and termination; also addresses third-party personnel security.

- **Risk Assessment (RA):** the process of identifying risks to operations, assets, or individuals by determining the probability of occurrence, the resulting impact, and additional security controls that would mitigate this impact.

- **System and Services Acquisition (SA):** allocation of resources for information system security to be maintained throughout the systems life cycle and the development of acquisition policies based on risk assessment results including requirements, design criteria, test procedures, and associated documentation.

- **System and Communications Protection (SC):** mechanisms for protecting both system and data transmission components.

- **System and Information Integrity (SI):** policies and procedures to protect information systems and their data from design flaws and data modification using functionality verification, data integrity checking, intrusion detection, malicious code detection, and security alert and advisory controls.

- **Program Management (PM):** provides security controls at the organizational rather than the information-system level.

Additionally, Appendix J of NIST SP 800-53 Rev. 4 includes a catalog of Privacy Controls. Privacy controls are the administrative, technical, and physical safeguards employed within organizations to protect and ensure the proper handling of personally identifiable information (PII).[18] The 8 privacy control families are each aligned with the Fair Information Practice Principles (FIPPS),[19] which are designed to build public trust in an organization's privacy practices and to help organizations avoid tangible costs and intangible damages stemming from privacy incidents.

---

[18] OMB Memorandum 07-16 defines PII as "information which can be used to distinguish or trace an individual's identity such as their name, social security number, biometric records, etc., alone, or when combined with other personal or identifying information which is linked or linkable to a specific individual, such as date and place of birth, mother's maiden name, etc." [86]. OMB Memorandum 10-22 reaffirmed this definition [87]. NIST Special Publication 800-122 defines PII as "any information about an individual [that is] maintained by an agency, including: (i) any information that can be used to distinguish or trace an individual's identity, such as name, social security number, date and place of birth, mother's maiden name, or biometric records; and (ii) any other information that is linked or linkable to an individual, such as medical, educational, financial, and employment information" [88].

[19] The FIPPs are widely accepted in the United States and internationally as a general framework for privacy and are reflected in other federal and international laws and policies. In a number of organizations, FIPPs serve as the basis for analyzing privacy risks and determining appropriate mitigation strategies. The Federal Enterprise Architecture Security and Privacy Profile (FEA-SPP) also provided information and materials in development of the privacy controls [89].

Sections 6.2.1 through 6.2.19 introduce each of the SP 800-53 control families and privacy controls, provide background information on the control family, as well as any ICS guidance and implementation considerations for ICS owners. ICS-specific recommendations and guidance, if available, is provided in an outlined box for each section. Much of the ICS-specific guidance was derived from ISA-62443 [34] and the EPRI report: *Supervisory Control and Data Acquisition (SCADA) Systems Security Guide* [62].

6.2.1 Access Control

The security controls that fall within the NIST SP 800-53 Access Control (AC) family provide policies and procedures for specifying the use of system resources by only authorized users, programs, processes, or other systems. This family specifies controls for managing information system accounts, including establishing, activating, modifying, reviewing, disabling, and removing accounts. Controls cover access and flow enforcement issues such as separation of duties, least privilege, unsuccessful login attempts, system use notification, previous logon notification, concurrent session control, session lock, and session termination. There are also controls to address the use of portable and remote devices and personally owned information systems to access the information system as well as the use of remote access capabilities and the implementation of wireless technologies. Access can take several forms, including viewing, using, and altering specific data or device functions.

Supplemental guidance for the AC controls can be found in the following documents:

- NIST SP 800-63 provides guidance on remote electronic authentication [53].

- NIST SP 800-48 provides guidance on wireless network security with particular emphasis on the IEEE 802.11b and Bluetooth standards 0.

- NIST SP 800-97 provides guidance on IEEE 802.11i wireless network security [64].

- FIPS 201 provides requirements for the personal identity verification of federal employees and contractors [65].

- NIST SP 800-96 provides guidance on PIV card to reader interoperability [66].

- NIST SP 800-73 provides guidance on interfaces for personal identity verification [49].

- NIST SP 800-76 provides guidance on biometrics for personal identity verification [50].

- NIST SP 800-78 provides guidance on cryptographic algorithms and key sizes for personal identity verification [67].

If the new federal Personal Identity Verification (PIV) is used as an identification token, the access control system should conform to the requirements of FIPS 201 and NIST SP 800-73 and employ either cryptographic verification or biometric verification. When token-based access control employs cryptographic verification, the access control system should conform to the requirements of NIST SP 800-78. When token-based access control employs biometric verification, the access control system should conform to the requirements of NIST SP 800-76.

Access control technologies are filter and blocking technologies designed to direct and regulate the flow of information between devices or systems once authorization has been determined. The following sections present several access control technologies and their use with ICS.

6.2.1.1 Role-based Access Control (RBAC)

RBAC is a technology that has the potential to reduce the complexity and cost of security administration in networks with large numbers of intelligent devices. Under RBAC, security administration is simplified through the use of roles, hierarchies, and constraints to organize user access levels. RBAC reduces costs within an organization because it accepts that employees change roles and responsibilities more frequently than the duties within roles and responsibilities.

ICS-specific Recommendations and Guidance

RBAC can be used to provide a uniform means to manage access to ICS devices while reducing the cost of maintaining individual device access levels and minimizing errors. RBAC should be used to restrict ICS user privileges to only those that are required to perform each person's job (i.e., configuring each role based on the principle of least privilege). The level of access can take several forms, including viewing, using, and altering specific ICS data or device functions.

RBAC tools can set, modify, or remove authorizations in applications, but they do not replace the authorization mechanism; they do not check and authenticate users every time a user wants to access an application. RBAC tools offer interfaces to authorization mechanisms for most current platforms in the IT arena. However, legacy ICS systems or specialized ICS equipment may require development of specialized interface software. This issue is a large problem for ICS that use a number of proprietary operating systems or customized operating system implementations and interfaces.

6.2.1.2 Web Servers

Web and Internet technologies are being added to a wide variety of ICS products because they make information more accessible and products more user-friendly and easier to configure remotely. However, they may also add cyber risks and create new security vulnerabilities that need to be addressed.

ICS-specific Recommendations and Guidance

SCADA and historian software vendors typically provide Web servers as a product option so that users outside the control room can access ICS information. In many cases, software components such as ActiveX controls or Java applets must be installed or downloaded onto each client machine accessing the Web server. Some products, such as PLCs and other control devices, are available with embedded Web, FTP, and email servers to make them easier to configure remotely and allow them to generate email notifications and reports when certain conditions occur. When feasible, use HTTPS rather than HTTP, use SFTP or SCP rather than FTP, block inbound FTP and email traffic, etc. Security appliances (or gateways) are beginning to appear with application proxies able to examine Web, FTP, and email traffic to block attacks and prevent downloading of ActiveX® controls or Java® applets.
Unless there is substantial benefit to connecting ICSs to the Internet, the systems are best left not connected.

6.2.1.3 Virtual Local Area Network (VLAN)

VLANs divide physical networks into smaller logical networks to increase performance, improve manageability, and simplify network design. VLANs are achieved through configuration of Ethernet switches. Each VLAN consists of a single broadcast domain that isolates traffic from other VLANs. Just as replacing hubs with switches reduces collisions, using VLANs limits the broadcast traffic, as well as allowing logical subnets to span multiple physical locations. There are two categories of VLANs:

- Static, often referred to as port-based, where switch ports are assigned to a VLAN so that it is transparent to the end user.

- Dynamic, where an end device negotiates VLAN characteristics with the switch or determines the VLAN based on the IP or hardware addresses.

Although more than one IP subnet may coexist on the same VLAN, the general recommendation is to use a one-to-one relationship between subnets and VLANs. This practice requires the use of a router or multi-layer switch to join multiple VLANs. Many routers and firewalls support tagged frames so that a single physical interface can be used to route between multiple logical networks.

VLANs are not typically deployed to address host or network vulnerabilities in the way that firewalls or IDS are deployed. However, when properly configured, VLANs do allow switches to enforce security policies and segregate traffic at the Ethernet layer. Properly segmented networks can also mitigate the risks of broadcast storms that may result from port scanning or worm activity.

Switches have been susceptible to attacks such as MAC spoofing, table overflows, and attacks against the spanning tree protocols, depending on the device and its configuration. VLAN hopping, the ability for an attack to inject frames to unauthorized ports, has been demonstrated using switch spoofing or double-encapsulated frames. These attacks cannot be conducted remotely and require local physical access to the switch. A variety of features such as MAC address filtering, port-based authentication using IEEE 802.1x, and specific vendor recommended practices can be used to mitigate these attacks, depending on the device and implementation.

ICS-specific Recommendations and Guidance

VLANs have been effectively deployed in ICS networks, with each automation cell assigned to a single VLAN to limit unnecessary traffic flooding and allow network devices on the same VLAN to span multiple switches [34].

6.2.1.4 Dial-up Modems

ICS systems have stringent reliability and availability requirements. When there is a need to troubleshoot and repair, the technical resources may not be physically located at the control room or facility. Therefore, ICS often use modems to enable vendors, system integrators, or control engineers maintaining the system to dial in and diagnose, repair, configure, and perform maintenance on the network or component. While this allows easy access for authorized personnel, if the dial-up modems are not properly secured, they can also provide backdoor entries for unauthorized use.

Dial-up often uses remote control software that gives the remote user powerful (administrative or root) access to the target system. Such software usually has security options that should be carefully reviewed and configured.

ICS-specific Recommendations and Guidance

- Consider using callback systems when dial-up modems are installed in an ICS. This ensures that a dialer is an authorized user by having the modem establish the working connection based on the dialer's information and a callback number stored in the ICS approved authorized user list.

- Ensure that default passwords have been changed and strong passwords are in place for each modem.

- Physically identify modems in use to the control room operators.

- Configure remote control software to use unique user names and passwords, strong authentication, encryption if determined appropriate, and audit logs. Use of this software by remote users should be monitored on an almost real-time frequency.

- If feasible, disconnect modems when not in use or consider automating this disconnection process by having modems disconnect after being on for a given amount of time. It should be noted that sometimes modem connections are part of the legal support service agreement with the vendor (e.g., 24x7 support with 15 minute response time). Personnel should be aware that disconnecting/removing the modems may require that contracts be renegotiated.

6.2.1.5 Wireless

The use of wireless within an ICS is a risk-based decision that has to be determined by the organization. Generally, wireless LANs should only be deployed where health, safety, environmental, and financial implications are low. NIST SP 800-48 and SP 800-97 provide guidance on wireless network security.

ICS-specific Recommendations and Guidance

Wireless LANs

- Prior to installation, a wireless survey should be performed to determine antenna location and strength to minimize exposure of the wireless network. The survey should take into account the fact that attackers can use powerful directional antennas, which extend the effective range of a wireless LAN beyond the expected standard range. Faraday cages and other methods are also available to minimize exposure of the wireless network outside of the designated areas.

- Wireless users' access should utilize IEEE 802.1x authentication using a secure authentication protocol (e.g., Extensible Authentication Protocol [EAP] with TLS [EAP-TLS]) that authenticates users via a user certificates or a Remote Authentication Dial In User Service (RADIUS) server.

- The wireless access points and data servers for wireless worker devices should be located on an isolated network with documented and minimal (single if possible) connections to the ICS network.

- Wireless access points should be configured to have a unique service set identifier (SSID), disable SSID broadcast, and enable MAC filtering at a minimum.

- Wireless devices, if being utilized in a Microsoft Windows ICS network, should be configured into a separate organizational unit of the Windows domain.

- Wireless device communications should be encrypted and integrity-protected. The encryption must not degrade the operational performance of the end device. Encryption at OSI Layer 2 should be considered, rather than at Layer 3 to reduce encryption latency. The use of hardware accelerators to perform cryptographic functions should also be considered.

For mesh networks, consider the use of broadcast key versus public key management implemented at OSI Layer 2 to maximize performance. Asymmetric cryptography should be used to perform administrative functions, and symmetric encryption should be used to secure each data stream as well as network control traffic. An adaptive routing protocol should be considered if the devices are to be used for wireless mobility. The convergence time of the network should be as fast as possible supporting rapid network recovery in the event of a failure or power loss. The use of a mesh network may provide fault tolerance thru alternate route selection and pre-emptive fail-over of the network.

Wireless field networks

The ISA100[20] Committee is working to establish standards, recommended practices, technical reports, and related information that will define procedures for implementing wireless systems in the automation and control environment with a focus on the field level (e.g., IEEE 802.15.4). Guidance is directed towards those responsible for the complete life cycle including the designing, implementing, on-going maintenance, scalability or managing industrial automation and control systems, and applies to users, system integrators, practitioners, and control systems manufacturers and vendors.

---

[20] Additional information on ISA100 at: http://www.isa.org/isa100.

6.2.2 Awareness and Training

The security controls that fall within the NIST SP 800-53 Awareness and Training (AT) family provide policy and procedures for ensuring that all users of an information system are provided basic information system security awareness and training materials before authorization to access the system is granted. Personnel training must be monitored and documented.

Supplemental guidance for the AT controls can be found in the following documents:

■ NIST SP 800-50 provides guidance on security awareness training [61].

■ NIST SP 800-100 provides guidance on information security governance and planning [27].

ICS-specific Recommendations and Guidance

For the ICS environment, this must include control system-specific information security awareness and training for specific ICS applications. In addition, an organization must identify, document, and train all personnel having significant ICS roles and responsibilities. Awareness and training must cover the physical process being controlled as well as the ICS.

Security awareness is a critical part of ICS incident prevention, particularly when it comes to social engineering threats. Social engineering is a technique used to manipulate individuals into giving away private information, such as passwords. This information can then be used to compromise otherwise secure systems.

Implementing an ICS security program may bring changes to the way in which personnel access computer programs, applications, and the computer desktop itself. Organizations should design effective training programs and communication vehicles to help employees understand why new access and control methods are required, ideas they can use to reduce risks, and the impact on the organization if control methods are not incorporated. Training programs also demonstrate management's commitment to, and the value of, a cybersecurity program. Feedback from staff exposed to this type of training can be a valuable source of input for refining the charter and scope of the security program.

6.2.3 Audit and Accountability

An audit is an independent review and examination of records and activities to assess the adequacy of system controls, to ensure compliance with established policies and operational procedures, and to recommend necessary changes in controls, policies, or procedures. The security controls that fall within the NIST SP 800-53 Audit and Accountability (AU) family provide policies and procedures for generating audit records, their content, capacity, and retention requirements. The controls also provide safeguards to react to problems such as an audit failure or audit log capacity being reached. Audit data should be protected from modification and be designed with non-repudiation capability.

Supplemental guidance for the AU controls can be found in the following documents:

■ NIST SP 800-61 provides guidance on computer security incident handling and audit log retention [59].

- NIST SP 800-92 provides guidance on log management (including audit logs) [68].

- NIST SP 800-100 provides guidance on information security governance and planning [27].

ICS-specific Recommendations and Guidance

It is necessary to determine that the system is performing as intended. Periodic audits of the ICS should be performed to validate the following items:

- The security controls present during system validation testing (e.g., factory acceptance testing and site acceptance testing) are still installed and operating correctly in the production system.

- The production system is free from security compromises and provides information on the nature and extent of compromises as feasible, should they occur.

- The management of change program is being rigorously followed with an audit trail of reviews and approvals for all changes.

The results from each periodic audit should be expressed in the form of performance against a set of predefined and appropriate metrics to display security performance and security trends. Security performance metrics should be sent to the appropriate stakeholders, along with a view of security performance trends.

Traditionally, the primary basis for audit in IT systems has been recordkeeping. Using appropriate tools within an ICS environment requires extensive knowledge from an IT professional familiar with the ICS, critical production and safety implications for the facility. Many of the process control devices that are integrated into the ICS have been installed for many years and do not have the capability to provide the audit records described in this section. Therefore, the applicability of these more modern tools for auditing system and network activity is dependent upon the capabilities of the components in the ICS.

The critical tasks in managing a network in an ICS environment are ensuring reliability and availability to support safe and efficient operation. In regulated industries, regulatory compliance can add complexity to security and authentication management, registry and installation integrity management, and all functions that can augment an installation and operational qualification exercise. Diligent use of auditing and log management tools can provide valuable assistance in maintaining and proving the integrity of the ICS from installation through the system life cycle. The value of these tools in this environment can be calculated by the effort required to re-qualify or otherwise retest the ICS where the integrity due to attack, accident, or error is in question. The system should provide reliable, synchronized time stamps in support of the audit tools.

Monitoring of sensors, logs, Intrusion Detection Systems (IDS), antivirus, patch management, policy management software, and other security mechanisms should be done on a real-time basis where feasible. A first-line monitoring service would receive alarms, do rapid initial problem determination and take action to alert appropriate facility personnel to intervene.

System auditing utilities should be incorporated into new and existing ICS projects. These auditing utilities should be tested (e.g., off-line on a comparable ICS) before being deployed on an operational ICS. These tools can provide tangible records of evidence and system integrity. Additionally, active log management utilities may actually flag an attack or event in progress and provide location and tracing information to help respond to the incident [34].

There should be a method for tracing all console activities to a user, either manually (e.g., control room sign in) or automatic (e.g., login at the application and/or OS layer). Policies and procedures for what is logged, how the logs are stored (or printed), how they are protected, who has access to the logs and how/when are they reviewed should be developed. These policies and procedures will vary with the ICS application and platform. Legacy systems typically employ printer loggers, which are reviewed by administrative, operational, and security staff. Logs maintained by the ICS application may be stored at various locations and may or may not be encrypted.

6.2.4　Security Assessment and Authorization

The security controls that fall within the NIST SP 800-53 Assessment and Authorization (CA) family provide the basis for performing periodic assessments and providing certification of the security controls implemented in the information system to determine if the controls are implemented correctly, operating as intended, and producing the desired outcome to meet the system security requirements. A senior organizational official is responsible for accepting residual risk and authorizing system operation. These steps constitute accreditation. In addition, all security controls should be monitored on an ongoing basis. Monitoring activities include configuration management and control of information system components, security impact analysis of changes to the system, ongoing assessment of security controls, and status reporting.

Supplemental guidance for the CA controls can be found in the following documents:

- NIST SP 800-53A provides guidance on security control assessments [23].

- NIST SP 800-37 provides guidance defining the information system boundary and security certification and accreditation of the information system [21].

- NIST SP 800-100 provides guidance on information security governance and planning [27].

6.2.5　Configuration Management

Configuration management policy and procedures are used to control modifications to hardware, firmware, software, and documentation to ensure that the information system is protected against improper modifications prior to, during, and after system implementation. The security controls that fall within the NIST SP 800-53 Configuration Management (CM) family provide policy and procedures for establishing baseline controls for information systems. Controls are also specified for maintaining, monitoring, and documenting configuration control changes. There should be restricted access to configuration settings, and security settings of IT products should be set to the most restrictive mode consistent with ICS operational requirements.

Supplemental guidance for the CM controls can be found in the following documents:

- NIST SP 800-70 provides guidance on configuration settings for IT products [26].

- NIST SP 800-100 provides guidance on information security governance and planning [27].

- NIST SP 800-128 provides guidance on implementation of a security-focused configuration management program [80].

ICS-specific Recommendations and Guidance

A formal change management program should be established and procedures used to insure that all modifications to an ICS network meet the same security requirements as the original components identified in the asset evaluation and the associated risk assessment and mitigation plans. Risk assessment should be performed on all changes to the ICS network that could affect security, including configuration changes, the addition of network components, and installation of software. Changes to policies and procedures may also be required. The current ICS network configuration and device configurations must always be known and documented.

6.2.6 Contingency Planning

Contingency plans are designed to maintain or restore business operations, including computer operations, possibly at an alternate location, in the event of emergencies, system failures, or disaster. The security controls that fall within the NIST SP 800-53 Contingency Planning (CP) family provide policies and procedures to implement a contingency plan by specifying roles and responsibilities, and assigning personnel and activities associated with restoring the information system after a disruption or failure. Along with planning, controls also exist for contingency training, testing, and plan update, and for backup information processing and storage sites.

Supplemental guidance for the CP controls can be found in the following documents:

■ NIST SP 800-34 provides guidance on contingency planning [52].

■ NIST SP 800-100 provides guidance on information security governance and planning [27].

ICS-specific Recommendations and Guidance

Contingency plans should cover the full range of failures or problems that could be caused by cyber incidents. Contingency plans should include procedures for restoring systems from known valid backups, separating systems from all non-essential interferences and connections that could permit cybersecurity intrusions, and alternatives to achieve necessary interfaces and coordination. Employees should be trained and familiar with the contents of the contingency plans. Contingency plans should be periodically reviewed with employees responsible for restoration of the ICS, and tested to ensure that they continue to meet their objectives. Organizations also have business continuity plans and disaster recovery plans that are closely related to contingency plans. Because business continuity and disaster recovery plans are particularly important for ICS, they are described in more detail in the sections to follow.

6.2.6.1 Business Continuity Planning

Business continuity planning addresses the overall issue of maintaining or reestablishing production in the case of an interruption. These interruptions may take the form of a natural disaster (e.g., hurricane, tornado, earthquake, flood), an unintentional man-made event (e.g., accidental equipment damage, fire or explosion, operator error), an intentional man-made event (e.g., attack by bomb, firearm or vandalism, attacker or virus), or an equipment failure. From a potential outage perspective, this may involve typical time spans of days, weeks, or months to recover from a natural disaster, or minutes or hours to recover from a malware infection or a mechanical/electrical failure. Because there is often a separate discipline that deals with reliability and electrical/mechanical maintenance, some organizations choose to define business continuity in a way that excludes these sources of failure. Because business continuity also deals primarily with the long-term implications of production outages, some organizations also choose to place a minimum interruption limit on the risks to be considered. For the purposes of ICS cybersecurity, it is recommended that neither of these constraints be made. Long-term outages (disaster recovery) and short-term outages (operational recovery) should both be considered. Because some of these potential interruptions involve man-made events, it is also important to work collaboratively with the physical security organization to understand the relative risks of these events and the physical security countermeasures that are in place to prevent them. It is also important for the physical security organization to understand which areas of a production site house data acquisition and control systems that might have higher-level risks.

Before creating a business continuity plan (BCP) to deal with potential outages, it is important to specify the recovery objectives for the various systems and subsystems involved based on typical business needs. There are two distinct types of objectives: system recovery and data recovery. System recovery involves the recovery of communication links and processing capabilities, and it is usually specified in terms of a Recovery Time Objective (RTO). This is defined as the time required to recover the required communication links and processing capabilities. Data recovery involves the recovery of data describing production or product conditions in the past and is usually specified in terms of a Recovery Point Objective (RPO). This is defined as the longest period of time for which an absence of data can be tolerated.

Once the recovery objectives are defined, a list of potential interruptions should be created and the recovery procedure developed and described. For most of the smaller scale interruptions, repair and replace activities based on a critical spares inventory will prove adequate to meet the recovery objectives. When this is not true, contingency plans need to be developed. Due to the potential cost and importance of these contingency plans, they should be reviewed with the managers responsible for business continuity planning to verify that they are justified. Once the recovery procedures are documented, a schedule should be developed to test part or all of the recovery procedures. Particular attention must be paid to the verification of backups of system configuration data and product or production data. Examples of system configuration data include computer configuration backups, application configuration backups, operational control limits, control bands and setpoints for pre-incident operation for all ICS programmable equipment. Not only should these be tested when they are produced, but the procedures followed for their storage should also be reviewed periodically to verify that the backups are kept in environmental conditions that will not render them unusable and that they are kept in a secure location, so they can be quickly obtained by authorized individuals when needed.

6.2.6.2 Disaster Recovery Planning

A disaster recovery plan (DRP) is a documented process or set of procedures to recover and protect an IT infrastructure in the event of a disaster. The DRP, ordinarily documented in written form, specifies procedures an organization is to follow in the event of a disaster. It is a comprehensive statement of consistent actions to be taken before, during and after a disaster. The disaster could be natural, environmental or man-made. Man-made disasters could be intentional or unintentional.

ICS-specific Recommendations and Guidance

A DRP is essential to continued availability of the ICS. The DRP should include the following items:

- Required response to events or conditions of varying duration and severity that would activate the recovery plan.

- Procedures for operating the ICS in manual mode with all external electronic connections severed until secure conditions can be restored.

- Roles and responsibilities of responders.

- Processes and procedures for the backup and secure storage of information.

- Complete and up-to-date logical network diagram.

- Personnel list for authorized physical and cyber access to the ICS.

- Communication procedure and list of personnel to contact in the case of an emergency including ICS vendors, network administrators, ICS support personnel, etc.

- Current configuration information for all components.

- Schedule for exercising the DRP.

The plan should also indicate requirements for the timely replacement of components in the case of an emergency. If possible, replacements for hard-to-obtain critical components should be kept in inventory.

The security plan should define a comprehensive backup and restore policy. In formulating this policy, the following should be considered:

- The speed at which data or the system must be restored. This requirement may justify the need for a redundant system, spare offline computer, or valid file system backups.

- The frequency at which critical data and configurations are changing. This will dictate the frequency and completeness of backups.

- The safe onsite and offsite storage of full and incremental backups.

- The safe storage of installation media, license keys, and configuration information.

- Identification of individuals responsible for performing, testing, storing, and restoring backups.

6.2.7   Identification and Authentication

Authentication describes the process of positively identifying potential network users, hosts, applications, services, and resources using a combination of identification factors or credentials. The result of this authentication process then becomes the basis for permitting or denying further actions (e.g., when an automatic teller machine asks for a PIN). Based on the authentication determination, the system may or may not allow the potential user access to its resources. Authorization is the process of determining who and what should be allowed to have access to a particular resource; access control is the mechanism for enforcing authorization. Access control is described in Section 6.2.1.

There are several possible factors for determining the authenticity of a person, device, or system, including something you know, something you have or something you are. For example, authentication could be based on something known (e.g., PIN number or password), something possessed (e.g., key, dongle, smart card), something you are such as a biological characteristic (e.g., fingerprint, retinal signature), a location (e.g., Global Positioning System [GPS] location access), the time a request is made, or a combination of these attributes. In general, the more factors that are used in the authentication process, the more robust the process will be. When two or more factors are used, the process is known generically as *multi-factor authentication*.

The security controls that fall within the NIST SP 800-53 Identification and Authentication (IA) family provide policy and guidance for the identification and authentication of users of and devices within the information system. These include controls to manage identifiers and authenticators within each technology used (e.g., tokens, certificates, biometrics, passwords, key cards).

Supplemental guidance for the IA controls can be found in the following documents:

- NIST SP 800-63 provides guidance on remote electronic authentication [53].

- NIST SP 800-73 provides guidance on interfaces for personal identity verification [49].

- NIST SP 800-76 provides guidance on biometrics for personal identity verification [50].

- NIST SP 800-100 provides guidance on information security governance and planning [27].

ICS-specific Recommendations and Guidance

Computer systems in ICS environments typically rely on traditional passwords for authentication. Control system suppliers often supply systems with default passwords. These passwords are factory set and are often easy to guess or are changed infrequently, which creates additional security risks. Also, protocols currently used in ICS environments generally have inadequate or no network service authentication. There are now several forms of authentication available in addition to traditional password techniques being used with ICS. Some of these, including password authentication, are presented in the following sections with discussions regarding their use with ICS.

6.2.7.1　Password Authentication

Password authentication technologies determine authenticity based on testing for something the device or human requesting access should know, such as a PIN number or password. Password authentication schemes are thought of as the simplest and most common forms of authentication.

Password vulnerabilities can be reduced by using an active password checker that prohibits weak, recently used, or commonly used passwords. Another weakness is the ease of third-party eavesdropping. Passwords typed at a keyboard are easily observed or recorded, especially in areas where adversaries could plant tiny wireless cameras or keystroke loggers. Network service authentication often transmits passwords as plaintext (unencrypted), allowing any network capture tool to expose the passwords.

ICS-specific Recommendations and Guidance

One problem with passwords unique to the ICS environment is that a user's ability to recall and enter a password may be impacted by the stress of the moment. During a major crisis when human intervention is critically required to control the process, an operator may panic and have difficulty remembering or entering the password and either be locked out completely or be delayed in responding to the event. If the password has been entered wrong and the system has a limit on allowed wrong password entries, the operator may be locked out permanently until an authorized employee can reset the account. Biometric identifiers may have similar drawbacks. Organizations should carefully consider the security needs and the potential ramifications of the use of authentication mechanisms on these critical systems.

In situations where the ICS cannot support, or the organization determines it is not advisable (e.g., performance, safety, or reliability are adversely impacted), to implement authentication mechanisms in an ICS, the organization uses compensating controls, such as rigorous physical security controls (e.g., control center keycard access for authorized users) to provide an equivalent security capability or level of protection for the ICS. This guidance also applies to the use of session lock and session termination in an ICS.

Special consideration must be made when pushing down policies based on login password authentication within the ICS environment. Without an exclusion list based on machine identification (ID), non-operator logon can result in policies being pushed down such as auto- logoff timeout and administrator password replacement that can be detrimental to the operation of the system.

Some ICS operating systems make setting secure passwords difficult, as the password size is very small and the system allows only group passwords at each level of access, not individual passwords. Some industrial (and Internet) protocols transmit passwords in plaintext, making them susceptible to interception. In cases where this practice cannot be avoided, it is important that users have different (and unrelated) passwords for use with encrypted and non-encrypted protocols.

The following are general recommendations and considerations with regards to the use of passwords.

- The length, strength, and complexity of passwords should balance security and operational ease of access within the capabilities of the software and underlying OS.

- Passwords should have appropriate length and complexity for the required security. In particular, they should not be able to be found in a dictionary or contain predictable sequences of numbers or letters.

- Passwords should be used with care on operator interface devices such as control consoles on critical processes. Using passwords on these consoles could introduce potential safety issues if operators are locked out or delayed access during critical events. Physical security should supplement operator control consoles when password protection is not feasible.

- The keeper of master passwords should be a trusted employee, available during emergencies. Any copies of the master passwords must be stored in a very secure location with limited access.

- The passwords of privileged users (such as network technicians, electrical or electronics technicians and management, and network designers/operators) should be most secure and be changed frequently. Authority to change master passwords should be limited to trusted employees. A password audit record, especially for master passwords, should be maintained separately from the control system.

- In environments with a high risk of interception or intrusion (such as remote operator interfaces in a facility that lacks local physical security access controls), organizations should consider supplementing password authentication with other forms of authentication such as multi-factor authentication using biometric or physical tokens.

- For user authentication purposes, password use is common and generally acceptable for users logging directly into a local device or computer. Passwords should not be sent across any network unless protected by some form of FIPS-approved encryption or salted cryptographic hash specifically designed to prevent replay attacks. It is assumed that the device used to enter a password is connected to the network in a secure manner.

- For network service authentication purposes, passwords should not be passed as plain text. There are more secure alternatives available, such as challenge/response or public key authentication.

6.2.7.2 Challenge/response Authentication

Challenge/response authentication requires that both the service requester and service provider know a "secret" code in advance. When service is requested, the service provider sends a random number or string as a challenge to the service requester. The service requester uses the secret code to generate a unique response for the service provider. If the response is as expected, it proves that the service requester has access to the "secret" without ever exposing the secret on the network.

Challenge/response authentication addresses the security vulnerabilities of traditional password authentication. When passwords (hashed or plain) are sent across a network, a portion of the actual "secret" itself is being sent, giving the secret to the remote device performs authentication. Therefore, traditional password exchange always suffers the risk of discovery or replay. Because the secret is known in advance and never sent in challenge/response systems, the risk of discovery is eliminated. If the service provider can never send the same challenge twice, and the receiver can detect all duplications, the risks of network capture and replay attacks are eliminated.

ICS-specific Recommendations and Guidance

For User Authentication, the direct use of challenge/response authentication may not be feasible for control system due to the possible latency that may be introduced in the necessary fast dynamics required for access to a control system or industrial network. For Network Service Authentication, the use of challenge/response authentication is preferable to more traditional password or source identity authentication schemes.

Challenge/response authentication provides more security than encrypted passwords for user authentication across a network. Managing master encryption algorithms and master passwords becomes increasing more complex as more parties are involved in the security processes and is an important consideration in the robustness of the security scheme.

6.2.7.3 Physical Token Authentication

Physical or token authentication is similar to password authentication, except that these technologies determine authenticity by testing for secret code or key produced by a device or token the person requesting access has in their possession, such as security tokens or smart cards. Increasingly, private keys are being embedded in physical devices such as USB dongles. Some tokens support single-factor authentication only, so that simply having possession of the token is sufficient to be authenticated. Others support multi-factor authentication that requires knowledge of a PIN or password in addition to possessing the token.

The primary vulnerability that token authentication addresses is easily duplicating a secret code or sharing it with others. It eliminates the all-too-common scenario of a password to a "secure" system being left on the wall next to a PC or operator station. The security token cannot be duplicated without special access to equipment and supplies.

A second benefit is that the secret within a physical token can be very large, physically secure, and randomly generated. Because it is embedded in metal or silicon, it does not have the same risks that manually entered passwords do. If a security token is lost or stolen, the authorized user loses access, unlike traditional passwords that can be lost or stolen without notice.

Common forms of physical/token authentication include:

- Traditional physical lock and keys.
- Security cards (e.g., magnetic, smart chip, optical coding).
- Radio frequency devices in the form of cards, key fobs, or mounted tags.
- Dongles with secure encryption keys that attach to the USB, serial, or parallel ports of computers.
- One-time authentication code generators (e.g., key fobs).

For single-factor authentication, the largest weakness is that physically holding the token means access is granted (e.g., anyone finding a set of lost keys now has access to whatever they open). Physical/token authentication is more secure when combined with a second form of authentication, such as a memorized PIN used along with the token.

ICS-specific Recommendations and Guidance

Multi-factor authentication is an accepted good practice for access to ICS applications from outside the ICS firewall.

Physical/token authentication has the potential for a strong role in ICS environments. An access card or other token can be an effective form of authentication for computer access, as long as the computer is in a secure area (e.g., once the operator has gained access to the room with appropriate secondary authentication, the card alone can be used to enable control actions).

6.2.7.4 Smart Card Authentication

Smart cards are similar to token authentication, but can provide additional functionality. Smart cards can be configured to run multiple on-board applications to support building access, computer dual-factor or triple-factor authentication and cashless vending on a single card, while also acting as the company photo ID for the individual.

Typically, smart cards come in a credit card size form-factor that can be printed, embossed, and individually personalized. Smart cards can be customized, individualized, and issued in-house or outsourced to service providers who typically issue hundreds of thousands of cards per day.
Smart cards enhance software-only solutions, such as password authentication, by offering an additional authentication factor and removing the human element in memorizing complex secrets. They also:

- Isolate security-critical computations, involving authentication, digital signatures, and key exchange from other parts of the system that do not have a need to know.
- Enable portability of credentials and other private information between multiple computer systems.
- Provide tamper-resistant storage for protecting private keys and other forms of personal information.

The majority of issues are logistical around issuing the cards, particularly to replace lost or stolen cards.

ICS-specific Recommendations and Guidance

Although smart cards are relatively inexpensive and offer useful functionality in an industrial control system context, their implementation must be done within the overall security context of the plant. The necessary identification of individuals, issuance of cards, revocation should compromise be suspected, and the assignment of authorizations to authenticated identities, represents a significant initial and on-going challenge. In some cases corporate IT or other resources may be available to assist in the deployment of smart card and public key based infrastructures.

If smart cards are implemented in an industrial control setting, provisions for management of lost or damaged cards should be considered, as well as the costs to incorporate a respective access control system and provide a management process for card distribution and retrieval.

6.2.7.5　Biometric Authentication

Biometric authentication technologies determine authenticity by determining presumably unique biological characteristics of the human requesting access. Usable biometric features include finger minutiae, facial geometry, retinal and iris signatures, voice patterns, typing patterns, and hand geometry.

Like physical tokens and smart cards, biometric authentication enhances software-only solutions, such as password authentication, by offering an additional authentication factor and removing the human element in memorizing complex secrets. In addition, because biometric characteristics are unique to a given individual, biometric authentication addresses the issues of lost or stolen physical tokens and smart cards.

Noted issues with biometric authentication include:

- Distinguishing a real object from a fake (e.g., how to distinguish a real human finger from a silicon-rubber cast of one or a real human voice from a recorded one).

- Generating type-I and type-II errors (the probability of rejecting a valid biometric image, and the probability of accepting an invalid biometric image, respectively). Biometric authentication devices should be configured to the lowest crossover between these two probabilities, also known as the crossover error rate.

- Handling environmental factors such as temperature and humidity to which some biometric devices are sensitive.

- Addressing industrial applications where employees may have on safety glasses and/or gloves and industrial chemicals may impact biometric scanners.

- Retraining biometric scanners that occasionally "drift" over time. Human biometric traits may also shift over time, necessitating periodic scanner retraining.

- Requiring face-to-face technical support and verification for device training, unlike a password that can be given over a phone or an access card that can be handed out by a receptionist.

- Denying needed access to the control system because of a temporary inability of the sensing device to acknowledge a legitimate user.

- Being socially acceptable. Users consider some biometric authentication devices more acceptable than others. For example, retinal scans may be considered very low on the scale of acceptability, while thumb print scanners may be considered high on the scale of acceptability. Users of biometric authentication devices will need to take social acceptability for their target group into consideration when selecting among various biometric authentication technologies.

ICS-specific Recommendations and Guidance

Biometric devices make a useful secondary check versus other forms of authentication that can become lost or borrowed. Using biometric authentication in combination with token-based access control or badge-operated employee time clocks increases the security level. A possible application is in a control room that is environmentally controlled and physically secured [34].

Biometrics can provide a valuable authentication mechanism, but need to be carefully assessed for industrial applications because physical and environmental issues within the installation environment may need to be restructured for reliable authorized authentication. The exact physical and environmental properties of an installation should be coordinated with a system vendor or manufacturer.

6.2.8 Incident Response

An incident response plan is documentation of a predetermined set of instructions or procedures to detect, respond to, and limit consequences of incidents against an organization's information systems. Response should be measured first and foremost against the "service being provided," not just the system that was compromised. If an incident is discovered, there should be a quick risk assessment performed to evaluate the effect of both the attack and the options to respond. For example, one possible response option is to physically isolate the system under attack. However, this may have such a dire impact on the service that it is dismissed as not viable.

The security controls that fall within the NIST SP 800-53 Incident Response (IR) family provide policies and procedures for incident response monitoring, handling, and reporting. The handling of a security incident includes preparation, detection and analysis, containment, eradication, and recovery. Controls also cover incident response training for personnel and testing the incident response capability for an information system.

Supplemental guidance for the IR controls can be found in the following documents:

■ NIST SP 800-61 provides guidance on incident handling and reporting [59].

■ NIST SP 800-83 provides guidance on malware incident prevention and handling [60].

■ NIST SP 800-100 provides guidance on information security governance and planning [27] .

ICS-specific Recommendations and Guidance

Regardless of the steps taken to protect an ICS, it is always possible that it may be compromised by an intentional or unintentional incident. The following symptoms can arise from normal network problems, but when several symptoms start to appear, a pattern may indicate the ICS is under attack and may be worth investigating further. If the adversary is skilled, it may not be very obvious that an attack is underway.

The symptoms of an incident could include any of the following:

■ Unusually heavy network traffic.

■ Out of disk space or significantly reduced free disk space.

■ Unusually high CPU usage.

■ Creation of new user accounts.

■ Attempted or actual use of administrator-level accounts.

■ Locked-out accounts.

■ Account in-use when the user is not at work.

■ Cleared log files.

■ Full log files with unusually large number of events.

- Antivirus or IDS alerts.

- Disabled antivirus software and other security controls.

- Unexpected patch changes.

- Machines connecting to outside IP addresses.

- Requests for information about the system (social engineering attempts).

- Unexpected changes in configuration settings.

- Unexpected system shutdown.

To minimize the effects of these intrusions, it is necessary to plan a response. Incident response planning defines procedures to be followed when an intrusion occurs. NIST SP 800-61 Revision 2, *Computer Security Incident Handling Guide* [59], provides guidance on incident response planning, which might include the following items:

- **Classification of Incidents.** The various types of ICS incidents should be identified and classified as to potential impact so that a proper response can be formulated for each potential incident.

- **Response Actions.** There are several responses that can be taken in the event of an incident. These range from doing nothing to full system shutdown (although full shutdown of an ICS is a highly unlikely response). The response taken will depend on the type of incident and its effect on the ICS system and the physical process being controlled. A written plan documenting the types of incidents and the response to each type should be prepared. This will provide guidance during times when there might be confusion or stress due to the incident. This plan should include step-by-step actions to be taken by the various organizations. If there are reporting requirements, these should be noted as well as where the report should be made and phone numbers to reduce reporting confusion.

- **Recovery Actions.** The results of the intrusion could be minor, or the intrusion could cause many problems in the ICS. Risk analysis should be conducted to determine the sensitivity of the physical system being controlled to failure modes in the ICS. In each case, step-by-step recovery actions should be documented so that the system can be returned to normal operations as quickly and safely as possible. Recovery actions for an intrusion that affects operation of the ICS will closely align with the system's Disaster Recovery Plan, and should take into account the planning and coordination already established.

During the preparation of the incident response plan, input should be obtained from the various stakeholders including operations, engineering, IT, system support vendors, management, organized labor, legal, and safety. These stakeholders should also review and approve the plan.

6.2.9 Maintenance

The security controls that fall within the NIST SP 800-53 Maintenance (MA) family provide policy and procedure for performing routine and preventative maintenance on the components of an information system. This includes the usage of maintenance tools (both local and remote) and management of maintenance personnel.

Supplemental guidance for the MA controls can be found in the following documents:

- NIST SP 800-63 provides guidance on electronic authentication for remote maintenance [53].

- NIST SP 800-100 provides guidance on information security governance and planning [27].

6.2.10 Media Protection

The security controls that fall within the NIST SP 800-53 Media Protection (MP) family provide policies and procedures for limiting the access to media to authorized users. Controls also exist for labeling media for distribution and handling requirements, as well as storage, transport, sanitization (removal of information from digital media), destruction, and disposal of the media.

Supplemental guidance for the MP controls can be found in the following documents:

- NIST SP 800-88 provides guidance on appropriate sanitization equipment, techniques, and procedures [78].

- NIST SP 800-100 provides guidance on information security governance and planning [27].

ICS-specific Recommendations and Guidance

Media assets include removable media and devices such as floppy disks, CDs, DVDs and USB memory sticks, as well as printed reports and documents. Physical security controls should address specific requirements for the safe and secure maintenance of these assets and provide specific guidance for transporting, handling, and erasing or destroying these assets. Security requirements could include safe storage from loss, fire, theft, unintentional distribution, or environmental damage.

If an adversary gains access to backup media associated with an ICS, it could provide valuable data for launching an attack. Recovering an authentication file from the backups might allow an adversary to run password cracking tools and extract usable passwords. In addition, the backups typically contain machine names, IP addresses, software version numbers, usernames, and other data useful in planning an attack.

The use of any unauthorized CDs, DVDs, floppy disks, USB memory sticks, or similar removable media on any node that is part of or connected to the ICS should not be permitted in order to prevent the introduction of malware or the inadvertent loss or theft of data. Where the system components use unmodified industry standard protocols, mechanized policy management software can be used to enforce media protection policy.

6.2.11 Physical and Environmental Protection

The security controls that fall within the NIST SP 800-53 Physical and Environmental Protection (PE) family provide policy and procedures for all physical access to an information system including designated entry/exit points, transmission media, and display media. These include controls for monitoring physical access, maintaining logs, and handling visitors. This family also includes controls for the deployment and management of emergency protection controls such as emergency shutdown of the IT system, backup for power and lighting, controls for temperature and humidity, and protection against fire and water damage.

Supplemental guidance for the PE controls can be found in the following documents:

- NIST SP 800-46 provides guidance on telecommuting and broadband communication security [51].

- NIST SP 800-100 provides guidance on information security governance and planning [27].

Physical security measures are designed to reduce the risk of accidental or deliberate loss or damage to plant assets and the surrounding environment. The assets being safeguarded may be physical assets such as tools and plant equipment, the environment, the surrounding community, and intellectual property, including proprietary data such as process settings and customer information. The deployment of physical security controls is often subject to environmental, safety, regulatory, legal, and other requirements that must be identified and addressed specific to a given environment. The subject of deploying physical security controls is vast and needs to be specific to the type of protection needed.

ICS-specific Recommendations and Guidance

The physical protection of the cyber components and data associated with the ICS must be addressed as part of the overall security of a plant. Security at many ICS facilities is closely tied to plant safety. A primary goal is to keep people out of hazardous situations without preventing them from doing their job or carrying out emergency procedures. Physical security controls are any physical measures, either active or passive, that limit physical access to any information assets in the ICS environment. These measures are employed to prevent many types of undesirable effects, including:

- Unauthorized physical access to sensitive locations.

- Physical modification, manipulation, theft or other removal, or destruction of existing systems, infrastructure, communications interfaces, personnel, or physical locations.

- Unauthorized observation of sensitive informational assets through visual observation, note taking, photographs, or other means.

- Prevention of unauthorized introduction of new systems, infrastructure, communications interfaces, or other hardware.

- Prevention of unauthorized introduction of devices intentionally designed to cause hardware manipulation, communications eavesdropping, or other harmful impact.

Gaining physical access to a control room or control system components often implies gaining logical access to the process control system as well. Likewise, having logical access to systems such as main servers and control room computers allows an adversary to exercise control over the physical process.

If computers are readily accessible, and they have removable media drives (e.g., floppy disks, compact discs, external hard drives) or USB ports, the drives can be fitted with locks or removed from the computers and USB ports disabled. Depending on security needs and risks, it might also be prudent to disable or physically protect power buttons to prevent unauthorized use. For maximum security, servers should be placed in locked areas and authentication mechanisms (such as keys) protected. Also, the network devices on the ICS network, including switches, routers, network jacks, servers, workstations, and controllers, should be located in a secured area that can only be accessed by authorized personnel. The secured area should also be compatible with the environmental requirements of the devices.

A defense-in-depth solution to physical security should include the following attributes:

- **Protection of Physical Locations**. Classic physical security considerations typically refer to a ringed architecture of layered security measures. Creating several physical barriers, both active and passive, around buildings, facilities, rooms, equipment, or other informational assets, establishes these physical security perimeters. Physical security controls meant to protect physical locations include fences, anti-vehicle ditches, earthen mounds, walls, reinforced barricades, gates, or other measures. Most organizations include this layered model by preventing access to the plant first by the use of fences, guard shacks, gates, and locked doors.

- **Access Control.** Access control systems should ensure that only authorized people have access to controlled spaces. An access control system should be flexible. The need for access may be based on time (day vs. night shift), level of training, employment status, work assignment, plant status, and a myriad of other factors. A system must be able to verify that persons being granted access are who they say they are (usually using something the person has, such as an access card or key; something they know, such as a personal identification number (PIN); or something they are, using a biometric device). Access control should be highly reliable, yet not interfere with the routine or emergency duties of plant personnel. Integration of access control into the process system allows a view into not only security access, but also physical and personnel asset tracking, dramatically accelerating response time in emergencies, helping to direct individuals to safe locations, and improving overall productivity. Within an area, access to network and computer cabinets should be limited to only those who have a need, such as network technicians and engineers, or computer maintenance staff. Equipment cabinets should be locked and wiring should be neat and within cabinets. Consider keeping all computers in secure racks and using peripheral extender technology to connect human-machine interfaces to the racked computers.

  Access Monitoring Systems. Access monitoring systems include still and video cameras, sensors, and various types of identification systems. Examples of these systems include cameras that monitor parking lots, convenience stores, or airline security. These devices do not specifically prevent access to a particular location; rather, they store and record either the physical presence or the lack of physical presence of individuals, vehicles, animals, or other physical entities. Adequate lighting should be provided based on the type of access monitoring device deployed.

  Access Limiting Systems. Access limiting systems may employ a combination of devices to physically control or prevent access to protected resources. Access limiting systems include both active and passive security devices such as fences, doors, safes, gates, and guards. They are often coupled with identification and monitoring systems to provide role-based access for specific individuals or groups of individuals.

- **People and Asset Tracking.** Locating people and vehicles in a large installation is important for safety reasons, and it is increasingly important for security reasons as well. Asset location technologies can be used to track the movements of people and vehicles within the plant, to ensure that they stay in authorized areas, to identify personnel needing assistance, and to support emergency response.

- **Environmental Factors.** In addressing the security needs of the system and data, it is important to consider environmental factors. For example, if a site is dusty, systems should be placed in a filtered environment. This is particularly important if the dust is likely to be conductive or magnetic, as in the case of sites that process coal or iron. If vibration is likely to be a problem, systems should be mounted on rubber bushings to prevent disk crashes and wiring connection problems. In addition, the environments containing systems and media (e.g., backup tapes, floppy disks) should have stable temperature and humidity. An alarm to the process control system should be generated when environmental specifications such as temperature and humidity are exceeded.

- **Environmental Control Systems.** Heating, ventilation, and air conditioning (HVAC) systems for control rooms must support plant personnel during normal operation and emergency situations, which could include the release of toxic substances. Fire systems must be carefully designed to avoid causing more harm than good (e.g., to avoid mixing water with incompatible products). HVAC and fire systems have significantly increased roles in security that arise from the interdependence of process control and security. For example, fire prevention and HVAC systems that support industrial control computers need to be protected against cyber incidents.

- **Power.** Reliable power for the ICS is essential, so an uninterruptible power supply (UPS) should be provided. If the site has an emergency generator, the UPS battery life may only need to be a few seconds; however, if the site relies on external power, the UPS battery life may need to be hours. It should be sized, at a minimum, so that the system can be shutdown safely.

6.2.11.1 Control Center/Control Room

ICS-specific Recommendations and Guidance

Providing physical security for the control center/control room is essential to reduce the potential of many threats. Control centers/control rooms frequently have consoles continuously logged onto the primary control server, where speed of response and continual view of the plant is of utmost importance. These areas will often contain the servers themselves, other critical computer nodes, and sometimes plant controllers. It is essential that access to these areas be limited to authorized users only, using authentication methods such as smart or magnetic identity cards or biometric devices. In extreme cases, it may be considered necessary to make the control center/control room blast-proof, or to provide an offsite emergency control center/control room so that control can be maintained if the primary control center/control room becomes uninhabitable.

6.2.11.2 Portable Devices

ICS-specific Recommendations and Guidance

Computers and computerized devices used for ICS functions (such as PLC programming) should never be allowed to leave the ICS area. Laptops, portable engineering workstations and handhelds (e.g., 375 HART communicator) should be tightly secured and should never be allowed to be used outside the ICS network. Antivirus and patch management should be kept current.

6.2.11.3 Cabling

ICS-specific Recommendations and Guidance

Cabling design and implementation for the control network should be addressed in the cybersecurity plan. Unshielded twisted pair communications cable, while acceptable for the office environment, is generally not suitable for the plant environment due to its susceptibility to interference from magnetic fields, radio waves, temperature extremes, moisture, dust, and vibration. Industrial RJ-45 connectors should be used in place of other types of twisted pair connectors to provide protection against moisture, dust and vibration. Fiber-optic cable and coaxial cable are often better network cabling choices for the control network because they are immune to many of the typical environmental conditions including electrical and radio frequency interference found in an industrial control environment. Cable and connectors should be color-coded and labeled so that the ICS and IT networks are clearly delineated and the potential for an inadvertent cross-connect is reduced. Cable runs should be installed so that access is minimized (i.e., limited to authorized personnel only) and equipment should be installed in locked cabinets with adequate ventilation and air filtration.

6.2.12 Planning

A security plan is a formal document that provides an overview of the security requirements for an information system and describes the security controls in place or planned for meeting those requirements. The security controls that fall within the NIST SP 800-53 Planning (PL) family provide the basis for developing a security plan. These controls also address maintenance issues for periodically updating a security plan. A set of rules describes user responsibilities and expected behavior regarding information system usage with provision for signed acknowledgement from users indicating that they have read, understand, and agree to abide by the rules of behavior before authorizing access to the information system.

Supplemental guidance for the PL controls can be found in the following documents:

- NIST SP 800-18 provides guidance on preparing rules of behavior [19].

- NIST SP 800-100 provides guidance on information security governance and planning [27].

ICS-specific Recommendations and Guidance

A security plan for an ICS should build on appropriate existing IT security experience, programs, and practices. However, the critical differences between IT and ICS addressed in Section 2.4 will influence how security will be applied to the ICS. A forward-looking plan is needed to provide a method for continuous security improvements. Whenever a new system is being designed and installed, it is imperative to take the time to address security throughout the lifecycle, from architecture to procurement to installation to maintenance to decommissioning. ICS security is a rapidly evolving field requiring the security planning process to constantly explore emerging ICS security capabilities as well as new threats that are identified by organizations such as the ICS-CERT.

6.2.13 Personnel Security

The security controls that fall within the NIST SP 800-53 Personnel Security (PS) family provide policies and procedures to reduce the risk of human error, theft, fraud, or other intentional or unintentional misuse of information systems.

Supplemental guidance for the PS controls can be found in the following documents:

- NIST SP 800-35 provides guidance on information technology security services [44].

- NIST SP 800-73 provides guidance on interfaces for personal identity verification [49].

- NIST SP 800-76 provides guidance on biometrics for personal identity verification [50].

- NIST SP 800-100 provides guidance on information security governance and planning [27].

Personnel security measures are meant to reduce the possibility and risk of human error, theft, fraud, or other intentional or unintentional misuse of informational assets. There are three main aspects to personnel security:

- **Hiring Policies.** This includes pre-employment screening such as background checks, the interview process, employment terms and conditions, complete job descriptions and detailing of duties, terms and condition of employment, and legal rights and responsibilities of employees or contractors.

- **Organization Policies and Practices.** These include security policies, information classification, document and media maintenance and handling policies, user training, acceptable usage policies for organization assets, periodic employee performance reviews, appropriate background checks, and any other policies and actions that detail expected and required behavior of organization employees, contractors, and visitors. Organization policies to be enforced should be written down and readily available to all workers through an employee handbook, distributed as email notices, located in a centralized resource area, or posted directly at a worker's area of responsibility.

- **Terms and Conditions of Employment.** This category includes job and position responsibilities, notification to employees of terminable offenses, disciplinary actions and punishments, and periodic employee performance reviews.

ICS-specific Recommendations and Guidance

Positions should be categorized with a risk designation and screening criteria, and individuals filling a position should be screened against this criteria as well as complete an access agreement before being granted access to an information system. Personnel should be screened for the critical positions controlling and maintaining the ICS.

Additionally, training programs should be carefully developed to ensure that each employee has received training relevant and necessary to his job functions. Further, ensure that the employees have demonstrated their competence in their job functions.

6.2.14 Risk Assessment

The security controls that fall within the NIST SP 800-53 Risk Assessment (RA) family provide policy and procedures to develop, distribute, and maintain a documented risk assessment policy that describes purpose, scope, roles, responsibilities, and compliance as well as policy implementation procedures. An information system and associated data is categorized based on the security objectives and a range of risk levels. A risk assessment is performed to identify risks and the magnitude of harm that could result from the unauthorized access, use, disclosure, disruption, modification, or destruction of an information system and data. Also included in these controls are mechanisms for keeping risk assessments up-to-date and performing periodic testing and vulnerability assessments.

Supplemental guidance for the RA controls can be found in the following documents:

- NIST SP 800-30 provides guidance on conducting risk assessments and updates [79].

- NIST SP 800-39 provides guidance on risk management at all organizational levels [20].

- NIST SP 800-40 provides guidance on handling security patches [40].

- NIST SP 800-115 provides guidance on network security testing [41].

- NIST SP 800-60 provides guidance on determining security categories for information types [25].

- NIST SP 800-100 provides guidance on information security governance and planning [27].

ICS-specific Recommendations and Guidance

Organizations must consider the potential consequences resulting from an incident on an ICS. Well-defined policies and procedures lead to mitigation techniques designed to thwart incidents and manage the risk to eliminate or minimize the consequences. The potential degradation of the physical plant, economic status, or stakeholder/national confidence could justify mitigation.

For an ICS, a very important aspect of the risk assessment is to determine the value of the data that is flowing from the control network to the corporate network. In instances where pricing decisions are determined from this data, the data could have a very high value. The fiscal justification for mitigation has to be derived by comparing the mitigation cost to the effects of the consequence. However, it is not possible to define a one-size-fits-all set of security requirements. A very high level of security may be achievable but undesirable in many situations because of the loss of functionality and other associated costs. A well-thought-out security implementation is a balance of risk versus cost. In some situations the risk may be safety, health, or environment-related rather than purely economic. The risk may result in an unrecoverable consequence rather than a temporary financial setback

---

6.2.15 System and Services Acquisition

The security controls that fall within the NIST SP 800-53 System and Services Acquisition (SA) family provide the basis for developing policies and procedures for acquisition of resources required to adequately protect an information system. These acquisitions are based on security requirements and security specifications. As part of the acquisition procedures, an information system is managed using a system development life cycle methodology that includes information security considerations. As part of acquisition, adequate documentation must be maintained on the information system and constituent components.

The SA family also addresses outsourced systems and the inclusion of adequate security controls by vendors as specified by the supported organization. Vendors are also responsible for configuration management and security testing for these outsourced information systems.

Supplemental guidance for the SA controls can be found in the following documents:

- NIST SP 800-23 provides guidance on the acquisition and use of tested/evaluated information technology products [42].

- NIST SP 800-27 provides guidance on engineering principles for information system security [43].

- NIST SP 800-35 provides guidance on information technology security services [44].

- NIST SP 800-36 provides guidance on the selection of information security products [45].

- NIST SP 800-64 provides guidance on security considerations in the system development life cycle [46].

- NIST SP 800-65 provides guidance on integrating security into the capital planning and investment control process [47].

- NIST SP 800-70 provides guidance on configuration settings for information technology products [26].

- NIST SP 800-100 provides guidance on information security governance and planning [27].

ICS-specific Recommendations and Guidance

The security requirements of an organization outsourcing the management and control of all or some of its information systems, networks, and desktop environments should be addressed in a contract agreed between the parties. External suppliers that have an impact on the security of the organization must be held to the same security policies and procedures to maintain the overall level of ICS security. Security policies and procedures of second and third-tier suppliers should also be in compliance with corporate cybersecurity policies and procedures in the case that they impact ICS security.

DHS has developed a procurement language document [48] for specifying security requirements when procuring new systems or maintaining existing systems.

6.2.16 System and Communications Protection

The security controls that fall within the NIST SP 800-53 System and Communications Protection (SC) family provide policy and procedures for protecting systems and data communications components.

Supplemental guidance for the SC controls can be found in the following documents:

- NIST SP 800-28 provides guidance on active content and mobile code [69].

- NIST SP 800-52 provides guidance on Transport Layer Security (TLS) Implementations [70].

- NIST SP 800-56 provides guidance on cryptographic key establishment [71].

- NIST SP 800-57 provides guidance on cryptographic key management [72].

- NIST SP 800-58 provides guidance on security considerations for VoIP technologies [73].

- NIST SP 800-63 provides guidance on remote electronic authentication [53].

- NIST SP 800-77 provides guidance on IPsec VPNs [74].

6.2.16.1 Encryption

Encryption is the cryptographic transformation of data (called plaintext) into a form (called ciphertext) that conceals the data's original meaning to prevent it from being known or used. If the transformation is reversible, the corresponding reversal process is called decryption, which is a transformation that restores encrypted data to its original state [75].

ICS-specific Recommendations and Guidance

Before deploying encryption, first determine if encryption is an appropriate solution for the specific ICS application, because authentication and integrity are generally the key security issues for ICS applications. Other cryptographic solutions such as cryptographic hashes should also be considered.

The use of encryption within an ICS environment could introduce communications latency due to the additional time and computing resources required to encrypt, decrypt, and authenticate each message. For ICS, any latency induced from the use of encryption, or any other security technique, must not degrade the operational performance of the end device or system. Before deploying encryption within an ICS environment, solutions should go through extensive performance testing. Encryption at OSI Layer 2 should be considered, rather than at Layer 3 to reduce encryption latency.

In addition, encrypted messages are often larger than unencrypted messages due to one or more of the following:

- Additional checksums to reduce errors.

- Protocols to control the cryptography.

- Padding (for block ciphers).

- Authentication procedures.

- Other required cryptographic processes.

Cryptography also introduces key management issues. Sound security policies require periodic key changes. This process becomes more difficult as the geographic size of the ICS increases, with extensive SCADA systems being the most severe example. Because site visits to change keys can be costly and slow, it is useful to be able to change keys remotely.

If cryptography is selected, the most effective safeguard is to use a complete cryptographic system approved by the NIST/ Communications Security Establishment (CSE) Cryptographic Module Validation Program (CMVP)[21]. Within this program standards are maintained to ensure that cryptographic systems were studied carefully for weaknesses by a wide range of experts, rather than being developed by a few engineers in a single organization. At a minimum, certification makes it probable that:

- Some method (such as counter mode) will be used to ensure that the same message does not

---

[21] Information on the CMVP can be found on the CMVP web site http://csrc.nist.gov/cryptval/cmvp.htm.

generate the same value each time.

- ICS messages are protected against replay and forging.

- Key management is secure throughout the life cycle of the key.

- The system is using an effective random number generator.

- The entire system has been implemented securely.

Even then, the technology is effective only if it is an integral part of an effectively enforced information security policy. American Gas Association (AGA) report 12-1 [5] contains an example of such a security policy. While it is directed toward a natural gas SCADA system, many of its policy recommendations could apply to any ICS.

For an ICS, encryption can be deployed as part of a comprehensive, enforced security policy. Organizations should select cryptographic protection based on a risk assessment and the identified value of the information being protected and ICS operating constraints. Specifically, a cryptographic key should be long enough so that guessing it or determining it through analysis takes more effort, time, and cost than the value of the protected asset.

The encryption hardware should be protected from physical tampering and uncontrolled electronic connections. Assuming cryptography is the appropriate solution, organizations should select cryptographic protection with remote key management if the units being protected are so numerous or geographically dispersed that changing keys is difficult or expensive.

Use separate plaintext and ciphertext ports unless the network absolutely requires the restriction to pass both plaintext and ciphertext through each port.

Use only modules that can be certified to comply with a standard, such as FIPS 140-2 [90] through the Cryptographic Module Validation Program (CMVP).

6.2.16.2 Virtual Private Network (VPN)

One method of encrypting communication data is through a VPN, which is a private network that operates as an overlay on a public infrastructure, so that the private network can function across a public network. The most common types of VPN technologies implemented today are:

- **Internet Protocol Security (IPsec).** IPsec is a set of standards defined by IETF to govern the secure communications of data across public networks at the IP layer. IPsec is included in many current operating systems. The intent of the standards is to guarantee interoperability across vendor platforms; however, the reality is that the determination of interoperability of multi-vendor implementations depends on specific implementation testing conducted by the end-user organization. IPsec supports two encryption modes: transport and tunnel. Transport mode encrypts only the data portion (payload) of each packet, but leaves the header untouched. The more secure tunnel mode adds a new header to each packet and encrypts both the original header and the payload. On the receiving side, an IPsec-compliant device decrypts each packet. The protocol has been continually enhanced to address specific requirements, such as extensions to the protocol to address individual user authentication and NAT device transversal. These extensions are typically vendor-specific and can lead to interoperability issues primarily in host-to-security gateway environments. NIST SP 800-77 provides guidance on IPsec VPNs [74].

■ **Secure Sockets Layer (SSL).** SSL provides a secure channel between two machines that encrypts the contents of each packet. The IETF made slight modifications to the SSL version 3 protocol and created a new protocol called Transport Layer Security (TLS). The terms "SSL" and "TLS" are often used interchangeably, and this document generically uses the SSL terminology. SSL is most often recognized for securing HTTP traffic; this protocol implementation is known as HTTP Secure (HTTPS). However, SSL is not limited to HTTP traffic; it can be used to secure many different application layer programs. SSL-based VPN products have gained acceptance because of the market for "clientless" VPN products. These products use standard Web browsers as clients, which have built-in SSL support. The "clientless" term means that there is no need to install or configure third-party VPN "client" software on users' systems. NIST SP 800-52 provides guidance on SSL configuration [70].

■ **Secure Shell (SSH).** SSH is a command interface and protocol for securely gaining access to a remote computer. It is widely used by network administrators to remotely control Web servers and other types of servers. The latest version, SSH2, is a proposed set of standards from the IETF. Typically, SSH is deployed as a secure alternative to a telnet application. SSH is included in most UNIX distributions, and is typically added to other platforms through a third-party package.

ICS-specific Recommendations and Guidance

VPNs are most often used in the ICS environment to provide secure access from an untrusted network to the ICS control network. Untrusted networks can range from the Internet to the corporate LAN. Properly configured, VPNs can greatly restrict access to and from control system host computers and controllers, thereby improving security. They can also potentially improve control network responsiveness by removing unauthorized non-essential traffic from the intermediary network.

Other possible deployments include using either host-based or mini-standalone security gateways, either interposed before or running on individual control devices. This technique of implementing VPNs on an individual device basis can have significant administration overhead.

VPN devices used to protect control systems should be thoroughly tested to verify that the VPN technology is compatible with the application and that implementation of the VPN devices does not unacceptably affect network traffic characteristics.

6.2.17 System and Information Integrity

Maintaining system and information integrity assures that sensitive data has not been modified or deleted in an unauthorized and undetected manner. The security controls that fall within the NIST SP 800-53 System and Information Integrity (SI) family provide policies and procedures for identifying, reporting, and correcting information system flaws. Controls exist for malicious code detection, spam and spyware protection, and intrusion detection, although they may not be appropriate for all ICS applications. Also provided are controls for receiving security alerts and advisories, and the verification of security functions on the information system. In addition, there are controls within this family to detect and protect against unauthorized changes to software and data, provide restrictions to data input and output, and check for the accuracy, completeness, and validity of data as well as handle error conditions, although they may not be appropriate for all ICS applications.

Supplemental guidance for the SI controls can be found in the following documents:

- NIST SP 800-40 provides guidance on security patch installation [40].

- NIST SP 800-94 provides guidance on Intrusion Detection and Prevention (IDP) Systems [55].

- NIST SP 800-100 provides guidance on information security governance and planning [27].

ICS-specific Recommendations and Guidance

Controls exist for malicious code detection, spam and spyware protection, and intrusion detection, although they may not be appropriate for all ICS applications. ICS-specific recommendations and guidance for these controls are included in Sections **Error! Reference source not found.**and 0.

6.2.17.1 Virus and Malicious Code Detection

Antivirus and malware code detection products evaluate files on a computer's storage devices against an inventory of known malware signature files. If one of the files on a computer matches the profile of a known virus, the virus is removed through a disinfection process (e.g., quarantine, deletion) so it cannot infect other local files or communicate across a network to infect other files. Antivirus software can be deployed on workstations, servers, firewalls and handheld devices.

ICS-specific Recommendations and Guidance

Antivirus tools only function effectively when installed, configured, running full-time, and maintained properly against the state of known attack methods and payloads. While antivirus tools are common security practice in IT computer systems, their use with ICS may require adopting special practices including compatibility checks, change management issues, and performance impact metrics. These special practices should be utilized whenever new signatures or new versions of antivirus software are installed.

Major ICS vendors recommend and even support the use of particular antivirus tools. In some cases, control system vendors may have performed regression testing across their product line for supported versions of a particular antivirus tool and also provide associated installation and configuration documentation. There is also an effort to develop a general set of guidelines and test procedures focused on ICS performance impacts to fill the gaps where ICS and antivirus vendor guidance is not available [56].

Generally:

- Windows, Unix, Linux systems, etc. used as consoles, engineering workstations, data historians, HMIs and general purpose SCADA and backup servers can be secured just like commercial IT equipment: install push- or auto-updated antivirus and patch management software with updates distributed via an antivirus server and patch management server located inside the process control network and auto-updated from the IT network.

- Follow vendor recommendations on all other servers and computers (DCS, PLC, instruments) that have time-dependent code, modified or extended the operating system or any other change that makes it different from any standard PC that one could buy at an office supply or computer store. Expect the vendor to make periodic maintenance releases that include security patches.

6.2.17.2 Intrusion Detection and Prevention

Intrusion detection systems (IDS) monitor events on a network, such as traffic patterns, or a system, such as log entries or file accesses, so that they can identify an intruder breaking into or attempting to break into a system [57]. IDS ensure that unusual activity such as new open ports, unusual traffic patterns, or changes to critical operating system files is brought to the attention of the appropriate security personnel.

The two most commonly used types of IDS are:

- **Network-Based IDS.** These systems monitor network traffic and generate alarms when they identify traffic that they deem to be an attack.

■ **Host-Based IDS.** This software monitors one or more types of characteristics of a system, such as application log file entries, system configuration changes, and access to sensitive data on a system and responds with an alarm or countermeasure when a user attempts to breach security.

ICS-specific Recommendations and Guidance

An effective IDS deployment typically involves both host-based and network-based IDS. In the current ICS environment, network-based IDS are most often deployed between the control network and the corporate network in conjunction with a firewall; host-based IDS are most often deployed on the computers that use general-purpose OSs or applications such as HMIs, SCADA servers, and engineering workstations. Properly configured, an IDS can greatly enhance the security management team's ability to detect attacks entering or leaving the system, thereby improving security. They can also potentially improve a control network's efficiency by detecting non-essential traffic on the network. However, even when IDS are implemented, security staff can primarily recognize individual attacks, as opposed to organized patterns of attacks over time. Network security monitoring and an understanding of the normal state of the ICS network can help distinguish attacks from transient conditions, and both trigger and provide information into events that are outside the normal state.

Current IDS and IPS products are effective in detecting and preventing well-known Internet attacks, but until recently they have not addressed ICS protocol attacks. IDS and IPS vendors are beginning to develop and incorporate attack signatures for various ICS protocols such as Modbus, DNP3, and ICCP [58].

6.2.17.3 Patch Management

Patches are additional pieces of code that have been developed to address specific problems or flaws in existing software. Vulnerabilities are flaws that can be exploited, enabling unauthorized access to IT systems or enabling users to have access to greater privileges than authorized.

A systematic approach to managing and using software patches can help organizations to improve the overall security of their IT systems in a cost-effective way. Organizations that actively manage and use software patches can reduce the chances that the vulnerabilities in their IT systems can be exploited; in addition, they can save time and money that might be spent in responding to vulnerability-related incidents.

NIST SP 800-40 Revision 3 [40] provides guidance for organizational security managers who are responsible for designing and implementing security patch and vulnerability management programs and for testing the effectiveness of the programs in reducing vulnerabilities. The guidance is also useful to system administrators and operations personnel who are responsible for applying and testing patches and for deploying solutions to vulnerability problems.

ICS-specific Recommendations and Guidance

Applying patches to OS components creates another situation where significant care should be exercised in the ICS environment. Patches should be adequately tested (e.g., off-line on a comparable ICS) to determine the acceptability of side effects. Regression testing is advised. It is not uncommon for patches to have an adverse effect on other software. A patch may remove a vulnerability, but it can

---

also introduce a greater risk from a production or safety perspective. Patching the vulnerability may also change the way the OS or application works with control applications, causing the control application to lose some of its functionality. Another issue is that many ICS utilize older versions of operating systems that are no longer supported by the vendor. Consequently, available patches may not be applicable. Organizations should implement a systematic, accountable, and documented ICS patch management process for managing exposure to vulnerabilities.

Once the decision is made to deploy a patch, there are other tools that automate this process from a centralized server and with confirmation that the patch has been deployed correctly. Consider separating the automated process for ICS patch management from the automated process for non-ICS applications. Patching should be scheduled to occur during planned ICS outages.

6.2.18 Program Management

The security controls that fall within the NIST SP 800-53 Program Management (PM) focus on the organization-wide information security requirements that are independent of any particular information system and are essential for managing information security programs.

Organizations document program management controls in the information security program plan. The organization-wide information security program plan supplements the individual security plans developed for each organizational information system. In addition to documenting the information security program management controls, the security program plan provides a vehicle for the organization, in a central repository, to document all security controls that have been designated as common controls (i.e., security controls inherited by organizational information systems).

6.2.19 Privacy Controls

Protecting the privacy of personally identifiable information (PII)[22] collected, used, maintained, shared, and disposed of by programs and information systems is critical given the advances in information technologies and applications of those technologies. Effective privacy for individuals depends on the safeguards employed within the organizational information systems that are processing, storing, and transmitting PII. Organizations cannot have effective privacy without a foundation of information security. However, privacy is more than security and includes, for example, the principles of transparency, notice, and choice.

The privacy controls focus on information privacy as a value distinct from, but highly interrelated with, information security. The privacy controls are based on the Fair Information Practice Principles (FIPPs) embodied in the Privacy Act of 1974, Section 208 of the E-Government Act of 2002, and related Office of Management and Budget (OMB) guidance. The FIPPs are designed to build public trust in an organization's privacy practices and to help organizations avoid tangible costs and intangible damages stemming from privacy incidents.

---

[22] OMB Memorandum 07-16 defines PII as "information which can be used to distinguish or trace an individual's identity such as their name, social security number, biometric records, etc., alone, or when combined with other personal or identifying information which is linked or linkable to a specific individual, such as date and place of birth, mother's maiden name, etc." [86]. OMB Memorandum 10-22 reaffirmed this definition [87]. NIST Special Publication 800-122 defines PII as "any information about an individual [that is] maintained by an agency, including: (i) any information that can be used to distinguish or trace an individual's identity, such as name, social security number, date and place of birth, mother's maiden name, or biometric records; and (ii) any other information that is linked or linkable to an individual, such as medical, educational, financial, and employment information" [88].

Privacy controls are the administrative, technical, and physical safeguards employed within organizations to protect and ensure the proper handling of PII. There are eight privacy control families with each family aligning with one of the FIPPs. The privacy control families can be implemented at the organization, department, agency, component, office, program, or information system level. The privacy controls are structured in a similar manner to the information system security controls in Appendix F of NIST SP 800-53.

The Privacy Appendix of NIST SP 800-53, Rev. 4 [22], provides a structured set of privacy controls, based on international standards and best practices to help organizations enforce requirements derived from federal privacy legislation, policies, regulations, directives, standards, and guidance. Additionally, it establishes a linkage and relationship between privacy and security controls for purposes of enforcing respective privacy and security requirements that may overlap in concept and in implementation within federal information systems, programs, and organizations.

The privacy controls are intended primarily for use by an organization's Senior Agency Official for Privacy (SAOP)/Chief Privacy Officer (CPO) when working with program managers, information system developers, and information security personnel to determine how best to incorporate effective privacy protections and practices within those programs and/or systems. These controls facilitate the organization's efforts to comply with privacy requirements affecting those programs and/or systems that collect, use, maintain, share, or dispose of PII. This promotes closer cooperation between privacy and security officials within the federal government to help achieve the objectives of senior leaders/executives in enforcing the requirements in federal privacy legislation, policies, regulations, directives, standards, and guidance.

The 8 privacy control families include:

- Authority and Purpose (AP).
- Accountability, Audit, and Risk Management (AR).
- Data Quality and Integrity (DI).
- Data Minimization and Retention (DM).
- Individual Participation and Redress (IP).
- Security (SE).
- Transparency (TR).
- Use Limitation (UL).

Appendix A—Acronyms and Abbreviations

Selected acronyms and abbreviations used in the *Guide to Industrial Control Systems (ICS) Security* are defined below.

AC	Alternating Current
ACL	Access Control List
AGA	American Gas Association
API	American Petroleum Institute
ARP	Address Resolution Protocol
BCP	Business Continuity Plan
CIDX	Chemical Industry Data Exchange
CIGRE	International Council on Large Electric Systems
CIP	Critical Infrastructure Protection
CMVP	Cryptographic Module Validation Program
COTS	Commercial Off-the-Shelf
CPNI	Centre for the Protection of National Infrastructure
CPU	Central Processing Unit
CSE	Communications Security Establishment
CSRC	Computer Security Resource Center
CSSC	Control System Security Center
CVE	Common Vulnerabilities and Exposures
DCOM	Distributed Component Object Model
DCS	Distributed Control System(s)
DETL	Distributed Energy Technology Laboratory
DHS	Department of Homeland Security
DMZ	Demilitarized Zone
DNP3	DNP3 Distributed Network Protocol (published as IEEE 1815)
DNS	Domain Name System
DOE	Department of Energy
DoS	Denial of Service
DRP	Disaster Recovery Plan
EAP	Extensible Authentication Protocol
EMS	Energy Management System
EPRI	Electric Power Research Institute
ERP	Enterprise Resource Planning
FIPS	Federal Information Processing Standards
FISMA	Federal Information Security Modernization Act
FTP	File Transfer Protocol
GAO	Government Accountability Office
GPS	Global Positioning System
HMI	Human-Machine Interface
HSPD	Homeland Security Presidential Directive
HTTP	Hypertext Transfer Protocol

HTTPS	Hypertext Transfer Protocol Secure
HVAC	Heating, Ventilation, and Air Conditioning
I/O	Input/Output
I3P	Institute for Information Infrastructure Protection
IACS	Industrial Automation and Control System
IAONA	Industrial Automation Open Networking Association
ICCP	Inter-control Center Communications Protocol
ICMP	Internet Control Message Protocol
ICS	Industrial Control System(s)
ICS-CERT	Industrial Control Systems - Cyber Emergency Response Team
IDS	Intrusion Detection System
IEC	International Electrotechnical Commission
IED	Intelligent Electronic Device
IEEE	Institute of Electrical and Electronics Engineers
IETF	Internet Engineering Task Force
IGMP	Internet Group Management Protocol
INL	Idaho National Laboratory
IP	Internet Protocol
IPS	Intrusion Prevention System
IPsec	Internet Protocol Security
ISA	International Society of Automation
ISID	Industrial Security Incident Database
ISO	International Organization for Standardization
IT	Information Technology
ITL	Information Technology Laboratory
LAN	Local Area Network
MAC	Media Access Control
MES	Manufacturing Execution System
MIB	Management Information Base
MTU	Master Terminal Unit (also Master Telemetry Unit)
NAT	Network Address Translation
NCCIC	National Cybersecurity and Communications Integration Center
NCSD	National Cyber Security Division
NERC	North American Electric Reliability Council
NFS	Network File System
NIC	Network Interface Card
NISCC	National Infrastructure Security Coordination Centre
NIST	National Institute of Standards and Technology
NSTB	National SCADA Testbed
OLE	Object Linking and Embedding
OMB	Office of Management and Budget
OPC	OLE for Process Control
OS	Operating System
OSI	Open Systems Interconnection

PCII	Protected Critical Infrastructure Information
PDA	Personal Digital Assistant
PIN	Personal Identification Number
PID	Proportional – Integral - Derivative
PIV	Personal Identity Verification
PLC	Programmable Logic Controller
PP	Protection Profile
PPP	Point-to-Point Protocol
R&D	Research and Development
RADIUS	Remote Authentication Dial In User Service
RBAC	Role-Based Access Control
RFC	Request for Comments
RMA	Reliability, Maintainability, and Availability
RMF	Risk Management Framework
RPC	Remote Procedure Call
RPO	Recovery Point Objective
RTO	Recovery Time Objective
RTU	Remote Terminal Unit (also Remote Telemetry Unit)
SC	Security Category
SCADA	Supervisory Control and Data Acquisition
SCP	Secure Copy
SFTP	Secure File Transfer Protocol
SIS	Safety Instrumented System
SMTP	Simple Mail Transfer Protocol
SNL	Sandia National Laboratories
SNMP	Simple Network Management Protocol
SP	Special Publication
SPP-ICS	System Protection Profile for Industrial Control Systems
SQL	Structured Query Language
SSH	Secure Shell
SSID	Service Set Identifier
SSL	Secure Sockets Layer
TCP	Transmission Control Protocol
TCP/IP	Transmission Control Protocol/Internet Protocol
TFTP	Trivial File Transfer Protocol
TLS	Transport Layer Security
UDP	User Datagram Protocol
UPS	Uninterruptible Power Supply
US-CERT	United States Computer Emergency Readiness Team
USB	Universal Serial Bus
VFD	Variable Frequency Drive
VLAN	Virtual Local Area Network
VPN	Virtual Private Network
WAN	Wide Area Network
XML	Extensible Markup Language

Appendix B—Glossary of Terms

Selected terms used in the *Guide to Industrial Control Systems (ICS) Security* are defined below. Source References for certain definitions are listed at the end of this appendix.

Alternating Current Drive	Synonymous with Variable Frequency Drive (VFD). SOURCE: NIST IR 6859 [2]
Access Control List (ACL)	A mechanism that implements access control for a system resource by enumerating the identities of the system entities that are permitted to access the resources. SOURCE: RFC 4949 [75]
Accreditation	The official management decision given by a senior agency official to authorize operation of an information system and to explicitly accept the risk to agency operations (including mission, functions, image, or reputation), agency assets, or individuals, based on the implementation of an agreed-upon set of security controls. SOURCE: NIST SP 800-53 [22]
Actuator	A device for moving or controlling a mechanism or system. It is operated by a source of energy, typically electric current, hydraulic fluid pressure, or pneumatic pressure, and converts that energy into motion. An actuator is the mechanism by which a control system acts upon an environment. The control system can be simple (a fixed mechanical or electronic system), software-based (e.g. a printer driver, robot control system), or a human or other agent.
Alarm	A device or function that signals the existence of an abnormal condition by making an audible or visible discrete change, or both, so as to attract attention to that condition. SOURCE: ANSI/ISA-5.1-2009
Antivirus Tools	Software products and technology used to detect malicious code, prevent it from infecting a system, and remove malicious code that has infected the system.
Application Server	A computer responsible for hosting applications to user workstations.
Attack	An attempt to gain unauthorized access to system services, resources, or information, or an attempt to compromise system integrity, availability, or confidentiality. SOURCE: CNSSI-4009

Authentication

Verifying the identity of a user, process, or device, often as a prerequisite to allowing access to resources in an information system.
SOURCE: NIST SP 800-53 [22]

Authorization

The right or a permission that is granted to a system entity to access a system resource.
SOURCE: RFC 4949 [75]

Backdoor

An undocumented way of gaining access to a computer system. A backdoor is a potential security risk.

Batch Process

A process that leads to the production of finite quantities of material by subjecting quantities of input materials to an ordered set of processing activities over a finite time using one or more pieces of equipment.
SOURCE: ANSI/ISA-88.01-1995

Broadcast

Transmission to all devices in a network without any acknowledgment by the receivers.
SOURCE: IEC/PAS 62410

Buffer Overflow

A condition at an interface under which more input can be placed into a buffer or data holding area than the capacity allocated, overwriting other information. Adversaries exploit such a condition to crash a system or to insert specially crafted code that allows them to gain control of the system.
SOURCE: NIST SP 800-28 [69]

Certification

A comprehensive assessment of the management, operational, and technical security controls in an information system, made in support of security accreditation, to determine the extent to which the controls are implemented correctly, operating as intended, and producing the desired outcome with respect to meeting the security requirements for the system.
SOURCE: NIST SP 800-37 [21]

Clear Text

Information that is not encrypted.

Communications Router

A communications device that transfers messages between two networks. Common uses for routers include connecting a LAN to a WAN, and connecting MTUs and RTUs to a long-distance network medium for SCADA communication.

Confidentiality

Preserving authorized restrictions on information access and disclosure, including means for protecting personal privacy and proprietary information.
SOURCE: NIST SP 800-53 [22]

Configuration (of a system or device)

Step in system design; for example, selecting functional units, assigning their locations, and defining their interconnections.
SOURCE: IEC/PAS 62409

Configuration Control

Process for controlling modifications to hardware, firmware, software, and documentation to ensure the information system is protected against improper modifications before, during, and after system implementation.
SOURCE: CNSSI-4009

Continuous Process

A process that operates on the basis of continuous flow, as opposed to batch, intermittent, or sequenced operations.

Control Algorithm

A mathematical representation of the control action to be performed.
SOURCE: The Automation, Systems, and Instrumentation Dictionary

Control

The part of the ICS used to perform the monitoring and control of the physical process. This includes all control servers, field devices, actuators, sensors, and their supporting communication systems.

Control Center

An equipment structure or group of structures from which a process is measured, controlled, and/or monitored.
SOURCE: ANSI/ISA-51.1-1979

Control Loop

A control loop consists of sensors for measurement, controller hardware such as PLCs, actuators such as control valves, breakers, switches and motors, and the communication of variables. Controlled variables are transmitted to the controller from the sensors. The controller interprets the signals and generates corresponding manipulated variables, based on set points, which it transmits to the actuators. Process changes from disturbances result in new sensor signals, identifying the state of the process, to again be transmitted to the controller.

Control Network

Those networks of an enterprise typically connected to equipment that controls physical processes and that is time or safety critical. The control network can be subdivided into zones, and there can be multiple separate control networks within one enterprise and site.
SOURCE: ISA99 [34]

Control Server

A controller that also acts as a server that hosts the control software that communicates with lower-level control devices, such as Remote Terminal Units (RTUs) and Programmable Logic Controllers (PLCs), over an ICS network. In a SCADA system, this is often called a SCADA server, MTU, or supervisory controller.

Control System   A system in which deliberate guidance or manipulation is used to achieve a prescribed value for a variable. Control systems include SCADA, DCS, PLCs and other types of industrial measurement and control systems.

Controlled Variable   The variable that the control system attempts to keep at the set point value. The set point may be constant or variable.
SOURCE: The Automation, Systems, and Instrumentation Dictionary

Controller   A device or program that operates automatically to regulate a controlled variable.
SOURCE: ANSI/ISA-51.1-1979

Cycle Time   The time, usually expressed in seconds, for a controller to complete one control loop where sensor signals are read into memory, control algorithms are executed, and corresponding control signals are transmitted to actuators that create changes the process resulting in new sensor signals.
SOURCE: The Automation, Systems, and Instrumentation Dictionary

Data Diode   A data diode (also referred to as a unidirectional gateway, deterministic one-way boundary device or unidirectional network) is a network appliance or device allowing data to travel only in one direction.

Database   A repository of information that usually holds plant-wide information including process data, recipes, personnel data, and financial data.
SOURCE: NIST IR 6859 [2]

Data Historian   A centralized database supporting data analysis using statistical process control techniques.

DC Servo Drive   A type of drive that works specifically with servo motors. It transmits commands to the motor and receives feedback from the servo motor resolver or encoder.
SOURCE: NIST IR 6859 [2]

Demilitarized Zone (DMZ)	An interface on a routing firewall that is similar to the interfaces found on the firewall's protected side. Traffic moving between the DMZ and other interfaces on the protected side of the firewall still goes through the firewall and can have firewall protection policies applied. SOURCE: SP 800-41 [85] A host or network segment inserted as a "neutral zone" between an organization's private network and the Internet. SOURCE: SP 800-45 [91] Perimeter network segment that is logically between internal and external networks. Its purpose is to enforce the internal network's Information Assurance policy for external information exchange and to provide external, untrusted sources with restricted access to releasable information while shielding the internal networks from outside attacks. SOURCE: CNSSI-4009
Denial of Service (DoS)	The prevention of authorized access to a system resource or the delaying of system operations and functions. SOURCE: RFC 4949 [75]
Diagnostics	Information concerning known failure modes and their characteristics. Such information can be used in troubleshooting and failure analysis to help pinpoint the cause of a failure and help define suitable corrective measures. SOURCE: The Automation, Systems, and Instrumentation Dictionary
Disaster Recovery Plan (DRP)	A written plan for processing critical applications in the event of a major hardware or software failure or destruction of facilities. SOURCE: NIST SP 800-34 [52]
Discrete Process	A type of process where a specified quantity of material moves as a unit (part or group of parts) between work stations and each unit maintains its unique identity. SOURCE: The Automation, Systems, and Instrumentation Dictionary
Distributed Control System (DCS)	In a control system, refers to control achieved by intelligence that is distributed about the process to be controlled, rather than by a centrally located single unit. SOURCE: The Automation, Systems, and Instrumentation Dictionary
Distributed Plant	A geographically distributed factory that is accessible through the Internet by an enterprise. SOURCE: NIST IR 6859 [2]

Disturbance

An undesired change in a variable being applied to a system that tends to adversely affect the value of a controlled variable.
SOURCE: ANSI/ISA-51.1-1979

Domain

An environment or context that includes a set of system resources and a set of system entities that have the right to access the resources as defined by a common security policy, security model, or security architecture. See Security Domain.
SOURCE: CNSSI-4009; SP 800-53 [22]; SP 800-37 [21]

Domain Controller

A server responsible for managing domain information, such as login identification and passwords.
SOURCE: NIST IR 6859 [2]

Encryption

Cryptographic transformation of data (called "plaintext") into a form (called "ciphertext") that conceals the data's original meaning to prevent it from being known or used. If the transformation is reversible, the corresponding reversal process is called "decryption," which is a transformation that restores encrypted data to its original state.
SOURCE: RFC 4949 [75]

Enterprise

An organization that coordinates the operation of one or more processing sites.
SOURCE: ANSI/ISA-88.01-1995

Enterprise Resource Planning (ERP) System

A system that integrates enterprise-wide information including human resources, financials, manufacturing, and distribution as well as connects the organization to its customers and suppliers.

Extensible Markup Language (XML)

A specification for a generic syntax to mark data with simple, human-readable tags, enabling the definition, transmission, validation, and interpretation of data between applications and between organizations.

Fault Tolerant

Of a system, having the built-in capability to provide continued, correct execution of its assigned function in the presence of a hardware and/or software fault.

Field Device

Equipment that is connected to the field side on an ICS. Types of field devices include RTUs, PLCs, actuators, sensors, HMIs, and associated communications.

Field Site

A subsystem that is identified by physical, geographical, or logical segmentation within the ICS. A field site may contain RTUs, PLCs, actuators, sensors, HMIs, and associated communications.

Fieldbus

A digital, serial, multi-drop, two-way data bus or communication path or link between low-level industrial field equipment such as sensors, transducers, actuators, local controllers, and even control room devices. Use of fieldbus technologies eliminates the need of point-to-point wiring between the controller and each device. A protocol is used to define messages over the fieldbus network with each message identifying a particular sensor on the network.

File Transfer Protocol (FTP)

FTP is an Internet standard for transferring files over the Internet. FTP programs and utilities are used to upload and download Web pages, graphics, and other files between local media and a remote server which allows FTP access.
SOURCE: API 1164

Firewall

An inter-network gateway that restricts data communication traffic to and from one of the connected networks (the one said to be "inside" the firewall) and thus protects that network's system resources against threats from the other network (the one that is said to be "outside" the firewall).
SOURCE: RFC 4949 [75]

An inter-network connection device that restricts data communication traffic between two connected networks. A firewall may be either an application installed on a general-purpose computer or a dedicated platform (appliance), which forwards or rejects/drops packets on a network. Typically firewalls are used to define zone borders. Firewalls generally have rules restricting which ports are open.
SOURCE: ISA-62443-1-1 [34]

Human-Machine Interface (HMI)

The hardware or software through which an operator interacts with a controller. An HMI can range from a physical control panel with buttons and indicator lights to an industrial PC with a color graphics display running dedicated HMI software.
SOURCE: NIST IR 6859 [2]

Software and hardware that allows human operators to monitor the state of a process under control, modify control settings to change the control objective, and manually override automatic control operations in the event of an emergency. The HMI also allows a control engineer or operator to configure set points or control algorithms and parameters in the controller. The HMI also displays process status information, historical information, reports, and other information to operators, administrators, managers, business partners, and other authorized users. Operators and engineers use HMIs to monitor and configure set points, control algorithms, send commands, and adjust and establish parameters in the controller. The HMI also displays process status information and historical information.

Identification

The process of verifying the identity of a user, process, or device, usually as a prerequisite for granting access to resources in an IT system.
SOURCE: NIST SP 800-47 [92]

Incident

An occurrence that actually or potentially jeopardizes the confidentiality, integrity, or availability of an information system or the information the system processes, stores, or transmits or that constitutes a violation or imminent threat of violation of security policies, security procedures, or acceptable use policies
SOURCE: FIPS 200 [16]; SP 800-53 [22]

Industrial Control System (ICS)

General term that encompasses several types of control systems, including supervisory control and data acquisition (SCADA) systems, distributed control systems (DCS), and other control system configurations such as Programmable Logic Controllers (PLC) often found in the industrial sectors and critical infrastructures. An ICS consists of combinations of control components (e.g., electrical, mechanical, hydraulic, pneumatic) that act together to achieve an industrial objective (e.g., manufacturing, transportation of matter or energy).

Information Security Program Plan

Formal document that provides an overview of the security requirements for an organization-wide information security program and describes the program management controls and common controls in place or planned for meeting those requirements.
SOURCE: NIST SP 800-53 [22]

Input/Output (I/O)

A general term for the equipment that is used to communicate with a computer as well as the data involved in the communications.
SOURCE: The Automation, Systems, and Instrumentation Dictionary

Insider

An entity inside the security perimeter that is authorized to access system resources but uses them in a way not approved by those who granted the authorization.
SOURCE: RFC 4949 [75]

Integrity

Guarding against improper information modification or destruction, and includes ensuring information non-repudiation and authenticity.
SOURCE: NIST SP 800-53 [22]

Intelligent Electronic Device (IED)

Any device incorporating one or more processors with the capability to receive or send data/control from or to an external source (e.g., electronic multifunction meters, digital relays, controllers).
SOURCE: AGA 12 [5]

Internet

The single interconnected world-wide system of commercial, government, educational, and other computer networks that share the set of protocols specified by the Internet Architecture Board (IAB) and the name and address spaces managed by the Internet Corporation for Assigned Names and Numbers (ICANN).
SOURCE: RFC 4949 [75]

Intrusion Detection System (IDS)	A security service that monitors and analyzes network or system events for the purpose of finding, and providing real-time or near real-time warning of, attempts to access system resources in an unauthorized manner. SOURCE: RFC 4949 [75]
Intrusion Prevention System (IPS)	A system that can detect an intrusive activity and can also attempt to stop the activity, ideally before it reaches its targets.
Jitter	The time or phase difference between the data signal and the ideal clock.
Key Logger	A program designed to record which keys are pressed on a computer keyboard used to obtain passwords or encryption keys and thus bypass other security measures.
Light Tower	A device containing a series of indicator lights and an embedded controller used to indicate the state of a process based on an input signal. SOURCE: NIST IR 6859 [2]
Local Area Network (LAN)	A group of computers and other devices dispersed over a relatively limited area and connected by a communications link that enables any device to interact with any other on the network.
Machine Controller	A control system/motion network that electronically synchronizes drives within a machine system instead of relying on synchronization via mechanical linkage.
Maintenance	Any act that either prevents the failure or malfunction of equipment or restores its operating capability. SOURCE: The Automation, Systems, and Instrumentation Dictionary
Malware	Software or firmware intended to perform an unauthorized process that will have adverse impact on the confidentiality, integrity, or availability of an information system. A virus, worm, Trojan horse, or other code-based entity that infects a host. Spyware and some forms of adware are also examples of malicious code (malware). SOURCE: NIST SP 800-53 [22]
Management Controls	The security controls (i.e., safeguards or countermeasures) for an information system that focus on the management of risk and the management of information security. SOURCE: NIST SP 800-18 [19]
Manipulated Variable	In a process that is intended to regulate some condition, a quantity or a condition that the control alters to initiate a change in the value of the regulated condition. SOURCE: The Automation, Systems, and Instrumentation Dictionary

Manufacturing Execution System (MES)	A system that uses network computing to automate production control and process automation. By downloading recipes and work schedules and uploading production results, a MES bridges the gap between business and plant-floor or process-control systems. SOURCE: NIST IR 6859 [2]
Master Terminal Unit (MTU)	See *Control Server*.
Modem	A device used to convert serial digital data from a transmitting terminal to a signal suitable for transmission over a telephone channel to reconvert the transmitted signal to serial digital data for the receiving terminal. SOURCE: NIST IR 6859 [2]
Motion Control Network	The network supporting the control applications that move parts in industrial settings, including sequencing, speed control, point-to-point control, and incremental motion. SOURCE: The Automation, Systems, and Instrumentation Dictionary
Network Interface Card (NIC)	A circuit board or card that is installed in a computer so that it can be connected to a network.
Object Linking and Embedding (OLE) for Process Control (OPC)	A set of open standards developed to promote interoperability between disparate field devices, automation/control, and business systems.
Operating System	An integrated collection of service routines for supervising the sequencing of programs by a computer. An operating system may perform the functions of input/output control, resource scheduling, and data management. It provides application programs with the fundamental commands for controlling the computer. SOURCE: The Automation, Systems, and Instrumentation Dictionary
Operational Controls	The security controls (i.e., safeguards or countermeasures) for an information system that are primarily implemented and executed by people (as opposed to systems). SOURCE: NIST SP 800-18 [19]
Password	A string of characters (letters, numbers, and other symbols) used to authenticate an identity or to verify access authorization.
Phishing	Tricking individuals into disclosing sensitive personal information by claiming to be a trustworthy entity in an electronic communication (e.g., internet web sites).

Photo Eye
A light sensitive sensor utilizing photoelectric control that converts a light signal into an electrical signal, ultimately producing a binary signal based on an interruption of a light beam.
SOURCE: NIST IR 6859 [2]

Plant
The physical elements necessary to support the physical process. This can include many of the static components not controlled by the ICS; however, the operation of the ICS may impact the adequacy, strength, and durability of the plant's components.

Port
The entry or exit point from a computer for connecting communications or peripheral devices.
SOURCE: The Automation, Systems, and Instrumentation Dictionary

Port Scanning
Using a program to remotely determine which ports on a system are open (e.g., whether systems allow connections through those ports).
SOURCE: NIST SP 800-61 [59]

Predisposing Condition
A condition that exists within an organization, a mission/business process, enterprise architecture, or information system including its environment of operation, which contributes to (i.e., increases or decreases) the likelihood that one or more threat events, once initiated, will result in undesirable consequences or adverse impact to organizational operations and assets, individuals, other organizations, or the Nation.
SOURCE: SP 800-30 [79]

Pressure Regulator
A device used to control the pressure of a gas or liquid.
SOURCE: NIST IR 6859 [2]

Pressure Sensor
A sensor system that produces an electrical signal related to the pressure acting on it by its surrounding medium. Pressure sensors can also use differential pressure to obtain level and flow measurements.
SOURCE: NIST IR 6859 [2]

Printer
A device that converts digital data to human-readable text on a paper medium.
SOURCE: NIST IR 6859 [2]

Process Controller
A type of computer system, typically rack-mounted, that processes sensor input, executes control algorithms, and computes actuator outputs.
SOURCE: NIST IR 6859 [2]

Programmable Logic Controller (PLC)	A solid-state control system that has a user-programmable memory for storing instructions for the purpose of implementing specific functions such as I/O control, logic, timing, counting, three mode (PID) control, communication, arithmetic, and data and file processing. SOURCE: The Automation, Systems, and Instrumentation Dictionary A small industrial computer originally designed to perform the logic functions executed by electrical hardware (relays, switches, and mechanical timer/counters). PLCs have evolved into controllers with the capability of controlling complex processes, and they are used substantially in SCADA systems and DCS. PLCs are also used as the primary controller in smaller system configurations. PLCs are used extensively in almost all industrial processes.
Protocol	A set of rules (i.e., formats and procedures) to implement and control some type of association (e.g., communication) between systems. SOURCE: RFC 4949 [75]
Protocol Analyzer	A device or software application that enables the user to analyze the performance of network data so as to ensure that the network and its associated hardware/software are operating within network specifications. SOURCE: The Automation, Systems, and Instrumentation Dictionary
Proximity Sensor	A non-contact sensor with the ability to detect the presence of a target within a specified range. SOURCE: NIST IR 6859 [2]
Proxy Server	A server that services the requests of its clients by forwarding those requests to other servers. SOURCE: CNSSI-4009
Real-Time	Pertaining to the performance of a computation during the actual time that the related physical process transpires so that the results of the computation can be used to guide the physical process. SOURCE: NIST IR 6859 [2]
Redundant Control Server	A backup to the control server that maintains the current state of the control server at all times. SOURCE: NIST IR 6859 [2]
Relay	An electromechanical device that completes or interrupts an electrical circuit by physically moving conductive contacts. The resultant motion can be coupled to another mechanism such as a valve or breaker. SOURCE: The Automation, Systems, and Instrumentation Dictionary

Remote Access   Access by users (or information systems) communicating external to an information system security perimeter.
SOURCE: NIST SP 800-53 [22]

Remote Access Point   Distinct devices, areas and locations of a control network for remotely configuring control systems and accessing process data. Examples include using a mobile device to access data over a LAN through a wireless access point, and using a laptop and modem connection to remotely access an ICS system.

Remote Diagnostics   Diagnostics activities conducted by individuals communicating external to an information system security perimeter.

Remote Maintenance   Maintenance activities conducted by individuals communicating external to an information system security perimeter.

Remote Terminal Unit (RTU)   A computer with radio interfacing used in remote situations where communications via wire is unavailable. Usually used to communicate with remote field equipment. PLCs with radio communication capabilities are also used in place of RTUs.

Special purpose data acquisition and control unit designed to support DCS and SCADA remote stations. RTUs are field devices often equipped with network capabilities, which can include wired and wireless radio interfaces to communicate to the supervisory controller. Sometimes PLCs are implemented as field devices to serve as RTUs; in this case, the PLC is often referred to as an RTU.

Resource Starvation   A condition where a computer process cannot be supported by available computer resources. Resource starvation can occur due to the lack of computer resources or the existence of multiple processes that are competing for the same computer resources.

Risk   The level of impact on agency operations (including mission, functions, image, or reputation), agency assets, or individuals resulting from the operation of an information system, given the potential impact of a threat and the likelihood of that threat occurring.
SOURCE: NIST SP 800-30 [79]

Risk Assessment   The process of identifying risks to agency operations (including mission, functions, image, or reputation), agency assets, or individuals by determining the probability of occurrence, the resulting impact, and additional security controls that would mitigate this impact. Part of risk management, synonymous with risk analysis. Incorporates threat and vulnerability analyses.
SOURCE: NIST SP 800-30 [79]

Risk Management	The process of managing risks to organizational operations (including mission, functions, image, reputation), organizational assets, individuals, other organizations, and the Nation, resulting from the operation of an information system, and includes: (i) the conduct of a risk assessment; (ii) the implementation of a risk mitigation strategy; and (iii) employment of techniques and procedures for the continuous monitoring of the security state of the information system. SOURCE: FIPS 200, Adapted [16]
Risk Management Framework	The Risk Management Framework (RMF), presented in NIST SP 800-37, provides a disciplined and structured process that integrates information security and risk management activities into the system development life cycle. SOURCE: SP 800-37 [21]
Router	A computer that is a gateway between two networks at OSI layer 3 and that relays and directs data packets through that inter-network. The most common form of router operates on IP packets. SOURCE: RFC 4949 [75]
Router Flapping	A router that transmits routing updates alternately advertising a destination network first via one route, then via a different route.
Safety Instrumented System (SIS)	A system that is composed of sensors, logic solvers, and final control elements whose purpose is to take the process to a safe state when predetermined conditions are violated. Other terms commonly used include emergency shutdown system (ESS), safety shutdown system (SSD), and safety interlock system (SIS). SOURCE: ANSI/ISA-84.00.01
SCADA Server	The device that acts as the master in a SCADA system. SOURCE: NIST IR 6859 [2]
Security Audit	Independent review and examination of a system's records and activities to determine the adequacy of system controls, ensure compliance with established security policy and procedures, detect breaches in security services, and recommend any changes that are indicated for countermeasures. SOURCE: ISO/IEC 7498
Security Controls	The management, operational, and technical controls (i.e., safeguards or countermeasures) prescribed for an information system to protect the confidentiality, integrity, and availability of the system and its information. SOURCE: FIPS PUB 199 [15]

Security Plan
Formal document that provides an overview of the security requirements for the information system and describes the security controls in place or planned for meeting those requirements.
SOURCE: NIST SP 800-53 [22]

Security Policy
Security policies define the objectives and constraints for the security program. Policies are created at several levels, ranging from organization or corporate policy to specific operational constraints (e.g., remote access). In general, policies provide answers to the questions "what" and "why" without dealing with "how." Policies are normally stated in terms that are technology-independent.
SOURCE: ISA99

Sensor
A device that produces a voltage or current output that is representative of some physical property being measured (e.g., speed, temperature, flow).
SOURCE: The Automation, Systems, and Instrumentation Dictionary

A device that measures a physical quantity and converts it into a signal which can be read by an observer or by an instrument. A sensor is a device, which responds to an input quantity by generating a functionally related output usually in the form of an electrical or optical signal.

Servo Valve
An actuated valve whose position is controlled using a servo actuator.
SOURCE: NIST IR 6859 [2]

Set Point
An input variable that sets the desired value of the controlled variable. This variable may be manually set, automatically set, or programmed.
SOURCE: The Automation, Systems, and Instrumentation Dictionary

Simple Network Management Protocol (SNMP)
A standard TCP/IP protocol for network management. Network administrators use SNMP to monitor and map network availability, performance, and error rates. To work with SNMP, network devices utilize a distributed data store called the Management Information Base (MIB). All SNMP-compliant devices contain a MIB which supplies the pertinent attributes of a device. Some attributes are fixed or "hard-coded" in the MIB, while others are dynamic values calculated by agent software running on the device.
SOURCE: API 1164

Single Loop Controller
A controller that controls a very small process or a critical process.
SOURCE: NIST IR 6859 [2]

Social Engineering
An attempt to trick someone into revealing information (e.g., a password) that can be used to attack systems or networks.
SOURCE: NIST SP 800-61 [59]

Solenoid Valve   A valve actuated by an electric coil. A solenoid valve typically has two states: open and closed.
SOURCE: NIST IR 6859 [2]

Spyware   Software that is secretly or surreptitiously installed onto an information system to gather information on individuals or organizations without their knowledge; a type of malicious code.
SOURCE: NIST SP 800-53 [22]

Statistical Process Control (SPC)   The use of statistical techniques to control the quality of a product or process.
SOURCE: The Automation, Systems, and Instrumentation Dictionary

Steady State   A characteristic of a condition, such as value, rate, periodicity, or amplitude, exhibiting only negligible change over an arbitrarily long period of time.
SOURCE: ANSI/ISA-51.1-1979

Supervisory Control   A term that is used to imply that the output of a controller or computer program is used as input to other controllers. See *Control Server*
SOURCE: The Automation, Systems, and Instrumentation Dictionary

Supervisory Control and Data Acquisition (SCADA)   A generic name for a computerized system that is capable of gathering and processing data and applying operational controls over long distances. Typical uses include power transmission and distribution and pipeline systems. SCADA was designed for the unique communication challenges (e.g., delays, data integrity) posed by the various media that must be used, such as phone lines, microwave, and satellite. Usually shared rather than dedicated.
SOURCE: The Automation, Systems, and Instrumentation Dictionary

System Security Plan   Formal document that provides an overview of the security requirements for a system and describes the security controls in place or planned for meeting those requirements.
SOURCE: NIST SP 800-18, Adapted [19]

Technical Controls   The security controls (i.e., safeguards or countermeasures) for an information system that are primarily implemented and executed by the information system through mechanisms contained in the hardware, software, or firmware components of the system.
SOURCE: NIST SP 800-18 [19]

Temperature Sensor   A sensor system that produces an electrical signal related to its temperature and, as a consequence, senses the temperature of its surrounding medium.
SOURCE: NIST IR 6859 [2]

Threat

Any circumstance or event with the potential to adversely impact agency operations (including mission, functions, image, or reputation), agency assets, or individuals through an information system via unauthorized access, destruction, disclosure, modification of information, and/or denial of service.
SOURCE: NIST SP 800-53 [22]

Threat Event

An event or situation that has the potential for causing undesirable consequences or impact.
SOURCE: SP 800-30 [79]

Threat Source

The intent and method targeted at the intentional exploitation of a vulnerability or a situation and method that may accidentally trigger a vulnerability. Synonymous with Threat Agent.
SOURCE: FIPS 200 [16]; SP 800-53 [22]; SP 800-53A [23]; SP 800-37 [21]

Transmission Control Protocol (TCP)

TCP is one of the main protocols in TCP/IP networks. Whereas the IP protocol deals only with packets, TCP enables two hosts to establish a connection and exchange streams of data. TCP guarantees delivery of data and also guarantees that packets will be delivered in the same order in which they were sent.
SOURCE: API 1164

Trojan Horse

A computer program that appears to have a useful function, but also has a hidden and potentially malicious function that evades security mechanisms, sometimes by exploiting legitimate authorizations of a system entity that invokes the program.
SOURCE: RFC 4949 [75]

Unauthorized Access

A person gains logical or physical access without permission to a network, system, application, data, or other resource.
SOURCE: NIST SP 800-61 [59]

Unidirectional Gateway

Unidirectional gateways are a combination of hardware and software. The hardware permits data to flow from one network to another, but is physically unable to send any information at all back into the source network. The software replicates databases and emulates protocol servers and devices.

Valve

An in-line device in a fluid-flow system that can interrupt flow, regulate the rate of flow, or divert flow to another branch of the system.
SOURCE: The Automation, Systems, and Instrumentation Dictionary

Variable Frequency Drive (VFD)

A type of drive that controls the speed, but not the precise position, of a non-servo, AC motor by varying the frequency of the electricity going to that motor. VFDs are typically used for applications where speed and power are important, but precise positioning is not.
SOURCE: NIST IR 6859 [2]

Virtual Private Network (VPN)	A restricted-use, logical (i.e., artificial or simulated) computer network that is constructed from the system resources of a relatively public, physical (i.e., real) network (such as the Internet), often by using encryption (located at hosts or gateways), and often by tunneling links of the virtual network across the real network. SOURCE: RFC 4949 [75]
Virus	A hidden, self-replicating section of computer software, usually malicious logic, that propagates by infecting (i.e., inserting a copy of itself into and becoming part of) another program. A virus cannot run by itself; it requires that its host program be run to make the virus active. SOURCE: RFC 4949 [75]
Virus Definitions	Predefined signatures for known malware used by antivirus detection algorithms.
Vulnerability	Weakness in an information system, system security procedures, internal controls, or implementation that could be exploited or triggered by a threat source. SOURCE: NIST SP 800-53 [22]
Whitelist	A list of discrete entities, such as hosts or applications that are known to be benign and are approved for use within an organization and/or information system. SOURCE: SP 800-128 [80]
Wide Area Network (WAN)	A physical or logical network that provides data communications to a larger number of independent users than are usually served by a local area network (LAN) and that is usually spread over a larger geographic area than that of a LAN. SOURCE: API 1164
Wireless Device	Any device that can connect to an ICS network via radio or infrared waves, usually to collect or monitor data, but also in some cases to modify control set points.
Workstation	A computer used for tasks such as programming, engineering, and design. SOURCE: NIST IR 6859 [2]
Worm	A computer program that can run independently, can propagate a complete working version of itself onto other hosts on a network, and may consume computer resources destructively. SOURCE: RFC 4949 [75]

Appendix C—Threat Sources, Vulnerabilities, and Incidents

Several terms are used to describe the inter-related concepts of threat, threat source, threat event, and incident. A *threat* is any circumstance or event with the potential to adversely impact organizational operations (including mission, functions, image, or reputation), organizational assets, individuals, other organizations, or the Nation through an information system via unauthorized access, destruction, disclosure, modification of information, and/or denial of service. Threats have some intent or method that may exploit of a vulnerability through either intentional or unintentional means, this intent or method referred to as the *threat source*. A *vulnerability* is a weakness in an information system (including an ICS), system security procedures, internal controls, or implementation that could be exploited or triggered by a threat source. A *threat event* is an event or situation that has the potential for causing undesirable consequences or impact. When a threat event occurs it becomes an *incident* that actually or potentially jeopardizes the confidentiality, integrity, or availability of an information system or the information the system processes, stores, or transmits or that constitutes a violation or imminent threat of violation of security policies, security procedures, or acceptable use policies. This section will explore ICS-specific threat sources, vulnerabilities, and incidents.

Threat Sources

Threats to ICS can come from numerous sources, which can be classified as adversarial, accidental, structural, and environmental. Table C-1 lists and defines known threats sources to ICS. It is necessary to create a risk management strategy for the ICS that protects the system against these possible threat sources. The threat source must be well understood in order to define and implement adequate protection. For example, environmental events (e.g. floods, earthquakes) are well understood, but may vary in their magnitude, frequency, and their ability to compound other interconnected events. However, adversarial threats depend on the resources available to the adversary and the emergence of previously unknown vulnerabilities or attacks.

Table C-1. Threats to ICS

Type of Threat Source	Description	Characteristics
ADVERSARIAL - Individual - Outsider - Insider - Trusted Insider - Privileged Insider - Group - Ad hoc - Established - Organization - Competitor - Supplier - Partner - Customer - Nation-State	Individuals, groups, organizations, or states that seek to exploit the organization's dependence on cyber resources (e.g., information in electronic form, information and communications technologies, and the communications and information-handling capabilities provided by those technologies)	Capability, Intent, Targeting
ACCIDENTAL - User - Privileged User/Administrator	Erroneous actions taken by individuals in the course of executing their everyday responsibilities.	Range of effects

Type of Threat Source	Description	Characteristics

STRUCTURAL
 	
- Information Technology (IT) Equipment
  - Storage
  - Processing
  - Communications
  - Display
  - Sensor
  - Controller
- Environmental Controls
  - Temperature/Humidity Controls
  - Power Supply
- Software
  - Operating System
  - Networking
  - General-Purpose Application
  - Mission-Specific Application
	Failures of equipment, environmental controls, or software due to aging, resource depletion, or other circumstances which exceed expected operating parameters.	Range of effects

ENVIRONMENTAL
- Natural or man-made disaster
  - Fire
  - Flood/Tsunami
  - Windstorm/Tornado
  - Hurricane
  - Earthquake
  - Bombing
  - Overrun
- Unusual Natural Event (e.g., sunspots)
- Infrastructure Failure/Outage
  - Telecommunications
  - Electrical Power
	Natural disasters and failures of critical infrastructures on which the organization depends, but which are outside the control of the organization.
	
	Note: Natural and man-made disasters can also be characterized in terms of their severity and/or duration. However, because the threat source and the threat event are strongly identified, severity and duration can be included in the description of the threat event (e.g., Category 5 hurricane causes extensive damage to the facilities housing mission-critical systems, making those systems unavailable for three weeks).
		Range of effects

Vulnerabilities and Predisposing Conditions

This section addresses vulnerabilities and predisposing conditions that may be found in typical ICS. *Vulnerabilities* are weaknesses in information systems, system procedures, controls, or implementations the can be exploited by a threat source. *Predisposing conditions* are properties of the organization, mission/business process, architecture, or information systems that contribute to the likelihood of a threat event. The order of these vulnerabilities and predisposing conditions does not necessarily reflect any priority in terms of likelihood of occurrence or severity of impact. Additionally, the vulnerabilities and predisposing conditions identified in this section should not be considered a complete list; it should also not be assumed that these issues are found within every ICS.

The vulnerabilities and predisposing conditions are grouped according to where they exist–such as in the organization's policy and procedures, or the inadequacy of security mechanisms implemented in hardware, firmware, and software. The former are referred to as being in the organization and the latter as being in the system. Understanding the source of vulnerabilities and predisposing conditions can assist in determining optimal mitigation strategies. The groups of vulnerabilities used in this appendix are:

- Policy and Procedure.
- Architecture and Design.
- Configuration and Maintenance.
- Physical.
- Software Development.
- Communication and Network.

Deeper analysis may uncover that causes and observations may not be one-to-one; that is, some underlying causes may exhibit multiple symptoms and some symptoms may come from more than one cause. SP 800-53 contains a taxonomy of security controls, or countermeasures, to mitigate vulnerabilities and predisposing conditions. These are categorized in families, where each family contains security controls related to the general security topic of the family. While the families and controls from 800-53 provide a more complete overview of the potential vulnerabilities and predisposing conditions within in an ICS, this section briefly reviews those issues known to be common within ICS.

Any given ICS will usually exhibit a subset of the identified vulnerabilities, but may also contain additional vulnerabilities and predisposing conditions unique to the particular ICS implementation that do not appear in this appendix. Specific current information on ICS vulnerabilities can be researched at the Industrial Control System Computer Emergency Response Team (ICS-CERT) Web site.[23]

Some vulnerabilities and predisposing conditions can be mitigated; others can only be accepted and controlled by appropriate countermeasures, but will result in some residual risk to the ICS. For example, some existing policies and procedures may be changed with a level of effort that the organization considers acceptable; others are more expeditiously dealt with by instituting additional policies and procedures.

Vulnerabilities in products and services acquired from outside the organization are rarely under the direct control of the organization. Changes may be influenced by market forces, but this is a slow and indirect approach. Instead, the organization may change predisposing conditions to reduce the likelihood that a systemic vulnerability will be exploited.

Policy and Procedure Vulnerabilities and Predisposing Conditions

Vulnerabilities and predisposing conditions are often introduced into the ICS because of incomplete, inappropriate, or nonexistent security policy, including its documentation, implementation guides (e.g., procedures), and enforcement. Management support of security policy and procedures is the cornerstone of any security program. Organization security policy can reduce vulnerabilities by mandating and enforcing proper conduct. Written policy and procedures are mechanisms for informing staff and stakeholders of decisions about behavior that is beneficial to the organization. From this perspective, policy is an educational and instructive way to reduce vulnerabilities. Enforcement is partner to policy, encouraging people to do the "right" thing. Various forms of corrective action are the usual consequences

---

[23]   http://ics-cert.us-cert.gov.http://ics-cert.us-cert.gov.

to personnel not following policy and procedures. Policies should be explicit about the consequences to individuals or organizations that do not conform.

There is usually a complex policy and procedure environment that includes laws and regulations, overlapping jurisdictions and spheres of influence, economics, custom, and history. The larger enterprise is often subdivided into organizational units that should work together to reduce vulnerabilities. The scope and hierarchical relationship among policies and procedures needs to be managed for maximum effectiveness.

Certain controls in SP 800-53 and the ICS overlay in Appendix G— specify responsibilities and requirements for the organization, while others focus on the capabilities and operation of the various systems within the organization. For example, the control AC-6, Least Privilege, states "The organization employs the principle of least privilege, allowing only authorized accesses for users (or processes acting on behalf of users) which are necessary to accomplish assigned tasks in accordance with organizational missions and business functions." The organization has to make decisions that get codified in policy and procedures. Some resulting artifacts, such as job descriptions that include roles, responsibilities, and authority, remain in a form suitable for people, while other artifacts, such as attributes, privileges, and access control rules, are implemented in IT.

Note that the ICS overlay follows SP 800-53 in employing the term "organization" very flexibly so that its guidance can be used by all sizes of organizational entities up and down an organization chart. Specific organizations should be identified, starting with the organization responsible for issuing and maintaining the policy or procedure.

Table C-2 presents examples of observed policy and procedure vulnerabilities for ICS.

Table C-2. Policy and Procedure Vulnerabilities and Predisposing Conditions

Vulnerability	Description
Inadequate security policy for the ICS	Vulnerabilities are often introduced into ICS due to inadequate policies or the lack of policies specifically for control system security. Every countermeasure should be traceable to a policy. This ensures uniformity and accountability. Policy must include portable and mobile devices used with ICS.
No formal ICS security training and awareness program	A documented formal security training and awareness policy and program is designed to keep staff up to date on organizational security policies and procedures as well as threats, industry cybersecurity standards, and recommended practices. Without training on specific ICS policies and procedures, staff cannot be expected to maintain a secure ICS environment.
Absent or deficient ICS equipment implementation guidelines	Equipment implementation guidelines should be kept up to date and readily available. These guidelines are an integral part of security procedures in the event of an ICS malfunction.
Lack of administrative mechanisms for security policy enforcement	Staff responsible for enforcing security should be held accountable for administering documented security policies and procedures.
Inadequate review of the effectiveness of the ICS security controls	Procedures and schedules should exist to determine the extent to which the security program and its constituent controls are implemented correctly, operating as intended, and producing the desired outcome with respect to meeting the security requirements for the ICS. The examination is sometimes called an "audit," "evaluation," or "assessment." Policy should address the stage of the life-cycle, purpose, technical expertise, methodology, and level of independence.

Vulnerability	Description
No ICS-specific contingency plan	A contingency plan should be prepared, tested and available in the event of a major hardware or software failure or destruction of facilities. Lack of a specific plan for the ICS could lead to extended downtimes and production loss.
Lack of configuration management policy	Lack of policy and procedures for ICS configuration change management can lead to unmanageable and highly vulnerable inventory of hardware, firmware, and software.
Lack of adequate access control policy	Access control enforcement depends of policy the correctly models roles, responsibilities, and authorizations. The policy model must enable the way the organization functions.
Lack of adequate authentication policy	Authentication policies are needed to define when authentication mechanisms (e.g., passwords, smart cards) must be used, how strong they must be, and how they must be maintained. Without policy, systems might not have appropriate authentication controls, making unauthorized access to systems more likely. Authentication policies should be developed as part of an overall ICS security program taking into account the capabilities of the ICS and its personnel to handle more complex passwords and other mechanisms.
Inadequate incident detection and response plan and procedures	Incident detection and response plans, procedures, and methods are necessary for rapidly detecting incidents, minimizing loss and destruction, preserving evidence for later forensic examination, mitigating the weaknesses that were exploited, and restoring ICS services. Establishing a successful incident response capability includes continually monitoring for anomalies, prioritizing the handling of incidents, and implementing effective methods of collecting, analyzing, and reporting data.
Lack of redundancy for critical components	Lack of redundancy in critical components could provide single point of failure possibilities

System Vulnerabilities and Predisposing Conditions

Security controls must clearly identify the systems to which they apply. Systems range widely in size, scope, and capability. At the small end of the spectrum, a system may be an individual hardware or software product or service. At the other end of the spectrum we find large complex systems, systems-of-systems, and networks, all of which incorporate hardware architecture and software framework (including application frameworks), where the combination supports the operation of the ICS.

System vulnerabilities can occur in the hardware, firmware, and software used to build the ICS. Sources of vulnerabilities include design flaws, development flaws, misconfigurations, poor maintenance, poor administration, and connections with other systems and networks. Many of the controls in the SP 800-53 and the ICS overlay in Appendix G— specify what the system must do to mitigate these vulnerabilities.

The potential vulnerabilities and predisposing conditions commonly found within ICS systems are categorized with the following tables:

■ Table C-3. Architecture and Design Vulnerabilities and Predisposing Conditions.

■ Table C-4. Configuration and Maintenance Vulnerabilities and Predisposing Conditions.

■ Table C-5. Physical Vulnerabilities and Predisposing Conditions.

- Table C-6. Software Development Vulnerabilities and Predisposing Conditions.

- Table C-7. Communication and Network Configuration Vulnerabilities and Predisposing Conditions.

Table C-3. Architecture and Design Vulnerabilities and Predisposing Conditions

Vulnerability	Description
Inadequate incorporation of security into architecture and design.	Incorporating security into the ICS architecture, design must start with budget, and schedule of the ICS. The security architecture is part of the Enterprise Architecture. The architectures must address the identification and authorization of users, access control mechanism, network topologies, and system configuration and integrity mechanisms.
Insecure architecture allowed to evolve	The network infrastructure environment within the ICS has often been developed and modified based on business and operational requirements, with little consideration for the potential security impacts of the changes. Over time, security gaps may have been inadvertently introduced within particular portions of the infrastructure. Without remediation, these gaps may represent backdoors into the ICS.
No security perimeter defined	If the ICS does not have a security perimeter clearly defined, then it is not possible to ensure that the necessary security controls are deployed and configured properly. This can lead to unauthorized access to systems and data, as well as other problems.
Control networks used for non-control traffic	Control and non-control traffic have different requirements, such as determinism and reliability, so having both types of traffic on a single network makes it more difficult to configure the network so that it meets the requirements of the control traffic. For example, non-control traffic could inadvertently consume resources that control traffic needs, causing disruptions in ICS functions.
Control network services not within the control network	Where IT services such as Domain Name System (DNS), and Dynamic Host Configuration Protocol (DHCP) are used by control networks, they are often implemented in the IT network, causing the ICS network to become dependent on the IT network that may not have the reliability and availability requirements needed by the ICS.
Inadequate collection of event data history	Forensic analysis depends on collection and retention of sufficient data. Without proper and accurate data collection, it might be impossible to determine what caused a security incident to occur. Incidents might go unnoticed, leading to additional damage and/or disruption. Regular security monitoring is also needed to identify problems with security controls, such as misconfigurations and failures.

Table C-4. Configuration and Maintenance Vulnerabilities and Predisposing Conditions

Vulnerability	Description
Hardware, firmware, and software not under configuration management.	The organization doesn't know what it has, what versions it has, where they are, or what their patch status is, resulting in an inconsistent, and ineffective defense posture. A process for controlling modifications to hardware, firmware, software, and documentation should be implemented to ensure an ICS is protected against inadequate or improper modifications before, during, and after system implementation. A lack of configuration change management procedures can lead to security oversights, exposures, and risks. To properly secure an ICS, there should be an accurate listing of the assets in the system and their current configurations. These procedures are critical to executing business continuity and disaster recovery plans.

Vulnerability	Description
OS and vendor software patches may not be developed until significantly after security vulnerabilities are found	Because of the tight coupling between ICS software and the underlying ICS, changes must undergo expensive and time-consuming comprehensive regression testing. The elapsed time for such testing and subsequent distribution of updated software provides a long window of vulnerability
OS and application security patches are not maintained or vendor declines to patch vulnerability	Out-of-date OSs and applications may contain newly discovered vulnerabilities that could be exploited. Documented procedures should be developed for how security patches will be maintained. Security patch support may not even be available for ICS that use outdated OSs, so procedures should include contingency plans for mitigating vulnerabilities where patches may never be available.
Inadequate testing of security changes	Modifications to hardware, firmware, and software deployed without testing could compromise normal operation of the ICS. Documented procedures should be developed for testing all changes for security impact. The live operational systems should never be used for testing. The testing of system modifications may need to be coordinated with system vendors and integrators.
Poor remote access controls	There are many reasons why an ICS may need to be remotely accessed, including vendors and system integrators performing system maintenance functions, and also ICS engineers accessing geographically remote system components. Remote access capabilities must be adequately controlled to prevent unauthorized individuals from gaining access to the ICS.
Poor configurations are used	Improperly configured systems may leave unnecessary ports and protocols open, these unnecessary functions may contain vulnerabilities that increase the overall risk to the system. Using default configurations often exposes vulnerabilities and exploitable services. All settings should be examined.
Critical configurations are not stored or backed up	Procedures should be available for restoring ICS configuration settings in the event of accidental or adversary-initiated configuration changes to maintain system availability and prevent loss of data. Documented procedures should be developed for maintaining ICS configuration settings.
Data unprotected on portable device	If sensitive data (e.g., passwords, dial-up numbers) is stored in the clear on portable devices such as laptops and mobile devices and these devices are lost or stolen, system security could be compromised. Policy, procedures, and mechanisms are required for protection.
Passwords generation, use, and protection not in accord with policy	There is a large body of experience with using passwords in IT that is applicable to ICS. Password policy and procedure must be followed to be effective. Violations of password policy and procedures can drastically increase ICS vulnerability.
Inadequate access controls applied	Access controls must be matched to the way the organization allocates responsibilities and privilege to its personnel. Poorly specified access controls can result in giving an ICS user too many or too few privileges. The following exemplify each case: • System configured with default access control settings gives an operator administrative privileges • System improperly configured results in an operator being unable to take corrective actions in an emergency situation
Improper data linking	ICS data storage systems may be linked with non-ICS data sources. An example of this is database links, which allow data from one database to be automatically replicated to others. Data linkage may create a vulnerability if it is not properly configured and may allow unauthorized data access or manipulation.
Malware protection not installed or up to date	Installation of malicious software, or malware, is a common attack. Malware protection software, such as antivirus software, must be kept current in a very dynamic environment. Outdated malware protection software and definitions leave the system open to new malware threats.

Vulnerability	Description
Malware protection implemented without sufficient testing	Malware protection software deployed without sufficient testing could impact normal operation of the ICS and block the system from performing necessary control actions.
Denial of service (DoS)	ICS software could be vulnerable to DoS attacks, resulting in the prevention of authorized access to a system resource or delaying system operations and functions.
Intrusion detection/prevention software not installed	Incidents can result in loss of system availability and integrity; the capture, modification, and deletion of data; and incorrect execution of control commands. IDS/IPS software may stop or prevent various types of attacks, including DoS attacks, and also identify attacked internal hosts, such as those infected with worms. IDS/IPS software must be tested prior to deployment to determine that it does not compromise normal operation of the ICS.
Logs not maintained	Without proper and accurate logs, it might be impossible to determine what caused a security event to occur.

Table C-5. Physical Vulnerabilities and Predisposing Conditions

Vulnerability	Description
Unauthorized personnel have physical access to equipment	Physical access to ICS equipment should be restricted to only the necessary personnel, taking into account safety requirements, such as emergency shutdown or restarts. Improper access to ICS equipment can lead to any of the following: • Physical theft of data and hardware • Physical damage or destruction of data and hardware • Unauthorized changes to the functional environment (e.g., data connections, unauthorized use of removable media, adding/removing resources) • Disconnection of physical data links • Undetectable interception of data (keystroke and other input logging)
Radio frequency, electromagnetic pulse (EMP), static discharge, brownouts and voltage spikes	The hardware used for control systems is vulnerable to radio frequency and electro-magnetic pulses (EMP), static discharge, brownouts and voltage spikes.. The impact can range from temporary disruption of command and control to permanent damage to circuit boards. Proper shielding, grounding, power conditioning, and/or surge suppression is recommended.
Lack of backup power	Without backup power to critical assets, a general loss of power will shut down the ICS and could create an unsafe situation. Loss of power could also lead to insecure default settings.
Loss of environmental control	Loss of environmental control (e.g., temperatures, humidity) could lead to equipment damage, such as processors overheating. Some processors will shut down to protect themselves; some may continue to operate but in a minimal capacity and may produce intermittent errors, continually reboot, or become permanently incapacitated.
Unsecured physical ports	Unsecured universal serial bus (USB) and PS/2 ports could allow unauthorized connection of thumb drives, keystroke loggers, etc.

Table C-6. Software Development Vulnerabilities and Predisposing Conditions

Vulnerability	Description
Improper Data Validation	ICS software may not properly validate user inputs or received data to ensure validity. Invalid data may result in numerous vulnerabilities including buffer overflows, command injections, cross-site scripting, and path traversals.
Installed security capabilities not enabled by default	Security capabilities that were installed with the product are useless if they are not enabled or at least identified as being disabled.
Inadequate authentication, privileges, and access control in software	Unauthorized access to configuration and programming software could provide the ability to corrupt a device.

Table C-7. Communication and Network Configuration Vulnerabilities and Predisposing Conditions

Vulnerability	Description
Data flow controls not employed	Data flow controls, based on data characteristics, are needed to restrict which information is permitted between systems. These controls can prevent exfiltration of information and illegal operations.
Firewalls nonexistent or improperly configured	A lack of properly configured firewalls could permit unnecessary data to pass between networks, such as control and corporate networks, allowing attacks and malware to spread between networks, making sensitive data susceptible to monitoring/eavesdropping, and providing individuals with unauthorized access to systems.
Inadequate firewall and router logs	Without proper and accurate logs, it might be impossible to determine what caused a security incident to occur.
Standard, well-documented communication protocols are used in plain text	Adversaries that can monitor the ICS network activity can use a protocol analyzer or other utilities to decode the data transferred by protocols such as telnet, File Transfer Protocol (FTP), Hypertext Transfer Protocol (HTTP), and Network File System (NFS). The use of such protocols also makes it easier for adversaries to perform attacks against the ICS and manipulate ICS network activity.
Authentication of users, data or devices is substandard or nonexistent	Many ICS protocols have no authentication at any level. Without authentication, there is the potential to replay, modify, or spoof data or to spoof devices such as sensors and user identities.
Use of unsecure industry-wide ICS protocols	ICS protocols often have few or no security capabilities, such as authentication and encryption, to protect data from unauthorized access or tampering. Additionally, incorrect implementation of the protocols can lead to additional vulnerabilities.
Lack of integrity checking for communications	There are no integrity checks built into most industrial control protocols; adversaries could manipulate communications undetected. To ensure integrity, the ICS can use lower-layer protocols (e.g., IPsec) that offer data integrity protection.
Inadequate authentication between wireless clients and access points	Strong mutual authentication between wireless clients and access points is needed to ensure that clients do not connect to a rogue access point deployed by an adversary, and also to ensure that adversaries do not connect to any of the ICS's wireless networks.
Inadequate data protection between wireless clients and access points	Sensitive data between wireless clients and access points should be protected using strong encryption to ensure that adversaries cannot gain unauthorized access to the unencrypted data.

Incidents

A threat event is an event or situations that could potentially cause an undesirable consequence or impact to the ICS resulting from some threat source. In NIST SP 800-30 Rev. 1, Appendix E identifies a broad set of threat events that could potentially impact information systems [79]. The properties of an ICS may also present unique threat events, specifically addressing how the threat events can manipulates the process of the ICS to cause physical damage. Table C-8 provides an overview of potential ICS threat events.

Table C-8. Example Adversarial Incidents

Threat Event	Description
Denial of Control Action	Control systems operation disrupted by delaying or blocking the flow of information, thereby denying availability of the networks to control system operators or causing information transfer bottlenecks or denial of service by IT-resident services (such as DNS)
Control Devices Reprogrammed	Unauthorized changes made to programmed instructions in PLCs, RTUs, DCS, or SCADA controllers, alarm thresholds changed, or unauthorized commands issued to control equipment, which could potentially result in damage to equipment (if tolerances are exceeded), premature shutdown of processes (such as prematurely shutting down transmission lines), causing an environmental incident, or even disabling control equipment
Spoofed System Status Information	False information sent to control system operators either to disguise unauthorized changes or to initiate inappropriate actions by system operators
Control Logic Manipulation	Control system software or configuration settings modified, producing unpredictable results
Safety Systems Modified	Safety systems operation are manipulated such that they either (1) do not operate when needed or (2) perform incorrect control actions that damage the ICS
Malware on Control Systems	Malicious software (e.g., virus, worm, Trojan horse) introduced into the system.

In addition, in control systems that cover a wide geographic area, the remote sites are often not staffed and may not be physically monitored. If such remote systems are physically breached, the adversaries could establish a connection back to the control network.

Sources of Incidents

An accurate accounting of cyber incidents on control systems is difficult to determine. However, individuals in the industry who have been focusing on this issue see similar growth trends between vulnerabilities exposed in traditional IT systems and those being found in control systems. ICS-CERT is a DHS organization that focuses on reducing the risk across critical infrastructure by identifying threats and vulnerabilities, while also providing mitigation strategies. ICS-CERT provides a trusted party where system owners and operators can report information about incidents within their ICS and obtain advice on mitigating their risk. Information submitted by infrastructure owners and operators is protected under the Critical Infrastructure Information Act of 2002 as Protected Critical Infrastructure Information (PCII) from disclosure under the Freedom of Information Act (FOIA), disclosure under state, tribal, and local disclosure laws, use in regulatory actions, and use in civil litigation. In the event of an incident at critical infrastructure facilities, ICS-CERT can also perform onsite deployments to respond to and analyze incidents. ICS-CERT publishes advisories of new security vulnerabilities discovered in common ICS platforms. Figure C-1 demonstrates (1) the number of ICS incidents reported, (2) the number of onsite

ICS deployments taken by ICS-CERT, and (3) number of ICS vulnerabilities reported between years 2010 and 2013[24].

Other sources of control system impact information show an increase in control system incidents as well. This information should not be assumed to contain all ICS related incidents or discovered vulnerabilities as some information may go unreported.

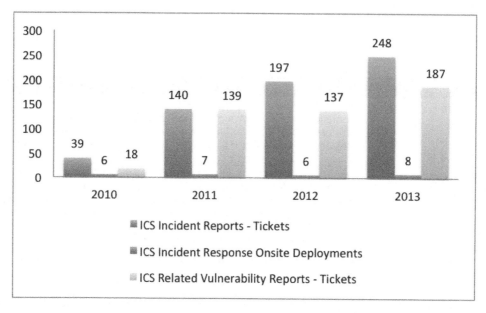

Figure C-1. ICS-CERT Reported Incidents by Year

Documented Incidents

Numerous ICS incidents have been reported that demonstrate how threat sources can negatively impact an ICS. These events help demonstrate the severity of the threat sources, vulnerabilities, and impacts within the ICS domain. As mentioned in Section C.2, the four broad categories of threat sources are adversarial, accidental, structural, and environmental. Often the incident can be the result of multiple threat sources (e.g. an environmental event causes a system failure, which is responded to incorrectly by an operator resulting in an accidental event). Reported incidents from these categories include the following:

Adversarial Events

■ **Worcester Air Traffic Communications**[25]. In March 1997, a teenager in Worcester, Massachusetts disabled part of the public switched telephone network using a dial-up modem connected to the system. This knocked out phone service at the control tower, airport security, the airport fire department, the weather service, and carriers that use the airport. Also, the tower's main radio transmitter and another transmitter that activates runway lights were shut down, as well as a printer that controllers use to monitor flight progress. The attack also knocked out phone service to 600 homes and businesses in the nearby town of Rutland.

---

[24] https://ics-cert.us-cert.gov/

[25] Additional information on the Worcester Air Traffic Communications incident can be found at:
   http://www.cnn.com/TECH/computing/9803/18/juvenile.hacker/index.html

- **Maroochy Shire Sewage Spill[26].** In the spring of 2000, a former employee of an Australian organization that develops manufacturing software applied for a job with the local government, but was rejected. Over a two-month period, the disgruntled rejected employee reportedly used a radio transmitter on as many as 46 occasions to remotely break into the controls of a sewage treatment system. He altered electronic data for particular sewerage pumping stations and caused malfunctions in their operations, ultimately releasing about 264 000 gallons of raw sewage into nearby rivers and parks.

- **Davis-Besse[27].** In August 2003, the Nuclear Regulatory Commission confirmed that in January 2003, the Microsoft SQL Server worm known as Slammer infected a private computer network at the idled Davis-Besse nuclear power plant in Oak Harbor, Ohio, disabling a safety monitoring system for nearly five hours. In addition, the plant's process computer failed, and it took about six hours for it to become available again. Slammer reportedly also affected communications on the control networks of at least five other utilities by propagating so quickly that control system traffic was blocked.

- **Zotob Worm[28].** In August 2005, a round of Internet worm infections knocked 13 of DaimlerChrysler's U.S. automobile manufacturing plants offline for almost an hour, stranding workers as infected Microsoft Windows systems were patched. Plants in Illinois, Indiana, Wisconsin, Ohio, Delaware, and Michigan were knocked offline. While the worm affected primarily Windows 2000 systems, it also affected some early versions of Windows XP. Symptoms include the repeated shutdown and rebooting of a computer. Zotob and its variations caused computer outages at heavy-equipment maker Caterpillar Inc., aircraft-maker Boeing, and several large U.S. news organizations.

- **Stuxnet Worm[29].** Stuxnet was a Microsoft Windows computer worm discovered in July 2010 that specifically targeted industrial software and equipment. The worm initially spread indiscriminately, but included a highly specialized malware payload that was designed to target only specific SCADA systems that were configured to control and monitor specific industrial processes

- **Brute Force Attacks on Internet-Facing Control Systems[30].** On February 22, 2013 ICS-CERT received a report from a gas compressor station owner about an increase in brute force attempts to access their process control network. The forensic evidence contained 10 separate IPs and additional calls of a similar nature from additional natural gas pipeline asset owners, which yielded 39 additional IPs of concern. Log analysis showed a date range from January 16, 2013 but there have been no reports since March 8, 2013.

- **Shamoon[31].** Saudi Aramco, which is the world's 8th largest oil refiner, experienced a malware attack that targeted their refineries and overwrote the attacked system's Master Boot Records (MBR), partition tables and other random data files. This caused the systems to become unusable.

---

[26] Additional information on the Maroochy Shire Sewage Spill incident can be found at:
http://csrc.nist.gov/groups/SMA/fisma/ics/documents/Maroochy-Water-Services-Case-Study_report.pdf and
http://www.theregister.co.uk/2001/10/31/hacker_jailed_for_revenge_sewage/ [each accessed 4/16/15].

[27] Additional information on the Davis-Besse incident can be found at:
http://www.securityfocus.com/news/6767 [accessed 4/16/15].

[28] Additional information on the Zotob Worm incident can be found at: http://www.eweek.com/c/a/Security/Zotob-PnP-Worms-Slam-13-DaimlerChrysler-Plants [accessed 4/16/15].

[29] Additional information on the Stuxnet worm can be found at: http://en.wikipedia.org/wiki/Stuxnet [accessed 4/16/15].

[30] Additional information on ICS-CERT reported incidents can be found at:
https://ics-cert.us-cert.gov/Information-Products [accessed 4/16/15].

[31] Additional information on Shamoon can be found at:
http://ics-cert.us-cert.gov/sites/default/files/Monitors/ICS-CERT_Monitor_Sep2012.pdf [accessed 4/16/15].

- **German Steel Mill Attack**[32]. In 2014, hackers manipulated and disrupted control systems to such a degree that a blast furnace could not be properly shut down, resulting in "massive"—though unspecified—damage.

Structural Events

- **CSX Train Signaling System**[33]. In August 2003, the Sobig computer virus was blamed for shutting down train signaling systems throughout the east coast of the U.S. The virus infected the computer system at CSX Corp.'s Jacksonville, Florida headquarters, shutting down signaling, dispatching, and other systems. According to Amtrak spokesman Dan Stessel, ten Amtrak trains were affected in the morning. Trains between Pittsburgh and Florence, South Carolina were halted because of dark signals, and one regional Amtrak train from Richmond, Virginia to Washington and New York was delayed for more than two hours. Long-distance trains were also delayed between four and six hours.

- **Northeast Power Blackout**[34]. In August 2003, failure of the alarm processor in First Energy's SCADA system prevented control room operators from having adequate *situational awareness* of critical operational changes to the electrical grid. Additionally, effective reliability oversight was prevented when the state estimator at the Midwest Independent System Operator failed due to incomplete information on topology changes, preventing contingency analysis. Several key 345 kV transmission lines in Northern Ohio tripped due to contact with trees. This eventually initiated cascading overloads of additional 345 kV and 138 kV lines, leading to an uncontrolled cascading failure of the grid. A total of 61 800 MW load was lost as 508 generating units at 265 power plants tripped.

- **Taum Sauk Water Storage Dam Failure**[35]. In December 2005, the Taum Sauk Water Storage Dam suffered a catastrophic failure releasing a billion gallons of water. The failure of the reservoir occurred as the reservoir was being filled to capacity or may have possibly been overtopped. The current working theory is that the reservoir's berm was overtopped when the routine nightly pump-back operation failed to cease when the reservoir was filled. According to the utility, the gauges at the dam read differently than the gauges at the Osage plant at the Lake of the Ozarks, which monitors and operates the Taum Sauk plant remotely. The stations are linked together using a network of microwave towers, and there are no operators on-site at Taum Sauk.

- **Bellingham, Washington Gasoline Pipeline Failure**[36]. In June 1999, 900 000 liters (237 000 gallons) of gasoline leaked from a 16 in. (40.64 cm) pipeline and ignited 1.5 hours later causing 3 deaths, 8 injuries, and extensive property damage. The pipeline failure was exacerbated by control systems not able to perform control and monitoring functions. "Immediately prior to and during the incident, the SCADA system exhibited poor performance that inhibited the pipeline controllers from seeing and reacting to the development of an abnormal pipeline operation." A key recommendation

---

[32] Additional information on the German steel mill incident can be found at: http://www.wired.com/2015/01/german-steel-mill-hack-destruction/ [accessed 4/16/15].

[33] Additional information on the CSX Train Signaling System incident can be found at: http://www.cbsnews.com/stories/2003/08/21/tech/main569418.shtml and http://www.informationweek.com/story/showArticle.jhtml?articleID=13100807 [each accessed 4/16/15].

[34] Additional information on the Northeast Power Blackout incident can be found at: http://energy.gov/sites/prod/files/oeprod/DocumentsandMedia/BlackoutFinalImplementationReport%282%29.pdf [accessed 4/16/15].http://www.oe.energy.gov/DocumentsandMedia/BlackoutFinal-Web.pdf

[35] Additional information on the Taum Sauk Water Storage Dam Failure incident can be found at: http://www.ferc.gov/industries/hydropower/safety/projects/taum-sauk/ipoc-rpt/full-rpt.pdf [accessed 4/16/15].

[36] Additional information on the Bellingham, Washington Gasoline Pipeline Failure incident can be found at http://csrc.nist.gov/groups/SMA/fisma/ics/documents/Bellingham_Case_Study_report%2020Sep071.pdf and http://www.ntsb.gov/investigations/AccidentReports/Reports/PAR0202.pdf [each accessed 4/16/15].

from the NTSB report issued October 2002 was to utilize an off-line development and testing system for implementing and testing changes to the SCADA database.

■ **Browns Ferry-3 PLC Failure**[37]. In August 2006, TVA was forced to manually shut down one of their plant's two reactors after unresponsive PLCs problems caused two water pumps to fail and threatened the stability of the plant itself. Although there were dual redundant PLCs, they were connected to the same Ethernet network. Later testing on the failed devices discovered that they would crash when they encountered excessive network traffic.

Environmental Events

■ **Fukushima Daiichi Nuclear Disaster**[38]. The Great East Japan Earthquake on 11 March 2011 struck off the coast of Japan, sending a massive tsunami inland towards the nuclear plant. The tsunami compromised the plants seawall, flooding much of the plant including the location housing the emergency generators. This emergency power was critical to operate the control rooms and also to provide coolant water for the reactors. The loss of coolant caused the reactor cores to overheat to the point where the fuel's zirconium cladding reacted with water, releasing hydrogen gas and fueling large explosions in three of the four reactor buildings. This resulted in large-scale radiation leakage that has impacted plant employees, nearby citizens, and the local environment. Post event analysis found that the plant's emergency response center had insufficient secure communication lines to provide other areas of the plant with information on key safety related instrumentation.

Accidental Events

■ **Vulnerability Scanner Incidents**[39]. While a ping sweep was being performed on an active SCADA network that controlled 3 meter (9 foot) robotic arms, it was noticed that one arm became active and swung around 180 degrees. The controller for the arm was in standby mode before the ping sweep was initiated. In a separate incident, a ping sweep was being performed on an ICS network to identify all hosts that were attached to the network, for inventory purposes, and it caused a system controlling the creation of integrated circuits in the fabrication plant to hang. This test resulted in the destruction of $50,000 worth of wafers.

■ **Penetration Testing Incident**[40]. A natural gas utility hired an IT security consulting organization to conduct penetration testing on its corporate IT network. The consulting organization carelessly ventured into a part of the network that was directly connected to the SCADA system. The penetration test locked up the SCADA system and the utility was not able to send gas through its pipelines for four hours. The outcome was the loss of service to its customer base for those four hours.

---

[37] Additional information on the Browns Ferry -3 PLC Failure incident can be found at:
http://www.nrc.gov/reading-rm/doc-collections/gen-comm/info-notices/2007/in200715.pdf [accessed 4/16/15].
[38] Additional information can be found at: http://www-pub.iaea.org/MTCD/meetings/PDFplus/2011/cn200/documentation/cn200_Final-Fukushima-Mission_Report.pdf and
http://pbadupws.nrc.gov/docs/ML1414/ML14140A185.pdf [each accessed 4/16/15].
[39] Additional information on the vulnerability scanner incidents can be found at: http://energy.sandia.gov/wp-content/gallery/uploads/sand_2005_2846p.pdfhttp://www.sandia.gov/scada/documents/sand_2005_2846p.pdf [accessed 4/16/15].
[40] Additional information on penetration testing incidents can be found at: http://energy.sandia.gov/wp-content/gallery/uploads/sand_2005_2846p.pdf [accessed 4/16/15].

Appendix D—Current Activities in Industrial Control System Security

This appendix contains abstracts of some of the many activities that are addressing ICS cybersecurity. Please be aware that organization descriptions and related information provided in this appendix has been drawn primarily from the listed organizations' Web sites and from other reliable public sources, but has not been verified. Readers are encouraged to contact the organizations directly for the most up-to-date and complete information.

American Gas Association (AGA) Standard 12, "Cryptographic Protection of SCADA Communications"

American Gas Association: **http://www.aga.org/**

The American Gas Association, representing 195 local energy utility organizations that deliver natural gas to more than 56 million homes, businesses, and industries throughout the United States, advocates the interests of its energy utility members and their customers, and provides information and services. The AGA 12 series of documents recommends practices designed to protect SCADA communications against cyber incidents. The recommended practices focus on ensuring the confidentiality of SCADA communications.

The purpose of the AGA 12 series is to save SCADA system owners' time and effort by recommending a comprehensive system designed specifically to protect SCADA communications using cryptography. The AGA 12 series may be applied to water, wastewater, and electric SCADA-based distribution systems because of their similarities with natural gas systems, however timing requirements may be different. Recommendations included in the series 12 documents may also apply to other ICS. Additional topics planned for future addendums in this series include key management, protection of data at rest, and security policies.

American Petroleum Institute (API) Standard 1164, "Pipeline SCADA Security"

American Petroleum Institute: **http://www.api.org/**

The American Petroleum Institute represents more than 400 members involved in all aspects of the oil and natural gas industry. API 1164 provides guidance to the operators of oil and natural gas pipeline systems for managing SCADA system integrity and security. The guideline is specifically designed to provide operators with a description of industry practices in SCADA security, and to provide the framework needed to develop sound security practices within the operator's individual organizations. It stresses the importance of operators understanding system vulnerability and risks when reviewing the SCADA system for possible system improvements. API 1164 provides a means to improve the security of SCADA pipeline operations by:

- Listing the processes used to identify and analyze the SCADA system's susceptibility to incidents.

- Providing a comprehensive list of practices to harden the core architecture.

- Providing examples of industry recommended practices.

The guideline targets small to medium pipeline operators with limited IT security resources. The guideline is applicable to most SCADA systems, not just oil and natural gas SCADA systems. The appendices of the document include a checklist for assessing a SCADA system and an example of a SCADA control system security plan.

Electric Power Research Institute (EPRI)

http://www.epri.com/Our-Work/Pages/Cyber-Security.aspx,
http://smartgrid.epri.com/NESCOR.aspx

The Electric Power Research Institute (EPRI) is a nonprofit center for public interest energy and environmental research. EPRI brings together member organizations, the Institute's scientists and engineers, and other leading experts to work collaboratively on solutions to the challenges of electric power. These solutions span nearly every area of power generation, delivery, and use, including health, safety, and environment. EPRI's members represent over 90% of the electricity generated in the United States.

Industrial Control Systems Cyber Emergency Response Team (ICS-CERT)

https://ics-cert.us-cert.gov/About-Industrial-Control-Systems-Cyber-Emergency-Response-Team

The Industrial Control Systems Cyber Emergency Response Team (ICS-CERT) operates within the National Cybersecurity and Integration Center (NCCIC), a division of the Department of Homeland Security's Office of Cybersecurity and Communications (DHS CS&C). NCCIC/ICS-CERT is a key component of the DHS Strategy for Securing Control Systems. The primary goal of the Strategy is to build a long-term common vision where effective risk management of control systems security can be realized through successful coordination efforts. ICS-CERT provides a control system security focus in collaboration with US-CERT to:

- Respond to and analyze control systems related incidents.

- Conduct vulnerability and malware analysis.

- Provide onsite support for incident response and forensic analysis.

- Provide situational awareness in the form of actionable intelligence.

- Coordinate the responsible disclosure of vulnerabilities/mitigations.

- Share and coordinate vulnerability information and threat analysis through information products and alerts.

ICS-CERT coordinates control systems-related security incidents and information sharing with Federal, State, and local agencies and organizations, the intelligence community, and private sector constituents, including vendors, owners and operators, and international and private sector CERTs. The focus on control systems cybersecurity provides a direct path for coordination of activities among all members of the critical infrastructure stakeholder community.

As a functional component of the NCCIC, ICS-CERT provides focused operational capabilities for defense of control system environments against emerging cyber threats.

ICS-CERT provides efficient coordination of control-systems-related security incidents and information sharing with federal, state, and local agencies and organizations, the Intelligence Community, private sector constituents including vendors, owners, and operators, and international and private sector computer security incident response teams (CSIRTs). The focus on control systems cybersecurity provides a direct path for coordination of activities for all members of the stakeholder community.

ICS-CERT Cyber Security Evaluation Tool (CSET®)

http://ics-cert.us-cert.gov/Assessments

The Cyber Security Evaluation Tool (CSET®) is a DHS product that assists organizations in protecting their key national cyber assets. It was developed under the direction of the DHS ICS-CERT by cybersecurity experts and with assistance from NIST. This tool provides users with a systematic and repeatable approach for assessing the security posture of their cyber systems and networks. It includes both high-level and detailed questions related to all industrial control and IT systems.

CSET is a desktop software tool that guides users through a step-by-step process to assess their control system and information technology network security practices against recognized industry standards. The output from CSET is a prioritized list of recommendations for improving the cybersecurity posture of the organization's enterprise and industrial control cyber systems. The tool derives the recommendations from a database of cybersecurity standards, guidelines, and practices. Each recommendation is linked to a set of actions that can be applied to enhance cybersecurity controls.

CSET has been designed for easy installation and use on a stand-alone laptop or workstation. It incorporates a variety of available standards from organizations such as NIST, NERC, Transportation Security Administration (TSA), U.S. Department of Defense (DoD), and others. When the tool user selects one or more of the standards, CSET will open a set of questions to be answered. The answers to these questions will be compared against a selected security assurance level, and a detailed report will be generated to show areas for potential improvement. CSET provides an excellent means to perform a self-assessment of the security posture of your control system environment.

ICS-CERT Recommended Practices

https://ics-cert.us-cert.gov/Introduction-Recommended-Practices

ICS-CERT works with the control systems community to ensure that recommended practices, which are made available, have been vetted by subject-matter experts in industry before being made publicly available in support of this program.

Recommended practices are developed to help users reduce their exposure and susceptibility to cyber attacks. These recommendations are based on understanding the cyber threats, control systems vulnerabilities and attack paths, and secure architecture design.

The recommended practices working group selects topics to be implemented in the recommended practices section. Additional supporting documents detailing a wide variety of control systems topics associated with cyber vulnerabilities and their mitigation have been developed and vetted by the working group for accuracy. These documents will be updated and topics added to address additional content and emerging issues.

Institute of Electrical and Electronics Engineers, Inc. (IEEE)

http://www.ieee.org

IEEE 1686-2007 – Standard for Substation IED Cybersecurity Capabilities. The functions and features to be provided in substation intelligent electronic devices (IEDs) to accommodate critical infrastructure protection programs are defined in this standard. Security regarding the access, operation, configuration, firmware revision, and data retrieval from an IED is addressed in this standard. Communications for the purpose of power system protection (teleprotection) is not addressed. Encryption for the secure transmission of data both within and external to the substation, including supervisory control and data acquisition, is not part of this standard as this is addressed in other efforts."

IEEE P1711 - Standard for a Cryptographic Protocol for Cybersecurity of Substation Serial Links. This standard defines a cryptographic protocol to provide integrity, and optional confidentiality, for cybersecurity of serial links. It does not address specific applications or hardware implementations, and is independent of the underlying communications protocol.

IEEE 1815-2012 - Standard for Electric Power System Communications-Distributed Network Protocol (DNP3). This standard describes the DNP3 SCADA protocol, incorporating version five of the application-layer authentication procedure called DNP3 Secure Authentication (DNP3-SAv5). DNP3-SAv5 uses a HMAC process to verify that data and commands are received (without tampering) from authorized individual users or devices while limiting computational and communications overhead. SAv5 supports remote update (add/change/revoke) of user credentials using either symmetric or PKI techniques. SAv5 authenticates but does not encrypt messages, hence it does not provide confidentiality. SAv5 can be used together with encryption techniques such as TLS or IEEE 1711 where confidentiality is required.

Institute for Information Infrastructure Protection (I3P)

http://www.thei3p.org/

The I3P is a consortium of leading national cybersecurity institutions, including academic research centers, government laboratories, and non-profit organizations. It was founded in September 2001 to help meet a well-documented need for improved research and development (R&D) to protect the nation's information infrastructure against catastrophic failures. The institute's main role is to coordinate a national cybersecurity R&D program and help build bridges between academia, industry, and government. The I3P continues to work toward identifying and addressing critical research problems in information infrastructure protection and opening information channels between researchers, policymakers, and infrastructure operators. Currently, the I3P does the following:

■ Fosters collaboration among academia, industry, and government on pressing cybersecurity problems.

■ Develops, manages, and supports national-scale research projects.

■ Provides research fellowship opportunities to qualified post-doctoral researchers, faculty, and research scientists.

■ Hosts workshops, meetings, and events on cybersecurity and information infrastructure protection issues.

■ Builds and supports a knowledge base as an online vehicle for sharing and distributing information to I3P members and others working on information security challenges.

International Electrotechnical Commission (IEC) Technical Committees 65 and 57

http://www.iec.ch/

IEC is a standards organization that prepares and publishes international standards for all electrical, electronic, and related technologies. These standards serve as a basis for creating national standards and as references for drafting international tenders and contracts. IEC's members include manufacturers, providers, distributors, vendors, consumers, and users, all levels of governmental agencies, professional societies, trade associations, and standards developers from over 60 countries.

In 2004 the IEC Technical Sub-Committee 65C (Industrial Networks), through its working group WG13 (cybersecurity), started to address security issues - within the IEC 61784 standard – for field buses and other industrial communication networks. Results of this work are outlined in part 4, entitled "Digital data communications for measurement and control – Profiles for secure communications in industrial networks."

TC65 WG10 is working to extend this field level communication to address security standards across common automation networking scenarios. The standard being drafted as a result of this work is IEC 62443, entitled "Security for industrial process measurement and control – Network and system security." It is based on a modular security architecture consisting of requirement sets. These modules are mapped into ICS component and network architecture. The resulting requirements can then be formulated for use as the basis for Requests for Proposals (RFP) for data communication standards, and security audits.

TC 57 is focused on Power Systems Management and Associated Information Exchange and is divided up into a series of working groups. Each working group is comprised of members of national standards committees from the countries that participate in the IEC. Each working group is responsible for the development of standards within its domain. The current working groups are:

■ WG 3: Telecontrol protocols.

■ WG 9: Distribution automation using distribution line carrier systems.

■ WG 10: Power system IED communication and associated data models.

■ WG 13: Energy management system application program interface (EMS-API).

■ WG 14: System interfaces for distribution management (SIDM).

■ WG 15: Data and communication security.

■ WG 16: Deregulated energy market communications.

■ WG 17: Communications Systems for Distributed Energy Resources (DER).

■ WG 18: Hydroelectric power plants – Communication for monitoring and control.

■ WG 19: Interoperability within TC 57 in the long term.

■ WG 20: Planning of (single-sideband) power line carrier systems (IEC 60495) Planning of (single-sideband) power line carrier systems (IEC 60663).

■ WG 21: Interfaces and protocol profiles relevant to systems connected to the electrical grid.

ISA99 Industrial Automation and Control Systems Security Standards

http://www.isa.org/isa99

The ISA99 standards development committee brings together industrial cybersecurity experts from across the globe to develop ISA standards on industrial automation and control system (IACS) security. This original and ongoing ISA99 work is being standardized by the IEC in producing the multi-standard IEC 62443 series. The committee's focus is to improve the confidentiality, integrity, and availability of components or systems used for automation or control and provides criteria for procuring and implementing secure control systems. Compliance with the committee's guidance will improve industrial automation and control system electronic security, and will help identify vulnerabilities and address them, thereby reducing the risk of compromising confidential information or causing industrial automation control system degradation or failure.

All ISA-62443 standards and technical reports are organized into four general categories called General, Policies and Procedures, System, and Component.

- General category includes common or foundational information such as concepts, models and terminology. Also included are work products that describe security metrics and security life cycles for IACS.

- Policies and Procedures category of work products targets the Asset Owner. These address various aspects of creating and maintaining an effective IACS security program.

- System category includes work products that describe system design guidance and requirements for the secure integration of control systems. Core in this is the zone and conduit design model.

- Component category includes work products that describe the specific product development and technical requirements of control system products. This is primarily intended for control product vendors, but can be used by integrator and asset owners for to assist in the procurement of secure products.

The current status of the ISA-62443 documents is provided on the ISA99 Wiki at http://isa99.isa.org/ISA99 Wiki/

General
- **ISA-62443-1-1 (IEC/TS 62443-1-1)** (formerly referred to as "ISA-99 Part 1") was originally published as ISA standard ANSI/ISA-99.00.01-2007, as well as an IEC technical specification IEC/TS 62443-1-1. The ISA99 committee is currently revising it to make it align with other documents in the series, and to clarify normative content.

- **ISA-TR62443-1-2 (IEC 62443-1-2)** is a master glossary of terms used by the ISA99 committee. This document is a working draft.

- **ISA-62443-1-3 (IEC 62443-1-3)** identifies a set of compliance metrics for IACS security. This document is currently under development and the committee will be releasing a draft for comment in 2013.

- **ISA-TR62443-1-4 (IEC/TS 62443-1-4)** defines the IACS security life cycle and use case. This work product has been proposed as part of the series, but as of January 2013 development had not yet started.

Policies and Procedures

■ **ISA-62443-2-1 (IEC 62443-2-1)** (formerly referred to as "ANSI/ISA 99.02.01-2009 or ISA-99 Part 2") addresses how to establish an IACS security program. This standard is approved and published the IEC as IEC 62443-2-1. It now being revised to permit closer alignment with the ISO 27000 series of standards.

■ **ISA-TR62443-2-2 (IEC 62443-2-2)** addresses how to operate an IACS security program. This standard is currently under development.

■ **ISA-TR62443-2-3 (IEC/TR 62443-2-3)** is a technical report on the subject of patch management in IACS environments. This report is currently under development.

■ **ISA-62443-2-4 (IEC 62443-2-4)** focuses on the certification of IACS supplier security policies and practices. This document was adopted from the WIB organization and is now a working product of the IEC TC65/WG10 committee. The proposed ISA version will be a U.S. national publication of the IEC standard.

System

■ **ISA-TR62443-3-1 (IEC/TR 62443-3-1)** is a technical report on the subject of suitable technologies for IACS security. This report is approved and published as ANSI/ISA-TR99.00.01-2007 and is now being revised.

■ **ISA-62443-3-2 (IEC 62443-3-2)** addresses how to define security assurance levels using the zones and conduits concept. This standard is currently under development.

■ **ISA-62443-3-3 (IEC 62443-3-3)** defines detailed technical requirements for IACS security. This standard has been published as ANSI/ISA-62443-3-3 (99.03.03)-2013. It was previously numbered as ISA-99.03.03.

Component

■ **ISA-62443-4-1 (IEC 62443-4-1)** addresses the requirements for the development of secure IACS products and solutions. This standard is currently under development.

■ **ISA-62443-4-2 (IEC 62443-4-2)** series address detailed technical requirements for IACS components level. This standard is currently under development.

ISA100 Wireless Systems for Automation

http://www.isa.org/isa100

The ISA100 Committee will establish standards, recommended practices, technical reports, and related information that will define procedures for implementing wireless systems in the automation and control environment with a focus on the field level. Guidance is directed towards those responsible for the complete life cycle including the designing, implementing, on-going maintenance, scalability or managing industrial automation and control systems, and shall apply to users, system integrators, practitioners, and control systems manufacturers and vendors.

ISO 27001

http://www.iso.org/, http://www.27000.org

ISO 27001 provides a model for establishing, implementing, operating, monitoring, reviewing, maintaining and improving an Information Security Management System. The objective of the standard itself is to "provide requirements for establishing, implementing, maintaining and continuously improving an Information Security Management System (ISMS)." Regarding its adoption, this should be a strategic decision. Further, "The design and implementation of an organization's information security management system is influenced by the organization's needs and objectives, security requirements, the organizational processes used and the size and structure of the organization." The content sections of the standard include:

- Context of the Organization.

- Information Security Leadership.

- Planning an ISMS.

- Support.

- Operation.

- Performance Evaluation.

- Improvement.

- Annex A – List of controls and their objectives.

The 2005 version of the standard heavily employed the Plan-Do-Check-Act model to structure the processes, and reflect the principles set out in the OECG guidelines (see oecd.org). However, the latest, 2013 version, places more emphasis on measuring and evaluating how well an organization's ISMS is performing.

ISO 27002

http://www.iso.org/, http://www.27000.org

ISO 27002 "established guidelines and general principles for initiating, implementing, maintaining, and improving information security management within an organization." The actual controls listed in the standard are intended to address the specific requirements identified via a formal risk assessment. The standard is also intended to provide a guide for the development of "organizational security standards and effective security management practices and to help build confidence in inter-organizational activities."[41]

In 2013 the current version was published. ISO 27002:2013 contains 114 controls, fewer than the 133 documented in the 2005 version. However for additional granularity, these are presented in 14 sections, rather than the original 11:

- Security Policy.

- Organization of Information Security.

- Human Resource Security.

- Asset Management.

- Access Control.

- Cryptography.

- Physical and Environmental Security.

- Operations Security.

- Communications Security.

- Information Systems Acquisition, Development, Maintenance.

- Supplier Relationships.

- Information Security Incident Management.

- Information Security Aspects of Business Continuity.

- Compliance.

---

[41] http://www.27000.org/iso-27002.htm.

International Council on Large Electric Systems (CIGRE)

http://www.cigre.org/

The International Council on Large Electric Systems (CIGRE) is a nonprofit international association based in France. It has established several study committees to promote and facilitate the international exchange of knowledge in the electrical industry by identifying recommended practices and developing recommendations. Three of its study committees focus on control systems:

- The objectives of the B3 Substations Committee include the adoption of technological advances in equipment and systems to achieve increased reliability and availability.

- The C2 System Operation and Control Committee focuses on the technical capabilities needed for the secure and economical operation of existing power systems including control centers and operators.

- The D2 Information Systems and Telecommunication for Power Systems Committee monitors emerging technologies in the industry and evaluates their possible impact. In addition, it focuses on the security requirements of the information systems and services of control systems.

LOGIIC – Linking the Oil and Gas Industry to Improve Cybersecurity

http://www.dhs.gov/csd-logiic

The LOGIIC (Linking the Oil and Gas Industry to Improve Cybersecurity) program is an ongoing collaboration of oil and natural gas companies and the DHS Science and Technology Directorate (S&T). LOGIIC was formed in 2004 to facilitate cooperative research, development, testing, and evaluation procedures to improve cybersecurity in petroleum industry digital control systems. The program undertakes collaborative R&D projects to improve the level of cybersecurity in critical systems of interest to the oil and natural gas sector. The program objective is to promote the interests of the sector while maintaining impartiality, the independence of the participants, and vendor neutrality. After a successful first project, the LOGIIC consortium was formally established as a collaboration between DHS, the Automation Federation, and five of the major oil and gas companies. The LOGIIC program has completed several R&D projects, and more projects are being planned and started.

National SCADA Test Bed (NSTB)

http://energy.sandia.gov/infrastructure-security/cyber/scada-systems/testbeds/national-scada-testbed/

The National Supervisory Control and Data Acquisition (SCADA) Test Bed is a DOE Office of Electricity Delivery and Energy Reliability (OE) -sponsored resource to help secure our nation's energy control systems. It combines state-of-the-art operational system testing facilities with research, development, and training to discover and address critical security vulnerabilities and threats to the energy sector.

Working in partnership with the energy sector, the National SCADA Test Bed seeks to:

- Identify and mitigate existing vulnerabilities.

- Facilitate development of security standards.

- Serve as an independent entity to test SCADA systems and related control system technologies.

- Identify and promote best cybersecurity practices.

- Increase awareness of control systems security within the energy sector.

- Develop advanced control system architectures and technologies that are more secure and robust.

Partners in the NSTB include Idaho National Laboratory, Sandia National Laboratories, Argonne National Laboratory, Pacific Northwest National Laboratory, and the National Institute of Standards and Technology.

NIST Special Publication 800 Series Security Guidelines

http://csrc.nist.gov/publications/nistpubs/index.html

The NIST Special Publication 800 series of documents on information technology reports on the NIST Information Technology Laboratory (ITL) research, guidance, and outreach efforts in computer security, and its collaborative activities with industry, government, and academic organizations. Focus areas include cryptographic technology and applications, advanced authentication, public key infrastructure, internetworking security, criteria and assurance, and security management and support. In addition to NIST SP 800-82, the following is a listing of some additional 800 series documents that have significant relevance to the ICS security community. These as well as many others are available through the URL listed above.

- NIST SP 800-18 Revision 1, *Guide for Developing Security Plans for Federal Information Systems* [19].

- NIST SP 800-30 Revision 1, *Guide for Conducting Risk Assessments* [79].

- NIST SP 800-37 Revision 1, *Guide for Applying the Risk Management Framework to Federal Information Systems: A Security Life Cycle Approach* [21].

- NIST SP 800-39, *Managing Information Security Risk: Organization, Mission, and Information System View* [20].

- NIST SP 800-40 Revision 3, *Guide to Enterprise Patch Management Technologies* [40].

- NIST SP 800-41 Revision 1, *Guidelines on Firewalls and Firewall Policy* [85].

- NIST SP 800-48 Revision 1, *Guide to Securing Legacy IEEE 802.11 Wireless Networks* 0.

- NIST SP 800-50, *Building an Information Technology Security Awareness and Training Program* [61].

- NIST SP 800-53 Revision 4, *Security and Privacy Controls for Federal Information Systems and Organizations* [22].

- NIST SP 800-53A Revision 4, *Assessing Security and Privacy Controls in Federal Information Systems and Organizations: Building Effective Security Assessment Plans* [23].

- NIST SP 800-61 Revision 2, *Computer Security Incident Handling Guide* [59].

- NIST SP 800-63-2, *Electronic Authentication Guideline* [53].

- NIST SP 800-64 Revision 2, *Security Considerations in the Information System Development Life Cycle* [46].

- NIST SP 800-70 Revision 2, *National Checklist Program for IT Products: Guidelines for Checklist Users and Developers* [26].

- NIST SP 800-77, *Guide to IPsec VPNs* [74].

- NIST SP 800-83 Revision 1, *Guide to Malware Incident Prevention and Handling for Desktops and Laptops* [60].

- NIST SP 800-86, *Guide to Integrating Forensic Techniques into Incident Response* [93].

- NIST SP 800-88 Revision 1, *Guidelines for Media Sanitization* [78].

- NIST SP 800-92, *Guide to Computer Security Log Management* [68].

- NIST SP 800-94, *Guide to Intrusion Detection and Prevention Systems (IDPS)* [55].

- NIST SP 800-97, *Establishing Robust Security Networks: a Guide to IEEE 802.11i* [64].

- NIST SP 800-100, *Information Security Handbook: A Guide for Managers* [27].

- NIST SP 800-111, *Guide to Storage Encryption Technologies for End User Devices* [94].

- NIST SP 800-115, *Technical Guide to Information Security Testing and Assessment* [41].

- NIST SP 800-123, *Guide to General Server Security* [95].

- NIST SP 800-127, *Guide to Securing WiMAX Wireless Communications* [96].

- NIST SP 800-128, *Guide for Security-Focused Configuration Management of Information Systems* [97].

- NIST SP 800-137, *Information Security Continuous Monitoring (ISCM) for Federal Information Systems and Organizations* [81].

NIST Cybersecurity Framework

http://www.nist.gov/cyberframework/index.cfm

Recognizing that the national and economic security of the United States depends on the reliable functioning of critical infrastructure, the President issued Executive Order 13636, Improving Critical Infrastructure Cybersecurity, in February 2013 [83]. It directed NIST to work with stakeholders to develop a voluntary framework – based on existing standards, guidelines, and practices – for reducing cyber risks to critical infrastructure.

NIST released the first version of the Framework for Improving Critical Infrastructure Cybersecurity on February 12, 2014 [83]. The Framework, created through collaboration between industry and government, consists of standards, guidelines, and practices to promote the protection of critical infrastructure. The prioritized, flexible, repeatable, and cost-effective approach of the Framework helps owners and operators of critical infrastructure to manage cybersecurity-related risk.

The Department of Homeland Security's Critical Infrastructure Cyber Community C³ Voluntary Program helps align critical infrastructure owners and operators with existing resources that will assist their efforts to adopt the Cybersecurity Framework and manage their cyber risks. Learn more about the C³ Voluntary Program by visiting: www.dhs.gov/ccubedvp.

NIST has also issued a companion Roadmap that discusses NIST's next steps with the Framework and identifies key areas of cybersecurity development, alignment, and collaboration.

NIST Industrial Control System Security Project

http://csrc.nist.gov/groups/SMA/fisma/ics/

As part of the continuing effort to provide effective security standards and guidance to federal agencies and their contractors in support of the Federal Information Security Management Act and as part of the effort to protect the nation's critical infrastructure, NIST continues to work with public and private sector entities on sector-specific security issues.

Industrial and process control systems are an integral part of the US critical infrastructure and the protection of those systems is a priority for the federal government. This project intends to build upon the current FISMA security standards and provide targeted extensions and/or interpretations of those standards for industrial and process controls systems where needed. Since many industrial and process controls systems are supporting private sector organizations, NIST will collaborate with ongoing standards efforts addressing these sector-specific types of systems.

NIST Cybersecurity for Manufacturing Systems Project

http://www.nist.gov/el/isd/cs/csms.cfm

Smart manufacturing systems need to be protected from vulnerabilities that may arise as a result of their increased connectivity, use of wireless networks and sensors, and use of widespread information technology. Manufacturers are hesitant to adopt common security technologies, such as encryption and device authentication, due to concern for potential negative performance impacts in their systems. This is exacerbated by a threat environment that has changed dramatically with the appearance of advanced persistent attacks specifically targeting industrial systems, such as Stuxnet. This project will develop a cybersecurity risk management framework with supporting guidelines, methods, metrics and tools to enable manufacturers, technology providers, and solution providers to assess and assure cybersecurity for smart manufacturing systems. The cybersecurity risk management framework and methodology will stimulate manufacturer adoption and enable effective use of security technologies, leading to smart manufacturing systems that offer security, reliability, resilience and continuity in the face of disruption and major incidents.

NIST Cybersecurity for Smart Grid Systems Project

http://www.nist.gov/el/smartgrid/cybersg.cfm

Smart grid cybersecurity must address not only deliberate attacks, such as from disgruntled employees, industrial espionage, and terrorists, but also inadvertent compromises of the information infrastructure due to user errors, equipment failures, and natural disasters. The Smart Grid Interoperability Panel (SGIP) Cybersecurity Committee (SGCC), which is led and managed by the NIST Information Technology Laboratory (ITL), Computer Security Division, is moving forward in fiscal year 2014 to address the critical cybersecurity needs in the areas of Advanced Metering Infrastructure (AMI) security requirements, cloud computing, supply chain, and privacy recommendations related to emerging standards. This project will provide foundational cybersecurity guidance, cybersecurity reviews of standards and requirements, outreach, and foster collaborations in the cross-cutting issue of cybersecurity in the smart grid.

NIST Smart Grid System Testbed Facility

http://www.nist.gov/el/smartgrid/sgtf.cfm

NIST is charged by the 2007 Energy Independence and Security Act (EISA) with facilitation of interoperability standards to enable successful implementation of the evolving cyber-physical national electric grid system known as the smart grid (SG). The Smart Grid Testbed Facility will create a unique set of interconnected and interacting labs in several key measurement areas—contiguously located on the NIST Gaithersburg site—that will accelerate the development of SG interoperability standards by providing a combined testbed platform for system measurements, characterization of smart grid protocols, and validation of SG standards, with particular emphasis on microgrids. (A microgrid is defined as a subset of the grid which has the capability of being quickly disconnected from, and functioning independently of, the larger grid.) Measurements will include eight areas: power conditioning, synchrophasor metrology, cybersecurity, precision time synchronization, electric power metering, modeling/evaluation of SG communications, sensor interfaces, and energy storage. The testbed will serve as a core Smart Grid Program research facility to address measurement needs of the evolving SG industrial community including the measurement and validation issues.

North American Electric Reliability Corporation (NERC)

http://www.nerc.com/

NERC's mission is to improve the reliability and security of the bulk power system in North America. To achieve that, NERC develops and enforces reliability standards; monitors the bulk power system; assesses future adequacy; audits owners, operators, and users for preparedness; and educates and trains industry personnel. NERC is a self-regulatory organization that relies on the diverse and collective expertise of industry participants. As the Electric Reliability Organization, NERC is subject to audit by the U.S. Federal Energy Regulatory Commission and governmental authorities in Canada

NERC has issued a set of cybersecurity standards to reduce the risk of compromise to electrical generation resources and high-voltage transmission systems above 100 kV, also referred to as bulk electric systems. Bulk electric systems include Balancing Authorities, Reliability Coordinators, Interchange Authorities, Transmission Providers, Transmission Owners, Transmission Operators, Generation Owners, Generation Operators, and Load Serving Entities. The cybersecurity standards include audit measures and levels of non-compliance that can be tied to penalties.

The set of NERC cybersecurity Standards includes the following:

- CIP-002, *Cyber Security - Critical Cyber Asset Identification.*

- CIP-003, *Cyber Security - Security Management Controls.*

- CIP-004, *Cyber Security - Personnel & Training.*

- CIP-005, *Cyber Security - Electronic Security Perimeter(s).*

- CIP-006, *Cyber Security - Physical Security of Critical Cyber Assets.*

- CIP-007, *Cyber Security - Systems Security Management.*

- CIP-008, *Cyber Security - Incident Reporting and Response Planning.*

- CIP-009, *Cyber Security - Recovery Plans for Critical Cyber Assets.*

SANS ICS Security Courses

http://ics.sans.org/

The ICS curriculum provides hands-on training courses focused on Attacking and Defending ICS environments. These courses equip both security professionals and control system engineers with the knowledge and skills they need to safeguard our critical infrastructures.

The Global Industrial Cyber Security Professional (GICSP) is the newest certification in the Global Information Assurance Certification (GIAC) family and focuses on the foundational knowledge of securing critical infrastructure assets. The GICSP bridges together IT, engineering and cybersecurity to achieve security for industrial control systems from design through retirement.

Smart Grid Interoperability Panel (SGIP) Cyber Security Working Group (CSWG)

http://collaborate.nist.gov/twiki-sggrid/bin/view/SmartGrid/CyberSecurityCTG

The primary goal of the working group is to develop an overall cybersecurity strategy for the Smart Grid that includes a risk mitigation strategy to ensure interoperability of solutions across different domains/components of the infrastructure. The cybersecurity strategy needs to address prevention, detection, response, and recovery. Implementation of a cybersecurity strategy requires the definition and implementation of an overall cybersecurity risk assessment process for the Smart Grid.

The working group's effort is documented in NIST Interagency Report (NISTIR) 7628 Revision 1, *Guidelines for Smart Grid Cybersecurity* [98].

Appendix E—ICS Security Capabilities and Tools

This section provides an overview of security capabilities that are available to or being developed in support of the ICS community. There are several security products that are marketed specifically for ICS, while others are general IT security products that are being used with ICS. Many of the products available offer "single point solutions," where a single security product offers multiple levels of protection. In addition to available products, this section also discusses some research and development work towards new products and technologies. Each organization should make a risk-based determination whether to employ the security capabilities and tools mentioned in this appendix.

Data Diode

A data diode (also referred to as a unidirectional gateway, deterministic one-way boundary device or unidirectional network) is a network appliance or device allowing data to travel only in one direction, used in guaranteeing information security or protection of critical digital systems, such as industrial control systems, from inbound cyber attacks. While use of these devices is common in high security environments such as defense, where they serve as connections between two or more networks of differing security classifications, the technology is also being used to enforce one-way communications outbound from critical digital systems to untrusted networks.

Encryption

Encryption protects the confidentiality of data by encoding the data to ensure that only the intended recipient can decode it. There are some commercially available encryption products designed specifically for ICS applications, as well as general encryption products that support basic serial and Ethernet-based communications.

Firewalls

Firewalls are commonly used to segregate networks to protect and isolate ICS. These implementations use commercially available firewalls that are focused on Internet and corporate application layer protocols and are not equipped to handle ICS protocols. Research was performed by an IT security vendor in 2003 to develop a Modbus-based firewall that allows policy decisions to be made on Modbus/TCP header values just as traditional firewalls filter on TCP/UDP ports and IP addresses [76]. There are currently several firewalls available for ICS.

Intrusion Detection and Prevention

Intrusion detection systems (IDS) and intrusion prevention systems (IPS) are being deployed on ICS networks and components to detect well-known cyber attacks. Network IDS products monitor network traffic and use various detection methods, such as comparing portions of the traffic to signatures of known attacks. In contrast, host intrusion detection uses software loaded on a host computer, often with attack signatures, to monitor ongoing events and data on a computer system for possible exploits. IPS products take intrusion detection a step further by automatically acting on detected exploits to attempt to stop them [57].

The required task of a security team to constantly monitor, evaluate, and quickly respond to intrusion detection events is sometimes contracted to a managed security service provider (MSSP). MSSPs have correlation and analysis engines to process and reduce the vast amounts of events logged per day to a small subset that needs to be manually evaluated. There are also correlation and analysis engine products available to large organizations wanting to perform this function in-house. Security information and event management (SIEM) products are used in some organizations to monitor, analyze, and correlate events from IDS and IPS logs, as well as audit logs from other computer systems, applications, infrastructure equipment, and other hardware and software, to look for intrusion attempts.

IDS and IPS vendors are developing and incorporating attack signatures for various ICS protocols such as Modbus, DNP3, and ICCP [58]. Snort rules have been developed for Modbus TCP, DNP3, and ICCP. Snort is an open source network intrusion detection and prevention system using a rule-driven language to perform signature, protocol, and anomaly-based inspections. Rules for DNP3 and Modbus protocols have also been added to the Bro IDS platform.

As with any software added to an ICS component, the addition of host IDS or IPS software could affect system performance. IPSs are commonplace in today's information security industry, but can be very resource intensive. These systems have the ability to automatically reconfigure systems if an intrusion attempt is identified. This automated and fast reaction is designed to prevent successful exploits; however, an automated tool such as this could be used by an adversary to adversely affect the operation on an ICS by shutting down segments of a network or server. False positives can also hinder ICS operation.

Malware/Antivirus Software

Because early malware threats were primarily viruses, the software to detect and remove malware has historically been called "antivirus software," even though it can detect many types of malware. Antivirus software is used to counter the threats of malware by evaluating files on a computer's storage devices (some tools also detect malware in real-time at the network perimeter and/or on the user's workstation) against an inventory of malware signature files. If one of the files on a computer matches the profile of known malware, the malware is removed through a disinfection process so it cannot infect other local files or communicate across a network to infect other files on other computers. There are also techniques available to identify unknown malware "in-the-wild" when a signature file is not yet available.

Many end-users and vendors of ICS are recommending the use of COTS antivirus software with their systems and have even developed installation and configuration guidance based on their own laboratory testing. Some ICS vendors recommend the use of antivirus software with their products, but offer little to no guidance. Some end users and vendors are hesitant to use antivirus software due to fears that its use would cause ICS performance problems or even failure. NIST and Sandia National Laboratories (SNL) conducted a study and produced a report aimed at helping ICS owners/operators to deploy antivirus software and to minimize and assess performance impacts of workstation and server-based antivirus products. This study assembled ICS-based antivirus knowledge and serves as a starting point or a secondary resource when installing, configuring, running, and maintaining antivirus software on an ICS [56]. In many cases, performance impacts can be reduced through configuration settings as well as antivirus scanning and maintenance scheduling outside of the antivirus software practices recommended for typical IT systems.

In summary, COTS antivirus software can be used successfully on most ICS components. However, special ICS specific considerations should be taken into account during the selection, installation, configuration, operational, and maintenance procedures. ICS end-users should consult with the ICS vendors regarding the use of antivirus software.

Vulnerability Assessment Tools

There are many tools available for performing network vulnerability assessments for typical IT networks; however, the impacts these tools may have on the operation of an ICS should be carefully considered [77]. The additional traffic and exploits used during active vulnerability and penetration testing, combined with the limited resources of many ICS, have been known to cause ICS to malfunction. As guidance in this area, SNL developed a preferred list of vulnerability and penetration testing techniques for ICS [77]. These are less intrusive methods, passive instead of active, to collect the majority of information that is often queried by automated vulnerability and penetration testing tools. These methods are intended to allow collection of the necessary vulnerability information without the risk of causing a failure while testing.

Sophia is a patent-pending, passive, real-time diagnostic and security tool designed and built specifically for control systems professionals. Sophia builds and maintains an ICS network fingerprint and continuously monitors activity against it, with white, gray and black-listing capabilities, alerting its managers of any abnormal activity for further investigation, monitoring and/or action. Beta testing conducted by the Battelle Energy Alliance (BEA) at the Idaho National Laboratories (INL) recently concluded with a group of over 30 participants, including major utilities and control system vendors. Those Beta participants reported immediate benefits in the fingerprinting process and longer-term benefits in monitoring, securing, and making on-going modifications to ICS configurations during the Beta testing period. Beta participants, as well as non-participants, who have been following the development of Sophia by BEA/INL, have long expressed interest in obtaining commercial grade Sophia software, services and support. Beta testing has proven that this suite of tools offers unique capabilities, including visualization of activity and tailored reporting to meet customer needs.

Shodan is a search engine that lets you find specific types of computers (routers, servers, etc.) on the Internet using a variety of filters. Some have also described it as a search engine of service banners, which are meta-data the server sends back to the client. This can be information about the server software, what options the service supports, a welcome message or anything else that the client can find out before interacting with the server. Shodan users are able to find systems including traffic lights, security cameras, home heating systems as well as control systems. Users can use Shodan to determine if any of the devices on their ICS are accessible from the internet.

The Cyber Security Evaluation Tool (CSET) is a Department of Homeland Security (DHS) product that assists organizations in protecting their key national cyber assets. It was developed under the direction of the DHS Industrial Control System Cyber Emergency Response Team (ICS-CERT) by cybersecurity experts and with assistance from NIST. This tool provides users with a systematic and repeatable approach for assessing the security posture of their cyber systems and networks. It includes both high-level and detailed questions related to all industrial control and IT systems. CSET is a desktop software tool that guides users through a step-by-step process to assess their control system and information technology network security practices against recognized industry standards. The output from CSET is a prioritized list of recommendations for improving the cybersecurity posture of the organization's enterprise and industrial control cyber systems. The tool derives the recommendations from a database of cybersecurity standards, guidelines, and practices. Each recommendation is linked to a set of actions that can be applied to enhance cybersecurity controls. CSET has been designed for easy installation and use on a stand-alone laptop or workstation. It incorporates a variety of available standards from organizations such as NIST, NERC, TSA, DoD, and others. When the tool user selects one or more of the standards, CSET will open a set of questions to be answered. The answers to these questions will be compared against a selected security assurance level, and a detailed report will be generated to show areas for potential improvement. CSET provides an excellent means to perform a self-assessment of the security posture of your control system environment.

SamuraiSTFU is the Samurai Project's Security Testing Framework for Utilities and takes best in breed security tools for traditional network and web penetration testing and adds specialized tools for embedded and RF testing and mixes in energy sector context, documentation and sample files. It also includes emulators for SCADA, Smart Meters, and other types of energy sector systems to provide leverage for a full test lab.

ICS owners must make the individuals using vulnerability assessment tools aware of the criticality of continuous operation and the risks involved with performing these tests on operational systems. It may be possible to mitigate these risks by performing tests on ICS components such as redundant servers or independent test systems in a laboratory setting. Laboratory tests can be used to screen out test procedures that might harm the operational system. Even with very good configuration management to assure that the test system is highly representative, tests on the actual system are likely to uncover flaws not represented in the laboratory.

Appendix F—References

[1]   Fraser, Roy E., *Process Measurement and Control: Introduction to Sensors, Communication, Adjustment, and Control*, Upper Saddle River, New Jersey: Prentice-Hall, Inc., 2001.

[2]   Falco, Joe, et al., *IT Security for Industrial Control Systems*, NIST Internal Report (NISTIR) 6859, February 2002, http://www.nist.gov/customcf/get_pdf.cfm?pub_id=821684 [accessed 4/16/15].

[3]   Bailey, David, and Edwin Wright, *Practical SCADA for Industry*, Vancouver: IDC Technologies, 2003.

[4]   Boyer, Stuart, *SCADA: Supervisory Control and Data Acquisition.* 4th ed. Research Triangle Park, North Carolina: International Society of Automation, 2010.

[5]   American Gas Association, AGA Report No. 12, *Cryptographic Protection of SCADA Communications, Part 1: Background, Policies and Test Plan*, September, March 14, 2006.

[6]   Erickson, Kelvin, and John Hedrick, *Plantwide Process Control*, New York: John Wiley & Sons, Inc., 1999.

[7]   Berge, Jonas, *Fieldbuses for Process Control: Engineering, Operation, and Maintenance*, Research Triangle Park, North Carolina: ISA, 2002.

[8]   Peerenboom, James, "Infrastructure Interdependencies: Overview of Concepts and Terminology," invited paper, *NSF/OSTP Workshop on Critical Infrastructure: Needs in Interdisciplinary Research and Graduate Training*, Washington, D.C., June 14-15, 2001.

[9]   Rinaldi, Steven, et al., "Identifying, Understanding, and Analyzing Critical Infrastructure Interdependencies," *IEEE Control Systems Magazine*, (December 2001), pp. 11-25, http://dx.doi.org/10.1109/37.969131.

[10] GAO-04-354, *Critical Infrastructure Protection: Challenges and Efforts to Secure Control Systems*, U.S. GAO, 2004, http://www.gao.gov/new.items/d04354.pdf.

[11] Weiss, Joseph, "Current Status of Cybersecurity of Control Systems," Presentation to Georgia Tech Protective Relay Conference, May 8, 2003.

[12] Keeney, Michelle et al., *Insider Threat Study: Computer System Sabotage in Critical Infrastructure Sectors*, United States Secret Service and Carnegie Mellon Software Institute, 2005, http://www.cert.org/archive/pdf/insidercross051105.pdf.

[13] Federal Information Security Management Act of 2002, Pub. L. 107-347 (Title III), 116 Stat 2946, http://www.gpo.gov/fdsys/pkg/PLAW-107publ347/pdf/PLAW-107publ347.pdf [accessed 4/16/15].

[14] Federal Information Security Management Act Implementation Project [Web site], http://csrc.nist.gov/groups/SMA/fisma/index.html [accessed 4/16/15].

[15] U.S. Department of Commerce, Federal Information Processing Standards (FIPS) Publication 199, *Standards for Security Categorization of Federal Information and Information Systems*, February 2004, http://csrc.nist.gov/publications/fips/fips199/FIPS-PUB-199-final.pdf [accessed 4/16/15].

[16] U.S. Department of Commerce, Federal Information Processing Standards (FIPS) Publication 200, *Minimum Security Requirements for Federal Information and Information Systems*, March 2006, http://csrc.nist.gov/publications/fips/fips200/FIPS-200-final-march.pdf [accessed 4/16/15].

[17] Knapp, Eric, *Industrial Network Security: Securing Critical Infrastructure Networks for Smart Grid, SCADA, and Other Industrial Control Systems*, Waltham, Massachusetts: Syngress, 2011.

[18] U.S. Government Accountability Office (GAO), GAO-15-6, *Federal Facility Cybersecurity: DHS and GSA Should Address Cyber Risk to Building and Access Control Systems*, December 12, 2014, http://www.gao.gov/products/GAO-15-6 [accessed 4/16/15].

[19] Swanson, Marianne, et al., NIST SP 800-18 Revision 1, *Guide for Developing Security Plans for Federal Information Systems*, February 2006, http://csrc.nist.gov/publications/PubsSPs.htmlhttp://csrc.nist.gov/publications/PubsSPs.html#800-18 [accessed 4/16/15].

[20] Joint Task Force Transformation Initiative, NIST SP 800-39, *Managing Information Security Risk: Organization, Mission, and Information System View*, March 2011, http://csrc.nist.gov/publications/PubsSPs.htmlhttp://csrc.nist.gov/publications/PubsSPs.html#800-39 [accessed 4/16/15].

[21] Joint Task Force Transformation Initiative, NIST SP 800-37 Revision 1, *Guide for Applying the Risk Management Framework to Federal Information Systems: a Security Life Cycle Approach*, February 2010 (updated June 5, 2014), http://dx.doi.org/10.6028/NIST.SP.800-37r1.

[22] Joint Task Force Transformation Initiative, NIST SP 800-53 Revision 4, *Security and Privacy Controls for Federal Information Systems and Organizations*, April 2013 (updated January 22, 2015), http://dx.doi.org/10.6028/NIST.SP.800-53r4.

[23] Joint Task Force Transformation Initiative, NIST SP 800-53A Revision 4, *Assessing Security and Privacy Controls in Federal Information Systems and Organizations: Building Effective Security Assessment Plans*, December 2014 (updated December 18, 2014),http://dx.doi.org/10.6028/NIST.SP.800-53Ar4.

[24] Barker, William, NIST SP 800-59, *Guideline for Identifying an Information System as a National Security System*, August 2003, http://csrc.nist.gov/publications/PubsSPs.htmlhttp://csrc.nist.gov/publications/PubsSPs.html#800-59 [accessed 4/16/15].

[25] Stine, Kevin, et al., NIST SP 800-60 Revision 1 (2 vols.), *Guide for Mapping Types of Information and Information systems to Security Categories*, August 2008, http://csrc.nist.gov/publications/PubsSPs.htmlhttp://csrc.nist.gov/publications/PubsSPs.html#800-60 [accessed 4/16/15].

[26] Quinn, Stephen, et al., NIST SP 800-70 Revision 2, *National Checklist Program for IT Products: Guidelines for Checklist Users and Developers*, February 2011, http://csrc.nist.gov/publications/PubsSPs.htmlhttp://csrc.nist.gov/publications/PubsSPs.html#800-70 [accessed 4/16/15].

[27] Bowen, Pauline, et al., NIST SP 800-100, *Information Security Handbook: A Guide for Managers*, October 2006 (updated March 7, 2007), http://csrc.nist.gov/publications/PubsSPs.htmlhttp://csrc.nist.gov/publications/PubsSPs.html#800-100 [accessed 4/16/15].

[28] NIST Security Configurations Checklists Program for IT Products [Web site], http://web.nvd.nist.gov/view/ncp/repository [accessed 4/16/15].

[29] Stamp, Jason, et al., *Common Vulnerabilities in Critical Infrastructure Control Systems*, Sandia National Laboratories, 2003, http://citeseerx.ist.psu.edu/viewdoc/download?doi=10.1.1.132.3264&rep=rep1&type=pdf.

[30] *SCADA Security - Advice for CEOs*, IT Security Expert Advisory Group (ITSEAG)

[31] Franz, Matthew, *Vulnerability Testing of Industrial Network Devices*, Critical Infrastructure Assurance Group, Cisco Systems, 2003, http://blogfranz.googlecode.com/files/franz-isa-device-testing-oct03.pdf.

[32] Duggan, David, et al., *Penetration Testing of Industrial Control Systems*, Sandia National Laboratories, Report No SAND2005-2846P, 2005.

[33] President's Critical Infrastructure Protection Board, and U.S. Department of Energy, Office of Energy Assurance, *21 Steps to Improve Cybersecurity of SCADA Networks*, [2002], http://energy.gov/sites/prod/files/oeprod/DocumentsandMedia/21_Steps_-_SCADA.pdf [accessed 4/16/15].

[34] ISA-62443[multiple parts], *Security for Industrial Automation and Control Systems*, Research Triangle Park, North Carolina: International Society of Automation, http://isa99.isa.org/ISA99%20Wiki/WP_List.aspx [accessed 4/16/15].

[35] Centre for the Protection of National Infrastructure (CPNI), *Firewall Deployment for SCADA and Process Control Networks: Good Practice Guide*, February 15, 2005, http://energy.gov/sites/prod/files/Good%20Practices%20Guide%20for%20Firewall%20Deployment.pdf [accessed 4/16/15].

[36] U.S. Department of Homeland Security, *Recommended Practice: Improving Industrial Control Systems Cybersecurity with Defense-in-Depth Strategies*, October 2009, https://ics-cert.us-cert.gov/sites/default/files/recommended_practices/Defense_in_Depth_Oct09.pdf [accessed 4/16/15].

[37] Industrial Automation Open Networking Association (IAONA), *The IAONA Handbook for Network Security*, Version 1.3, 2005, http://www.iaona.org/pictures/files/1122888138-IAONA_HNS_1_3-reduced_050725.pdf [accessed 4/16/15].

[38] U.S. Department of Homeland Security, *Common Cybersecurity Vulnerabilities in Industrial Control Systems*, May 2011, https://ics-cert.us-cert.gov/sites/default/files/recommended_practices/DHS_Common_Cybersecurity_Vulnerabilities_ICS_2010.pdf [accessed 4/16/15].

[39] NIST SP 800-12, *An Introduction to Computer Security: The NIST Handbook*, 1995, http://csrc.nist.gov/publications/PubsSPs.html.

[40] Souppaya, Murugiah, and Karen Scarfone, NIST SP 800-40 Revision 3, *Guide to Enterprise Patch Management Technologies*, July 2013, http://dx.doi.org/10.6028/NIST.SP.800-40r3.

[41] Scarfone, Karen, et al., NIST SP 800-115, *Technical Guide to Information Security Testing and Assessment*, September 2008, http://csrc.nist.gov/publications/PubsSPs.htmlhttp://csrc.nist.gov/publications/PubsSPs.html#800-115 [accessed 4/16/15].

[42] Roback, Edward, NIST SP 800-23, *Guidelines to Federal Organizations on Security Assurance and Acquisition/ Use of Tested/Evaluated Products*, August 2000, http://csrc.nist.gov/publications/PubsSPs.htmlhttp://csrc.nist.gov/publications/PubsSPs.html#800-23 [accessed 4/16/15].

[43] Stoneburner, Gary, et al., NIST SP 800-27 Revision A, *Engineering Principles for Information Technology Security (A Baseline for Achieving Security)*, June 2004, http://csrc.nist.gov/publications/PubsSPs.htmlhttp://csrc.nist.gov/publications/PubsSPs.html#800-27A [accessed 4/16/15].

[44] Grance, Tim, et al., NIST SP 800-35, *Guide to Information Technology Security Services*, October 2003, http://csrc.nist.gov/publications/PubsSPs.htmlhttp://csrc.nist.gov/publications/PubsSPs.html#800-35 [accessed 4/16/15].

[45] Grance, Tim, et al., NIST SP 800-36, *Guide to Selecting Information Technology Security Products*, October 2003, http://csrc.nist.gov/publications/PubsSPs.htmlhttp://csrc.nist.gov/publications/PubsSPs.html#800-36 [accessed 4/16/15].

[46] Grance, Tim, et al., NIST SP 800-64 Revision 2, *Security Considerations in the System Development Life Cycle*, October 2008, http://csrc.nist.gov/publications/PubsSPs.htmlhttp://csrc.nist.gov/publications/PubsSPs.html#800-64 [accessed 4/16/15].

[47] Hash, Joan, et al., NIST SP 800-65, *Integrating IT Security into the Capital Planning and Investment Control Process*, January 2005, http://csrc.nist.gov/publications/PubsSPs.htmlhttp://csrc.nist.gov/publications/PubsSPs.html#800-65 [accessed 4/16/15].

[48] U.S. Department of Homeland Security, *Department of Homeland Security: Cyber Security Procurement Language for Control Systems*, September 2009 https://ics-cert.us-cert.gov/sites/default/files/documents/Procurement_Language_Rev4_100809.pdf [accessed 4/16/15].

[49] Dray, James, et al., NIST SP 800-73-3, *Interfaces for Personal Identity Verification* (4 parts), February 2010, http://csrc.nist.gov/publications/PubsSPs.htmlhttp://csrc.nist.gov/publications/PubsSPs.html#800-73 [accessed 4/16/15].

[50] Grother, Patrick, et al., NIST SP 800-76-2, *Biometric Data Specification for Personal Identity Verification*, July 2013, http://dx.doi.org/10.6028/NIST.SP.800-76-2.

[51] Kuhn, D. Richard, et al., NIST SP 800-46 Revision 1, *Guide to Enterprise Telework and Remote Access Security*, June 2009, http://csrc.nist.gov/publications/PubsSPs.htmlhttp://csrc.nist.gov/publications/PubsSPs.html#800-46 [accessed 4/16/15].

[52] Swanson, Marianne, et al., NIST SP 800-34 Revision 1, *Contingency Planning Guide for Federal Information Systems*, May 2010, http://csrc.nist.gov/publications/PubsSPs.htmlhttp://csrc.nist.gov/publications/PubsSPs.html#800-34 [accessed 4/16/15].

[53] Burr, William, et al., NIST SP 800-63-2, *Electronic Authentication Guideline*, August 2013, http://dx.doi.org/10.6028/NIST.SP.800-63-2.

[54] Bace, Rebecca, and Mell, Peter, NIST SP 800-31, *Intrusion Detection Systems*, 2001, http://csrc.nist.gov/publications/PubsSPs.html.

[55] Scarfone, Karen, and Peter Mell, NIST SP 800-94, *Guide to Intrusion Detection and Prevention Systems (IDPS)*, February 2007, http://csrc.nist.gov/publications/PubsSPs.htmlhttp://csrc.nist.gov/publications/PubsSPs.html#800-94 [accessed 4/16/15].

[56] Falco, Joe, et al., NIST SP 1058, *Using Host-based Anti-virus Software on Industrial Control Systems: Integration Guidance and a Test Methodology for Assessing Performance Impacts*, September 18, 2006, http://www.nist.gov/manuscript-publication-search.cfm?pub_id=823596 [accessed 4/16/15].

[57] Peterson, Dale, "Intrusion Detection and Cyber Security Monitoring of SCADA and DCS Networks," *ISA Automation West (AUTOWEST 2004)*, Long Beach, California, April 2004, http://citeseerx.ist.psu.edu/viewdoc/download?doi=10.1.1.121.3420&rep=rep1&type=pdf [accessed 4/16/15].

[58] Symantec Corporation, "Symantec Expands SCADA Protection for Electric Utilities," [press release], September 14, 2005, http://www.symantec.com/about/news/release/article.jsp?prid=20050914_01 [accessed 4/16/15].

[59] Grance, Tim, et al., NIST SP 800-61 Revision 2, *Computer Security Incident Handling Guide*, August 2012, http://dx.doi.org/10.6028/NIST.SP.800-61r2.

[60] Mell, Peter, et al., NIST SP 800-83 Revision 1, *Guide to Malware Incident Prevention and Handling for Desktops and Laptops*, July 2013, http://dx.doi.org/10.6028/NIST.SP.800-83r1.

[61] Wilson, Mark, and Joan Hash, NIST SP 800-50, *Building an Information Technology Security Awareness and Training Program*, October 2003, http://csrc.nist.gov/publications/PubsSPs.htmlhttp://csrc.nist.gov/publications/PubsSPs.html#800-50 [accessed 4/16/15].

[62] Mix, S., *Supervisory Control and Data Acquisition (SCADA) Systems Security Guide*, Electric Power Research Institute (EPRI), 2003.

[63] Scarfone, Karen, et al., NIST SP 800-48 Revision 1, *Guide to Securing Legacy IEEE 802.11 Wireless Networks*, July 2008, http://csrc.nist.gov/publications/PubsSPs.htmlhttp://csrc.nist.gov/publications/PubsSPs.html#800-48 [accessed 4/16/15].

[64] Frankel, Sheila, et al, NIST SP 800-97, *Establishing Wireless Robust Security Networks: a Guide to IEEE 802.11i*, February 2007, http://csrc.nist.gov/publications/PubsSPs.htmlhttp://csrc.nist.gov/publications/PubsSPs.html#800-97 [accessed 4/16/15].

[65] U.S. Department of Commerce, Federal Information Processing Standards (FIPS) Publication 201-2, *Personal Identity Verification (PIV) of Federal Employees and Contractors*, August 2013, http://dx.doi.org/10.6028/NIST.FIPS.201-2.

[66] Dray, James, et al, NIST SP 800-96, *PIV Card to Reader Interoperability Guidelines*, September 2006, http://csrc.nist.gov/publications/PubsSPs.htmlhttp://csrc.nist.gov/publications/PubsSPs.html#800-96 [accessed 4/16/15].

[67] Polk, W. Timothy, et al, NIST SP 800-78-3, *Cryptographic Algorithms and Key Sizes for Personal Identity Verification*, December 2010, http://csrc.nist.gov/publications/PubsSPs.htmlhttp://csrc.nist.gov/publications/PubsSPs.html#800-78 [accessed 4/16/15].

[68] Kent, Karen, and Murugiah Souppaya, NIST SP 800-92, *Guide to Computer Security Log Management*, September 2006, http://csrc.nist.gov/publications/PubsSPs.htmlhttp://csrc.nist.gov/publications/PubsSPs.html#800-92 [accessed 4/16/15].

[69] Jansen, Wayne, et al., NIST SP 800-28 Version 2, *Guidelines on Active Content and Mobile Code*, March 2008, http://csrc.nist.gov/publications/PubsSPs.htmlhttp://csrc.nist.gov/publications/PubsSPs.html#800-28 [accessed 4/16/15].

[70] Polk, Tim, et al., NIST SP 800-52 Revision 1, *Guidelines for the Selection, Configuration, and Use of Transport Layer Security (TLS) Implementations*, April 2014, http://dx.doi.org/10.6028/NIST.SP.800-52r1.

[71] Barker, Elaine, et al., NIST SP 800-56A Revision 2, *Recommendation for Pair-Wise Key Establishment Schemes Using Discrete Logarithm Cryptography*, May 2013, http://dx.doi.org/10.6028/NIST.SP.800-56Ar2.

[72] Baker, Elaine, et al., NIST SP 800-57 (3 parts), *Recommendation for Key Management*: Part 1 Revision 3, *General,* July 2012 http://csrc.nist.gov/publications/PubsSPs.htmlhttp://csrc.nist.gov/publications/PubsSPs.html#800-57pt1; Part 2, *Best Practices for Key Management Organization*, August 2005, http://csrc.nist.gov/publications/PubsSPs.htmlhttp://csrc.nist.gov/publications/PubsSPs.html#800-57pt2; Part 3 Revision 1, *Application-Specific Key Management Guidance*, January 2015, http://dx.doi.org/10.6028/NIST.SP.800-57pt3r1.

[73] Kuhn, D. Richard, et al., NIST SP 800-58, *Security Considerations for Voice Over IP Systems,* January 2005, http://csrc.nist.gov/publications/PubsSPs.htmlhttp://csrc.nist.gov/publications/PubsSPs.html#800-58 [accessed 4/16/15].

[74] Frankel, Sheila, et al., NIST SP 800-77, *Guide to IPsec VPNs*, December 2005, http://csrc.nist.gov/publications/PubsSPs.htmlhttp://csrc.nist.gov/publications/PubsSPs.html#800-77 [accessed 4/16/15].

[75] Shirey, R., *Internet Security Glossary, Version 2*, RFC 4949, August 2007, http://www.rfc-editor.org/rfc/rfc4949.txt [accessed 4/16/15].

[76] Franz, Matthew, and Venkat Pothamsetty, *ModbusFW: Deep Packet Inspection for Industrial Ethernet*, Critical Infrastructure Assurance Group, Cisco Systems, 2004, http://blogfranz.googlecode.com/files/franz-niscc-modbusfw-may04.pdf [accessed 4/16/15].

[77] Duggan, David, *Penetration Testing of Industrial Control Systems*, SAND2005-2846P, Sandia National Laboratories, March 2005, http://energy.sandia.gov/wp/wp-content/gallery/uploads/sand_2005_2846p.pdf [accessed 4/16/15].

[78] Kissel, Richard, et al., NIST SP 800-88 Revision 1, *Guidelines for Media Sanitization,* December 2014, http://dx.doi.org/10.6028/NIST.SP.800-88r1.

[79] Joint Task Force Transformation Initiative, NIST SP 800-30 Revision 1, *Guide for Conducting Risk Assessments*, September 2012, http://csrc.nist.gov/publications/PubsSPs.htmlhttp://csrc.nist.gov/publications/PubsSPs.html#800-30 [accessed 4/16/15].

[80] Johnson, Arnold, et al., NIST SP 800-128, *Guide for Security-Focused Configuration Management of Information Systems*, August 2011, http://csrc.nist.gov/publications/PubsSPs.htmlhttp://csrc.nist.gov/publications/PubsSPs.html#800-128 [accessed 4/16/15].

[81] Dempsey, Kelley, et al., NIST SP 800-137, *Information Security Continuous Monitoring (ISCM) for Federal Information Systems and Organizations*, September 2011, http://csrc.nist.gov/publications/PubsSPs.htmlhttp://csrc.nist.gov/publications/PubsSPs.html#800-137 [accessed 4/16/15].

[82] Waltermire, David, et al., NIST SP 800-126 Revision 2, *The Technical Specification for the Security Content Automation Protocol (SCAP): SCAP Version 1.2*, September 2011 (updated March 19, 2012), http://csrc.nist.gov/publications/PubsSPs.htmlhttp://csrc.nist.gov/publications/PubsSPs.html#800-126-rev2 [accessed 4/16/15].

[83] Executive Order no. 13636, Improving Critical Infrastructure Cybersecurity, DCPD-201300091, February 12, 2013, http://www.gpo.gov/fdsys/pkg/FR-2013-02-19/pdf/2013-03915.pdf [accessed 4/16/15].

[84] National Institute of Standards and Technology, *Framework for Improving Critical Infrastructure Cybersecurity*, version 1.0, February 12, 2014, http://www.nist.gov/cyberframework/upload/cybersecurity-framework-021214.pdf [accessed 4/16/15].

[85] Scarfone, Karen, and Paul Hoffman, NIST SP 800-41 Revision 1, *Guidelines on Firewalls and Firewall Policy*, September 2009, http://csrc.nist.gov/publications/PubsSPs.html#800-41 [accessed 4/16/15].

[86] Office of Management and Budget, OMB Memorandum M-07-16, *Safeguarding Against and Responding to the Breach of Personally Identifiable Information*, May 22, 2007, https://www.whitehouse.gov/sites/default/files/omb/memoranda/fy2007/m07-16.pdf [accessed 4/16/15].

[87] Office of Management and Budget, OMB Memorandum M-10-22, *Guidance for Online Use of Web Measurement and Customization Technologies*, June 25, 2010, https://www.whitehouse.gov/sites/default/files/omb/assets/memoranda_2010/m10-22.pdf [accessed 4/16/15].

[88] McCallister, Erika, et al., NIST SP 800-122, *Guide to Protecting the Confidentiality of Personally Identifiable Information (PII)*, April 2010, http://csrc.nist.gov/publications/PubsSPs.html#800-122 [accessed 4/16/15].

[89] *Federal Enterprise Architecture Security and Privacy Profile, Version 3.0*, September 2010, https://cio.gov/wp-content/uploads/downloads/2012/09/FEA-Security-Privacy-Profile-v3-09-30-2010.pdf [accessed 4/16/15].

[90] U.S. Department of Commerce, Federal Information Processing Standards (FIPS) Publication 140-2, *Security Requirements for Cryptographic Modules*, May 25, 2001 (Change Notice 2, 12/3/2002), http://csrc.nist.gov/publications/PubsFIPS.html#140-2 [accessed 4/16/15].

[91] Tracy, Miles, et al., NIST SP 800-45 Version 2, Guidelines on Electronic Mail Security, February 2007, http://csrc.nist.gov/publications/PubsSPs.html#800-45 [accessed 4/16/15].

[92] Grance, Tim, et al., NIST SP 800-47, Security Guide for Interconnecting Information Technology Systems, August 2002, http://csrc.nist.gov/publications/PubsSPs.html#800-47 [accessed 4/16/15].

[93] Kent, Karen, et al., NIST SP 800-86, Guide to Integrating Forensic Techniques into Incident Response, August 2006, http://csrc.nist.gov/publications/PubsSPs.html#800-86 [accessed 4/16/15].

[94] Scarfone, Karen, et al., NIST SP 800-111, Guide to Storage Encryption Technologies for End User Devices, November 2007, http://csrc.nist.gov/publications/PubsSPs.html#800-111 [accessed 4/16/15].

[95] Scarfone, Karen, et al., NIST SP 800-123, Guide to General Server Security, July 2008, http://csrc.nist.gov/publications/PubsSPs.html#800-123 [accessed 4/16/15].

[96] Scarfone, Karen, et al., NIST SP 800-127, Guide to Securing WiMAX Wireless Communications, September 2010, http://csrc.nist.gov/publications/PubsSPs.html#800-127 [accessed 4/16/15].

[97] Johnson, Arnold, et al., NIST SP 800-128, Guide for Security-Focused Configuration Management of Information Systems, August 2011, http://csrc.nist.gov/publications/PubsSPs.html#800-128 [accessed 4/16/15].

[98] Smart Grid Interoperability Panel, Smart Grid Cybersecurity Committee, NISTIR 7628 Revision 1, Guidelines for Smart Grid Cybersecurity, September 2014, http://dx.doi.org/10.6028/NIST.IR.7628r1 [accessed 4/16/15].

[99] Kissel, Richard (ed.), NISTIR 7298 Revision 2, Glossary of Key Information Security Terms, May 2013, http://dx.doi.org/10.6028/NIST.IR.7298r2 [accessed 4/16/15].

Appendix G—ICS Overlay

NOTE TO READERS

The ICS overlay is a partial tailoring of the controls and control baselines in SP 800-53, Revision 4, and adds supplementary guidance specific to ICS. The concept of overlays is introduced in Appendix I of SP 800-53, Revision 4. The ICS overlay is intended to be applicable to all ICS systems in all industrial sectors. Further tailoring can be performed to add specificity to a particular sector (e.g., pipeline, energy). Ultimately, an overlay may be produced for a specific system (e.g., the XYZ company). This ICS overlay constitutes supplemental guidance and tailoring for SP 800-53, Revision 4. Please be sure you are looking at the correct version of SP 800-53. Duplicating Appendix F of SP 800-53 would increase the size of this Appendix by over 65 pages. Therefore, the drafting committee has decided to not duplicate Appendix F. The reader should have SP 800-53, Revision 4 available. The authoring team also considered that this ICS overlay may serve as a model for other overlays. Feedback on this Appendix's structure would be appreciated, especially in the following areas: the level of abstraction and whether the examples provided in the supplemental guidance are sufficient/beneficial for implementation.

Since the ICS overlay exists in the context of SP 800-53, Revision 4, it is important to review that context. SP 800-53, Revision 4, Security and Privacy Controls for Federal Information Systems and Organizations, represents the most comprehensive update to the security controls catalog since its inception in 2005. This update was motivated principally by the expanding threat space—characterized by the increasing sophistication of cyber attacks and the operations tempo of adversaries (i.e., the frequency of such attacks, the professionalism of the attackers, and the persistence of targeting by attackers). State-of-the-practice security controls and control enhancements have been developed and integrated into the catalog addressing such areas as: mobile and cloud computing; applications security; trustworthiness, assurance, and resiliency of information systems; insider threat; supply chain security; and the advanced persistent threat.

To take advantage of the expanded set of security and privacy controls, and to give organizations greater flexibility and agility in defending their information systems, the concept of overlays was introduced in this revision. Overlays provide a structured approach to help organizations tailor security control baselines and develop specialized security plans that can be applied to specific missions/business functions, environments of operation, and/or technologies. This specialization approach is important as the number of threat-driven controls and control enhancements in the catalog increases and organizations develop risk management strategies to address their specific protection needs within defined risk tolerances.

Identification

This overlay may be referenced as the NIST Special Publication 800-82 Revision 2 Industrial Control System Overlay ("NIST SP 800-82 Rev 2 ICS Overlay"). It is based on NIST SP 800-53 Revision 4 [22].

NIST developed this overlay in furtherance of its statutory responsibilities under the Federal Information Security Modernization Act (FISMA) of 2014 (Public Law 113-283), Presidential Policy Directive (PPD)-21 and Executive Order 13636. NIST is responsible for developing standards and guidelines, including minimum requirements, for providing adequate information security for all agency operations and assets, but such standards and guidelines shall not apply to national security systems without the express approval of appropriate federal officials exercising policy authority over such systems. Comments may be directed to icsoverlaycomments@nist.gov.

Overlay Characteristics

Industrial Control Systems (ICS) are typically used in industries such as electric, water and wastewater, oil and natural gas, transportation, chemical, pharmaceutical, pulp and paper, food and beverage, and discrete manufacturing (e.g., automotive, aerospace, and durable goods). Supervisory control and data acquisition (SCADA) systems are generally used to control dispersed assets using centralized data acquisition and supervisory control. Distributed Control Systems (DCS) are generally used to control production systems within a local area such as a factory using supervisory and regulatory control. Programmable Logic Controllers (PLCs) are generally used for discrete control for specific applications and generally provide regulatory control. These control systems are vital to the operation of the U.S. critical infrastructures that are often highly interconnected and mutually dependent systems. It is important to note that approximately 90 percent of the nation's critical infrastructures are privately owned and operated. Federal agencies also operate many of the ICS mentioned above; other examples include air traffic control and materials handling (e.g., Postal Service mail handling.)

Applicability

The purpose of this overlay is to provide guidance for securing ICS, including SCADA and DCS systems, PLCs, and other systems performing industrial control functions. This overlay has been prepared for use by federal agencies. It may be used by nongovernmental organizations on a voluntary basis.

Overlay Summary

Table G-1 provides a summary of the security controls and control enhancements from NIST SP 800-53 Appendix F [22, App. F] that have been allocated to the initial security control baselines (i.e., Low, Moderate, and High) along with indications of ICS Supplemental Guidance and ICS tailoring. Controls and control enhancements for which there is ICS Supplemental Guidance are **bolded**. If the control baselines are supplemented by the addition of a control to the baseline, the control or control enhancement is underlined. If a control or control enhancement is removed from the baseline, the control or control enhancement is ~~struck out~~.

Example:

AU-4	Audit Storage Capacity	AU-4 **(1)**	AU-4 **(1)**	AU-4 **(1)**

In this example, ICS Supplemental Guidance was added to Control Enhancement 1 of AU-4 (bolded). In addition, Control Enhancement 1 of AU-4 was added to the Low, Moderate (Mod), and High baselines (underlined).

Table G-1 Security Control Baselines

CNTL NO.	CONTROL NAME	INITIAL CONTROL BASELINES		
		LOW	MOD	HIGH
AC-1	Access Control Policy and Procedures	**AC-1**	**AC-1**	**AC-1**
AC-2	Account Management	**AC-2**	**AC-2 (1) (2) (3) (4)**	**AC-2 (1) (2) (3) (4) (5)** (11) (12) (13)
AC-3	Access Enforcement	**AC-3**	**AC-3**	**AC-3**
AC-4	Information Flow Enforcement	Not Selected	AC-4	AC-4
AC-5	Separation of Duties	Not Selected	**AC-5**	**AC-5**
AC-6	Least Privilege	Not Selected	**AC-6 (1) (2) (5) (9) (10)**	**AC-6 (1) (2) (3) (5) (9) (10)**
AC-7	Unsuccessful Logon Attempts	**AC-7**	**AC-7**	**AC-7**
AC-8	System Use Notification	**AC-8**	**AC-8**	**AC-8**
AC-10	Concurrent Session Control	Not Selected	Not Selected	**AC-10**
AC-11	Session Lock	Not Selected	**AC-11 (1)**	**AC-11 (1)**
AC-12	Session Termination	Not Selected	**AC-12**	**AC-12**
AC-14	Permitted Actions without Identification or Authentication	AC-14	AC-14	AC-14
AC-17	Remote Access	**AC-17**	**AC-17 (1) (2) (3) (4)**	**AC-17 (1) (2) (3) (4)**
AC-18	Wireless Access	**AC-18**	**AC-18 (1)**	**AC-18 (1) (4) (5)**
AC-19	Access Control for Mobile Devices	**AC-19**	**AC-19** (5)	**AC-19** (5)
AC-20	Use of External Information Systems	**AC-20**	**AC-20** (1) (2)	**AC-20** (1) (2)
AC-21	Collaboration and Information Sharing	<u>**AC-21**</u>	**AC-21**	**AC-21**
AC-22	Publicly Accessible Content	**AC-22**	**AC-22**	**AC-22**
AT-1	Security Awareness and Training Policy and Procedures	**AT-1**	**AT-1**	**AT-1**
AT-2	Security Awareness Training	**AT-2**	**AT-2** (2)	**AT-2** (2)
AT-3	Role-Based Security Training	**AT-3**	**AT-3**	**AT-3**
AT-4	Security Training Records	AT-4	AT-4	AT-4
AU-1	Audit and Accountability Policy and Procedures	**AU-1**	**AU-1**	**AU-1**
AU-2	Audit Events	**AU-2**	**AU-2** (3)	**AU-2** (3)
AU-3	Content of Audit Records	**AU-3**	**AU-3** (1)	**AU-3** (1) (2)
AU-4	Audit Storage Capacity	AU-4 **(1)**	AU-4 **(1)**	AU-4 **(1)**
AU-5	Response to Audit Processing Failures	AU-5	AU-5	AU-5 (1) (2)
AU-6	Audit Review, Analysis, and Reporting	AU-6	AU-6 **(1)** (3)	AU-6 **(1)** (3) (5) (6)
AU-7	Audit Reduction and Report Generation	Not Selected	AU-7 (1)	AU-7 (1)
AU-8	Time Stamps	**AU-8**	**AU-8 (1)**	**AU-8 (1)**
AU-9	Protection of Audit Information	AU-9	AU-9 (4)	AU-9 (2) (3) (4)
AU-10	Non-repudiation	Not Selected	Not Selected	**AU-10**
AU-11	Audit Record Retention	AU-11	AU-11	AU-11

AU-12	Audit Generation	AU-12	AU-12	AU-12 **(1) (3)**
CA-1	Security Assessment and Authorization Policies and Procedures	**CA-1**	**CA-1**	**CA-1**
CA-2	Security Assessments	**CA-2**	**CA-2** (1)	**CA-2** (1) **(2)**
CA-3	System Interconnections	**CA-3**	**CA-3** (5)	**CA-3** (5)
CA-5	Plan of Action and Milestones	CA-5	CA-5	CA-5
CA-6	Security Authorization	CA-6	CA-6	CA-6
CA-7	Continuous Monitoring	**CA-7**	**CA-7** (1)	**CA-7** (1)
CA-8	Penetration Testing	Not Selected	Not Selected	**CA-8**
CA-9	Internal System Connections	**CA-9**	**CA-9**	**CA-9**
CM-1	Configuration Management Policy and Procedures	**CM-1**	**CM-1**	**CM-1**
CM-2	Baseline Configuration	CM-2	CM-2 (1) (3) (7)	CM-2 (1) (2) (3) (7)
CM-3	Configuration Change Control	Not Selected	CM-3 (2)	CM-3 (1) (2)
CM-4	Security Impact Analysis	**CM-4**	**CM-4**	**CM-4** (1)
CM-5	Access Restrictions for Change	Not Selected	CM-5	CM-5 **(1) (2) (3)**
CM-6	Configuration Settings	CM-6	CM-6	CM-6 (1) (2)
CM-7	Least Functionality	**CM-7** <u>**(1)**</u>	**CM-7** (1) (2) ~~(4)~~ <u>(5)</u>	**CM-7** (1) (2) (5)
CM-8	Information System Component Inventory	CM-8	CM-8 (1) (3) (5)	CM-8 (1) (2) (3) (4) (5)
CM-9	Configuration Management Plan	Not Selected	CM-9	CM-9
CM-10	Software Usage Restrictions	**CM-10**	**CM-10**	**CM-10**
CM-11	User-Installed Software	CM-11	CM-11	CM-11
CP-1	Contingency Planning Policy and Procedures	**CP-1**	**CP-1**	**CP-1**
CP-2	Contingency Plan	**CP-2**	**CP-2 (1) (3) (8)**	**CP-2 (1) (2) (3) (4) (5) (8)**
CP-3	Contingency Training	CP-3	CP-3	CP-3 (1)
CP-4	Contingency Plan Testing	CP-4	CP-4 (1)	CP-4 (1) (2)
CP-6	Alternate Storage Site	Not Selected	CP-6 (1) (3)	CP-6 (1) (2) (3)
CP-7	Alternate Processing Site	Not Selected	CP-7 (1) (2) (3)	CP-7 (1) (2) (3) (4)
CP-8	Telecommunications Services	Not Selected	**CP-8** (1) (2)	**CP-8** (1) (2) (3) (4)
CP-9	Information System Backup	CP-9	CP-9 (1)	CP-9 (1) (2) (3) (5)
CP-10	Information System Recovery and Reconstitution	**CP-10**	**CP-10** (2)	**CP-10** (2) (4)
CP-12	Safe Mode	<u>**CP-12**</u>	<u>**CP-12**</u>	<u>**CP-12**</u>
IA-1	Identification and Authentication Policy and Procedures	**IA-1**	**IA-1**	**IA-1**
IA-2	Identification and Authentication (Organizational Users)	**IA-2 (1) (12)**	**IA-2 (1) (2) (3) (8)** (11) **(12)**	**IA-2 (1) (2) (3) (4) (8) (9)** (11) **(12)**
IA-3	Device Identification and Authentication	<u>**IA-3**</u>	IA-3 <u>(1) (4)</u>	**IA-3** <u>(1) (4)</u>
IA-4	Identifier Management	IA-4	IA-4	IA-4
IA-5	Authenticator Management	**IA-5** (1) (11)	**IA-5** (1) (2) (3) (11)	**IA-5** (1) (2) (3) (11)

IA-6	Authenticator Feedback	**IA-6**	**IA-6**	**IA-6**
IA-7	Cryptographic Module Authentication	IA-7	IA-7	IA-7
IA-8	Identification and Authentication (Non-Organizational Users)	**IA-8 (1) (2) (3) (4)**	**IA-8 (1) (2) (3) (4)**	**IA-8 (1) (2) (3) (4)**
IR-1	Incident Response Policy and Procedures	**IR-1**	**IR-1**	**IR-1**
IR-2	Incident Response Training	IR-2	IR-2	IR-2 (1) (2)
IR-3	Incident Response Testing	Not Selected	IR-3 (2)	IR-3 (2)
IR-4	Incident Handling	IR-4	IR-4 (1)	IR-4 (1) (4)
IR-5	Incident Monitoring	IR-5	IR-5	IR-5 (1)
IR-6	Incident Reporting	**IR-6**	**IR-6 (1)**	**IR-6 (1)**
IR-7	Incident Response Assistance	IR-7	IR-7 (1)	IR-7 (1)
IR-8	Incident Response Plan	IR-8	IR-8	IR-8
MA-1	System Maintenance Policy and Procedures	**MA-1**	**MA-1**	**MA-1**
MA-2	Controlled Maintenance	MA-2	MA-2	MA-2 (2)
MA-3	Maintenance Tools	Not Selected	MA-3 (1) (2)	MA-3 (1) (2) (3)
MA-4	Nonlocal Maintenance	MA-4	MA-4 (2)	MA-4 (2) **(3)**
MA-5	Maintenance Personnel	MA-5	MA-5	MA-5 (1)
MA-6	Timely Maintenance	Not Selected	MA-6	MA-6
MP-1	Media Protection Policy and Procedures	**MP-1**	**MP-1**	**MP-1**
MP-2	Media Access	MP-2	MP-2	MP-2
MP-3	Media Marking	Not Selected	MP-3	MP-3
MP-4	Media Storage	Not Selected	MP-4	MP-4
MP-5	Media Transport	Not Selected	MP-5 (4)	MP-5 (4)
MP-6	Media Sanitization	MP-6	MP-6	MP-6 (1) (2) (3)
MP-7	Media Use	MP-7	MP-7 (1)	MP-7 (1)
PE-1	Physical and Environmental Protection Policy and Procedures	**PE-1**	**PE-1**	**PE-1**
PE-2	Physical Access Authorizations	PE-2	PE-2	PE-2
PE-3	Physical Access Control	PE-3	PE-3	PE-3 (1)
PE-4	Access Control for Transmission Medium	Not Selected	PE-4	PE-4
PE-5	Access Control for Output Devices	Not Selected	PE-5	PE-5
PE-6	Monitoring Physical Access	**PE-6**	**PE-6** (1) **(4)**	**PE-6** (1) **(4)**
PE-8	Visitor Access Records	PE-8	PE-8	PE-8 (1)
PE-9	Power Equipment and Cabling	Not Selected	PE-9 (1)	PE-9 (1)
PE-10	Emergency Shutoff	Not Selected	PE-10	PE-10
PE-11	Emergency Power	PE-11 (1)	PE-11 (1)	PE-11 (1) (2)
PE-12	Emergency Lighting	PE-12	PE-12	PE-12
PE-13	Fire Protection	**PE-13**	**PE-13** (3)	**PE-13** (1) (2) (3)
PE-14	Temperature and Humidity Controls	PE-14	PE-14	PE-14
PE-15	Water Damage Protection	**PE-15**	**PE-15**	**PE-15** (1)
PE-16	Delivery and Removal	PE-16	PE-16	PE-16
PE-17	Alternate Work Site	Not Selected	PE-17	PE-17
PE-18	Location of Information System Components	Not Selected	Not Selected	PE-18
PL-1	Security Planning Policy and Procedures	**PL-1**	**PL-1**	**PL-1**
PL-2	System Security Plan	PL-2 (3)	PL-2 (3)	PL-2 (3)
PL-4	Rules of Behavior	PL-4	PL-4 (1)	PL-4 (1)
PL-7	Security Concept of Operations		PL-7	PL-7

PL-8	Information Security Architecture	Not Selected	PL-8	PL-8
PS-1	Personnel Security Policy and Procedures	**PS-1**	**PS-1**	**PS-1**
PS-2	Position Risk Designation	PS-2	PS-2	PS-2
PS-3	Personnel Screening	PS-3	PS-3	PS-3
PS-4	Personnel Termination	PS-4	PS-4	PS-4 (2)
PS-5	Personnel Transfer	PS-5	PS-5	PS-5
PS-6	Access Agreements	PS-6	PS-6	PS-6
PS-7	Third-Party Personnel Security	PS-7	PS-7	PS-7
PS-8	Personnel Sanctions	PS-8	PS-8	PS-8
RA-1	Risk Assessment Policy and Procedures	**RA-1**	**RA-1**	**RA-1**
RA-2	Security Categorization	RA-2	RA-2	RA-2
RA-3	Risk Assessment	RA-3	RA-3	RA-3
RA-5	Vulnerability Scanning	**RA-5**	**RA-5** (1) (2) (5)	**RA-5** (1) (2) (4) (5)
SA-1	System and Services Acquisition Policy and Procedures	**SA-1**	**SA-1**	**SA-1**
SA-2	Allocation of Resources	SA-2	SA-2	SA-2
SA-3	System Development Life Cycle	SA-3	SA-3	SA-3
SA-4	Acquisition Process	**SA-4 (10)**	**SA-4 (1) (2) (9) (10)**	**SA-4 (1) (2) (9) (10)**
SA-5	Information System Documentation	SA-5	SA-5	SA-5
SA-8	Security Engineering Principles	Not Selected	SA-8	SA-8
SA-9	External Information System Services	SA-9	SA-9 (2)	SA-9 (2)
SA-10	Developer Configuration Management	Not Selected	SA-10	SA-10
SA-11	Developer Security Testing and Evaluation	Not Selected	SA-11	SA-11
SA-12	Supply Chain Protection	Not Selected	Not Selected	SA-12
SA-15	Development Process, Standards, and Tools	Not Selected	Not Selected	SA-15
SA-16	Developer-Provided Training	Not Selected	Not Selected	SA-16
SA-17	Developer Security Architecture and Design	Not Selected	Not Selected	SA-17
SC-1	System and Communications Protection Policy and Procedures	**SC-1**	**SC-1**	**SC-1**
SC-2	Application Partitioning	Not Selected	**SC-2**	**SC-2**
SC-3	Security Function Isolation	Not Selected	Not Selected	**SC-3**
SC-4	Information in Shared Resources	Not Selected	**SC-4**	**SC-4**
SC-5	Denial of Service Protection	**SC-5**	**SC-5**	**SC-5**
SC-7	Boundary Protection	SC-7	SC-7 (3) (4) (5) (7) **(18)**	SC-7 (3) (4) (5) (7) (8) **(18)** (21)
SC-8	Transmission Confidentiality and Integrity	Not Selected	SC-8 **(1)**	SC-8 **(1)**
SC-10	Network Disconnect	Not Selected	**SC-10**	**SC-10**
SC-12	Cryptographic Key Establishment and Management	**SC-12**	**SC-12**	**SC-12** (1)
SC-13	Cryptographic Protection	SC-13	SC-13	SC-13
SC-15	Collaborative Computing Devices	SC-15	SC-15	SC-15
SC-17	Public Key Infrastructure Certificates	Not Selected	SC-17	SC-17
SC-18	Mobile Code	Not Selected	SC-18	SC-18
SC-19	Voice Over Internet Protocol	Not Selected	**SC-19**	**SC-19**
SC-20	Secure Name /Address Resolution Service (Authoritative Source)	**SC-20**	**SC-20**	**SC-20**

SC-21	Secure Name /Address Resolution Service (Recursive or Caching Resolver)	SC-21	SC-21	SC-21
SC-22	Architecture and Provisioning for Name/Address Resolution Service	**SC-22**	**SC-22**	**SC-22**
SC-23	Session Authenticity	Not Selected	**SC-23**	**SC-23**
SC-24	Fail in Known State	Not Selected	**SC-24**	**SC-24**
SC-28	Protection of Information at Rest	Not Selected	**SC-28**	**SC-28**
SC-39	Process Isolation	**SC-39**	**SC-39**	**SC-39**
SC-41	Port and I/O Device Access	**SC-41**	**SC-41**	**SC-41**
SI-1	System and Information Integrity Policy and Procedures	**SI-1**	**SI-1**	**SI-1**
SI-2	Flaw Remediation	**SI-2**	**SI-2 (2)**	**SI-2** (1) **(2)**
SI-3	Malicious Code Protection	**SI-3**	**SI-3 (1) (2)**	**SI-3 (1) (2)**
SI-4	Information System Monitoring	**SI-4**	**SI-4 (2) (4) (5)**	**SI-4 (2) (4) (5)**
SI-5	Security Alerts, Advisories, and Directives	**SI-5**	**SI-5**	**SI-5** (1)
SI-6	Security Function Verification	Not Selected	Not Selected	**SI-6**
SI-7	Software, Firmware, and Information Integrity	Not Selected	**SI-7 (1) (7)**	**SI-7 (1) (2) (5) (7)** (14)
SI-8	Spam Protection	Not Selected	**SI-8 (1) (2)**	**SI-8 (1) (2)**
SI-10	Information Input Validation	Not Selected	SI-10	SI-10
SI-11	Error Handling	Not Selected	SI-11	SI-11
SI-12	Information Handling and Retention	SI-12	SI-12	SI-12
SI-13	Predictable Failure Prevention	Not Selected	Not Selected	**SI-13**
SI-14	Non-Persistence	Not Selected	Not Selected	Not Selected
SI-15	Information Output Filtering	Not Selected	Not Selected	Not Selected
SI-16	Memory Protection	Not Selected	SI-16	SI-16
SI-17	Fail-Safe Procedures	SI-17	SI-17	SI-17

The PM-family is deployed organization-wide, supporting the information security program. It is not associated with security control baselines and is independent of any system impact level.

PM-1	Information Security Program Plan	**PM-1**
PM-2	Senior Information Security Officer	PM-2
PM-3	Information Security Resources	**PM-3**
PM-4	Plan of Action and Milestones Process	**PM-4**
PM-5	Information System Inventory	PM-5
PM-6	Information Security Measures of Performance	PM-6
PM-7	Enterprise Architecture	**PM-7**
PM-8	Critical Infrastructure Plan	**PM-8**
PM-9	Risk Management Strategy	**PM-9**
PM-10	Security Authorization Process	**PM-10**
PM-11	Mission/Business Process Definition	**PM-11**
PM-12	Insider Threat Program	PM-12
PM-13	Information Security Workforce	**PM-13**
PM-14	Testing, Training, and Monitoring	PM-14
PM-15	Contacts with Security Groups and Associations	PM-15
PM-16	Threat Awareness Program	PM-16

Tailoring Considerations

Due to the unique characteristics of ICS, these systems may require a greater use of compensating security controls than is the case for general purpose information systems. Compensating controls are not exceptions or waivers to the baseline controls; rather, they are alternative safeguards and countermeasures employed within the ICS that accomplish the intent of the original security controls that could not be effectively employed. See "Selecting Compensating Security Controls" in section 3.2 of NIST SP 800-53 Rev. 4 [22].

In situations where the ICS cannot support, or the organization determines it is not advisable to implement, particular security controls or control enhancements in an ICS (e.g., performance, safety, or reliability are adversely impacted), the organization provides a complete and convincing rationale for how the selected compensating controls provide an equivalent security capability or level of protection for the ICS and why the related baseline security controls could not be employed.

In accordance with the Technology-related Considerations of the Scoping Guidance in NIST SP 800-53 Rev. 4, section 3.2, if automated mechanisms are not readily available, cost-effective, or technically feasible in the ICS, compensating security controls, implemented through nonautomated mechanisms or procedures are employed [22].

Compensating controls are alternative security controls employed by organizations in lieu of specific controls in the baselines—controls that provide equivalent or comparable protection for organizational information systems and the information processed, stored, or transmitted by those systems.[42] This may occur, for example, when organizations are unable to effectively implement specific security controls in the baselines or when, due to the specific nature of the ICS or environments of operation, the controls in the baselines are not a cost-effective means of obtaining the needed risk mitigation. Compensating controls may include control enhancements that supplement the baseline. Using compensating controls may involve a trade-off between additional risk and reduced functionality. Every use of compensating controls should involve a risk-based determination of: (i) how much residual risk to accept, and (ii) how much functionality should be reduced. Compensating controls may be employed by organizations under the following conditions:

- Organizations select compensating controls from NIST SP 800-53 Rev. 4, Appendix F. If appropriate compensating controls are not available, organizations adopt suitable compensating controls from other sources.[43]

- Organizations provide supporting rationale for how compensating controls provide equivalent security capabilities for organizational information systems and why the baseline security controls could not be employed.

- Organizations assess and accept the risk associated with implementing compensating controls in ICS.

Organizational decisions on the use of compensating controls are documented in the security plan for the ICS.

---

[42] More than one compensating control may be required to provide the equivalent protection for a particular security control in Appendix F. For example, organizations with significant staff limitations may compensate for the separation of duty security control by strengthening the audit, accountability, and personnel security controls.

[43] Organizations should make every attempt to select compensating controls from the security control catalog in Appendix F. Organization-defined compensating controls are employed *only* when organizations determine that the security control catalog does not contain suitable compensating controls.

Controls that contain assignments (e.g., *Assignment: organization-defined conditions or trigger events*) may be tailored out of the baseline. This is equivalent to assigning a value of "none." The assignment may take on different values for different impact baselines.

Non-Addressable and Non-Routable Communications

The unique network properties within ICS warrant specific attention when applying certain security controls. Many of the controls in NIST SP 800-53 Rev. 4 that pertain to communication, devices, and interfaces implicitly assume the applicability of addressable and routable protocols such as the TCP/IP Internet protocol suite[44] or layers 1, 2, and 3 of the Open Systems Interconnection (OSI) model (ISO/IEC 7498-1). Some devices, or subsystems, used in ICS are exceptions to this assumption. This section addresses how the controls may be appropriately tailored. Tailoring is primarily required due to the following situations:

- *Capabilities not present.* The intent of certain controls may be more easily achieved through compensating controls due to certain network properties or capabilities not existing in the ICS subsystem. For example, physical protections (e.g., locked cabinets) may be used to secure an entire point-to-point communication channel as a means to compensate for a lack of protocols that support authentication. Security controls may warrant additional supplemental guidance to help ensure the implementation of the control or compensating control provides the appropriate level of protection.

- *Non-applicable security controls.* Many communication protocols found within an ICS may have limited functionality (e.g., not addressable or routable). Security controls dealing with addressing and routing may not be applicable to these protocols.

Security controls for devices that communicate point-to-point using standards and protocols that do not include addressing generally require tailoring. A modem connected to a computer through an RS-232 interface is an example. RS-232 was commonly employed in ICS equipment that is currently in use, even if it has been superseded in newer equipment. In telecommunications, RS-232 is the traditional name for a series of standards for serial binary single-ended data and control signals connecting between *DTE* (data terminal equipment) and *DCE* (data circuit-terminating equipment, originally defined as *data communication equipment*). The current version of the standard is Telecommunications Industry Association *(TIA)-232-F, Interface Between Data Terminal Equipment and Data Circuit-Terminating Equipment Employing Serial Binary Data Interchange*, issued in 1997.

An RS-232 serial port was once a standard feature of small computing devices, such as ICS subsystems, used for connections to peripheral devices. However, the low transmission speed, large voltage swing, and large standard connectors motivated development of the Universal Serial Bus (USB), which has displaced RS-232 from most of its peripheral interface roles. RS-232 devices are still found, especially in industrial machines, networking equipment, and scientific instruments.

Layered Network Models

The layered network models used in both TCP/IP and OSI can provide a basis for understanding the various properties of network communications and will help identify how security controls can be appropriately applied to systems and networks. The following table introduces key properties about the physical, data link, and network layers regarding the application of security controls.

---

[44] Currently, the Internet Engineering Task Force, or IETF, manages the TCP/IP protocol suite.

Network Layer	Layer properties
Physical	*Physical Medium* – A network's physical medium, specifically whether it's wired or wireless can drive the application/tailoring of certain controls. Wireless connections cannot be physically protected; therefore, compensating controls focusing on physical security cannot be used. *Topology* – The physical topologies may also determine how controls are tailored. For example point-to-point topologies (e.g., RS-232) generally do not need physically addressable interfaces, while multipoint topologies (e.g., IEEE 802.3 Ethernet) do require physically addressable interfaces.
Data link	*Physically Addressable* – Multipoint protocols require physically addressable interfaces to allow for multiple systems to communicate. Systems that are not physically addressable can only be accessed by those systems with which it shared point-to-point connections.
Network	*Network Addressable/Routable* – Network addressable/routable systems can be accessed by any system on an internetwork. That is, communications can be routed between networks. If a system is not network addressable/routable, it can only be accessed by systems with which it shares a local network connection.

Definitions

Terms used in this overlay are defined in Appendix B— or in NIST Internal Report (NISTIR) 7298 Revision 2, *Glossary of Key Information Security Terms* [99].

Additional Information or Instructions

None at this time. Organizations may provide any additional information or instructions relevant to the overlay not covered in the previous sections.

Detailed Overlay Control Specifications

This Overlay is based on the NIST SP 800-53 Rev. 4, *Security and Privacy Controls for Federal Information Systems and Organizations*, which provides a catalog of security and privacy controls for federal information systems and organizations and a process for selecting controls to protect organizational operations (including mission, functions, image, and reputation), organizational assets, individuals, other organizations, and the Nation from a diverse set of threats including hostile cyber attacks, natural disasters, structural failures, and human errors (both intentional and unintentional). The security and privacy controls are customizable and implemented as part of an organization-wide process that manages information security and privacy risk. The controls address a diverse set of security and privacy requirements across the federal government and critical infrastructure, derived from legislation, Executive Orders, policies, directives, regulations, standards, and/or mission/business needs. The publication also describes how to develop specialized sets of controls, or overlays, tailored for specific types of missions/business functions, technologies, or environments of operation. Finally, the catalog of security controls addresses security from both a functionality perspective (the strength of security functions and mechanisms provided) and an assurance perspective (the measures of confidence in the implemented security capability). Addressing both security functionality and assurance helps to ensure that information technology component products and the information systems built from those products using sound system and security engineering principles are sufficiently trustworthy.

In preparation for selecting and specifying the appropriate security controls for organizational information systems and their respective environments of operation, organizations first determine the criticality and sensitivity of the information to be processed, stored, or transmitted by those systems. This process is known as security categorization. FIPS 199 [15] enables federal agencies to establish security categories for both information and information systems. Other documents, such as those produced by ISA and CNSS, also provide guidance for defining low, moderate, and high levels of security based on impact. The security categories are based on the potential impact on an organization or on people (employees and/or the public) should certain events occur which jeopardize the information and information systems needed by the organization to accomplish its assigned mission, protect its assets, fulfill its legal responsibilities, maintain its day-to-day functions, and protect individuals' safety, health and life. Security categories are to be used in conjunction with vulnerability and threat information in assessing the risk to an organization.

This overlay provides ICS Supplemental Guidance for the security controls and control enhancements prescribed for an information system or an organization designed to protect the confidentiality, integrity, and availability of its information and to meet a set of defined security requirements. This overlay contains a tailoring of the security control baselines; its specification may be more stringent or less stringent than the original security control baseline specification and can be applied to multiple information systems. This overlay is high-level, applicable to all ICS; it may be used as the basis for more specific overlays. Use cases for specific systems in specific environments may be separately published (e.g., as a NISTIR).

Figure G-1 uses the AU-4 control as an example of the format and content of the detailed overlay control specifications.

❶ Control number and title.
❷ Column for control and control enhancement number.
❸ Column for control and control enhancement name.
❹ Columns for baselines. If the baselines have been supplemented, then SUPPLEMENTED appears.
❺ A row for each control or control enhancement.
❻ Columns for LOW, MODERATE, and HIGH baselines.
❼ "Selected" indicates the control is selected in NIST SP 800-53 Rev. 4. "Added" indicates the control is added to a baseline in the ICS overlay.
    A blank cell indicates the control is not selected.
    "Removed" indicates the control is removed from the baseline.
❽ The ICS Supplemental Guidance. If there is none, that is stated.
❾ The Control Enhancement ICS Supplemental Guidance. If there is none, that is stated.
❿ The rationale for changing the presence of a control or control enhancement in the baseline.

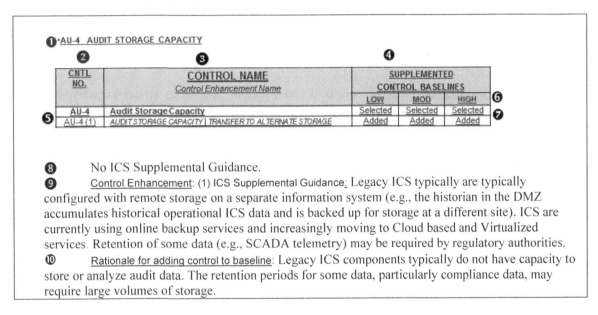

Figure G-1 Detailed Overlay Control Specifications Illustrated

NIST SP 800-53 Rev. 4, Appendix F, contains Supplemental Guidance for all Controls and Control Enhancements [22]. ICS Supplemental Guidance in this overlay provides organizations with additional information on the application of the security controls and control enhancements in NIST SP 800-53 Rev. 4, Appendix F, to ICS and the environments in which these specialized systems operate. The ICS Supplemental Guidance also provides information as to why a particular security control or control enhancement may not be applicable in some ICS environments and may be a candidate for tailoring (i.e., the application of scoping guidance and/or compensating controls).

ACCESS CONTROL – AC

Tailoring Considerations for Access Control Family

Before implementing controls in the AC family, consider the tradeoffs among security, privacy, latency, performance, throughput, and reliability. For example, the organization considers whether latency induced from the use of confidentiality and integrity mechanisms employing cryptographic mechanisms would adversely impact the operational performance of the ICS.

In situations where the ICS cannot support the specific Access Control requirements of a control, the organization employs compensating controls in accordance with the general tailoring guidance. Examples of compensating controls are given with each control, as appropriate.

Supplemental Guidance

Supplemental Guidance for all Controls and Control Enhancements in NIST SP 800-53 Rev. 4, Appendix F, should be used in conjunction with the ICS Supplemental Guidance in this overlay, if any.

AC-1   ACCESS CONTROL POLICY AND PROCEDURES

CNTL NO.	CONTROL NAME *Control Enhancement Name*	CONTROL BASELINES		
		LOW	MOD	HIGH
AC-1	**Access Control Policy and Procedures**	Selected	Selected	Selected

ICS Supplemental Guidance: The policy specifically addresses the unique properties and requirements of ICS and the relationship to non-ICS systems. ICS access by vendors and maintenance staff can occur over a very large facility footprint or geographic area and into unobserved spaces such as mechanical/electrical rooms, ceilings, floors, field substations, switch and valve vaults, and pump stations.

AC-2   ACCOUNT MANAGEMENT

CNTL NO.	CONTROL NAME *Control Enhancement Name*	CONTROL BASELINES		
		LOW	MOD	HIGH
AC-2	**Account Management**	Selected	Selected	Selected
AC-2 (1)	*ACCOUNT MANAGEMENT	AUTOMATED SYSTEM ACCOUNT MANAGEMENT*		Selected	Selected
AC-2 (2)	*ACCOUNT MANAGEMENT	REMOVAL OF TEMPORARY / EMERGENCY ACCOUNTS*		Selected	Selected
AC-2 (3)	*ACCOUNT MANAGEMENT	DISABLE INACTIVE ACCOUNTS*		Selected	Selected
AC-2 (4)	*ACCOUNT MANAGEMENT	AUTOMATED AUDIT ACTIONS*		Selected	Selected
AC-2 (5)	*ACCOUNT MANAGEMENT	INACTIVITY LOGOUT / TYPICAL USAGE MONITORING*			Selected
AC-2 (11)	*ACCOUNT MANAGEMENT	USAGE CONDITIONS*			Selected
AC-2 (12)	*ACCOUNT MANAGEMENT	ACCOUNT MONITORING / ATYPICAL USAGE*			Selected
AC-2 (13)	*ACCOUNT MANAGEMENT	ACCOUNT REVIEWS*			Selected

ICS Supplemental Guidance: Example compensating controls include providing increased physical security, personnel security, intrusion detection, auditing measures.

Control Enhancement: (1, 3, 4) ICS Supplemental Guidance: Example compensating controls include employing nonautomated mechanisms or procedures.

Control Enhancement: (2) ICS Supplemental Guidance: In situations where the ICS (e.g., field devices) cannot support temporary or emergency accounts, this enhancement does not apply. Example compensating controls include employing nonautomated mechanisms or procedures.

Control Enhancement: (5) ICS Supplemental Guidance: Example compensating controls include employing nonautomated mechanisms or procedures.

Control Enhancement: (11, 12, 13) No ICS Supplemental Guidance.

AC-3   ACCESS ENFORCEMENT

CNTL NO.	CONTROL NAME *Control Enhancement Name*	CONTROL BASELINES		
		LOW	MOD	HIGH
AC-3	**Access Enforcement**	Selected	Selected	Selected

ICS Supplemental Guidance: The organization ensures that access enforcement mechanisms do not adversely impact the operational performance of the ICS. Example compensating controls include encapsulation. Policy for logical access control to Non-Addressable and Non-Routable system resources and the associated information is made explicit. Access control mechanisms include hardware, firmware, and software that controls or has device access, such as device drivers and communications controllers. Physical access control may serve as a compensating control for logical access control, however, it may not provide sufficient granularity in situations where users require access to different functions. Logical access enforcement may be implemented in encapsulating hardware and software.

AC-4   INFORMATION FLOW ENFORCEMENT

CNTL NO.	CONTROL NAME *Control Enhancement Name*	CONTROL BASELINES		
		LOW	MOD	HIGH
AC-4	**Information Flow Enforcement**		Selected	Selected

ICS Supplemental Guidance: Physical addresses (e.g., a serial port) may be implicitly or explicitly associated with labels or attributes (e.g., hardware I/O address). Manual methods are typically static. Label or attribute policy mechanisms may be implemented in hardware, firmware, and software that controls or has device access, such as device drivers and communications controllers. Information flow policy may be supported by labeling or coloring physical connectors as an aid to manual hookup. Inspection of message content may enforce information flow policy. For example, a message containing a command to an actuator may not be permitted to flow between the control network and any other network.

AC-5   SEPARATION OF DUTIES

CNTL NO.	CONTROL NAME *Control Enhancement Name*	CONTROL BASELINES		
		LOW	MOD	HIGH
AC-5	**Separation of Duties**		Selected	Selected

ICS Supplemental Guidance: Example compensating controls include providing increased personnel security and auditing. The organization carefully considers the appropriateness of a single individual performing multiple critical roles.

AC-6   LEAST PRIVILEGE

CNTL NO.	CONTROL NAME *Control Enhancement Name*	CONTROL BASELINES		
		LOW	MOD	HIGH
AC-6	**Least Privilege**		Selected	Selected
AC-6 (1)	*LEAST PRIVILEGE | AUTHORIZE ACCESS TO SECURITY FUNCTIONS*		Selected	Selected
AC-6 (2)	*LEAST PRIVILEGE | NON-PRIVILEGED ACCESS FOR NONSECURITY FUNCTIONS*		Selected	Selected
AC-6 (3)	*LEAST PRIVILEGE | NETWORK ACCESS TO PRIVILEGED COMMANDS*			Selected
AC-6 (5)	*LEAST PRIVILEGE | PRIVILEGED ACCOUNTS*		Selected	Selected
AC-6 (9)	*LEAST PRIVILEGE | AUDITING USE OF PRIVILEGED FUNCTIONS*		Selected	Selected
AC-6 (10)	*LEAST PRIVILEGE | PROHIBIT NON-PRIVILEGED USERS FROM EXECUTING PRIVILEGED FUNCTIONS*		Selected	Selected

ICS Supplemental Guidance: Example compensating controls include providing increased personnel security and auditing. The organization carefully considers the appropriateness of a single individual having multiple critical privileges. System privilege models may be tailored to enforce integrity and availability (e.g., lower privileges include read access and higher privileges include write access).

Control Enhancement: (1) ICS Supplemental Guidance: In situations where the ICS cannot support access control to security functions, the organization employs nonautomated mechanisms or procedures as compensating controls in accordance with the general tailoring guidance.

Control Enhancement: (2) ICS Supplemental Guidance: In situations where the ICS cannot support access control to nonsecurity functions, the organization employs nonautomated mechanisms or procedures as compensating controls in accordance with the general tailoring guidance.

Control Enhancement: (3) ICS Supplemental Guidance: In situations where the ICS cannot support network access control to privileged commands, the organization employs nonautomated mechanisms or procedures as compensating controls in accordance with the general tailoring guidance.

Control Enhancement: (5) ICS Supplemental Guidance: In situations where the ICS cannot support access control to privileged accounts, the organization employs nonautomated mechanisms or procedures as compensating controls in accordance with the general tailoring guidance.

Control Enhancement: (9) ICS Supplemental Guidance: In general, audit record processing is not performed on the ICS, but on a separate information system. Example compensating controls include providing an auditing capability on a separate information system.

Control Enhancement: (10) ICS Supplemental Guidance: Example compensating controls include enhanced auditing.

AC-7   UNSUCCESSFUL LOGIN ATTEMPTS

CNTL NO.	CONTROL NAME *Control Enhancement Name*	CONTROL BASELINES		
		LOW	MOD	HIGH
AC-7	Unsuccessful Login Attempts	Selected	Selected	Selected

ICS Supplemental Guidance: Many ICS must remain continuously on and operators remain logged onto the system at all times. A "log-over" capability may be employed. Example compensating controls include logging or recording all unsuccessful login attempts and alerting ICS security personnel though alarms or other means when the number of organization-defined consecutive invalid access attempts is exceeded.

AC-8   SYSTEM USE NOTIFICATION

CNTL NO.	CONTROL NAME *Control Enhancement Name*	CONTROL BASELINES		
		LOW	MOD	HIGH
AC-8	System Use Notification	Selected	Selected	Selected

ICS Supplemental Guidance: Many ICS must remain continuously on and system use notification may not be supported or effective. Example compensating controls include posting physical notices in ICS facilities.

AC-10   CONCURRENT SESSION CONTROL

CNTL NO.	CONTROL NAME *Control Enhancement Name*	CONTROL BASELINES		
		LOW	MOD	HIGH
AC-10	Concurrent Session Control			Selected

ICS Supplemental Guidance: The number, account type, and privileges of concurrent sessions takes into account the roles and responsibilities of the affected individuals. Example compensating controls include providing increased auditing measures.

AC-11   SESSION LOCK

CNTL NO.	CONTROL NAME *Control Enhancement Name*	CONTROL BASELINES		
		LOW	MOD	HIGH
AC-11	**Session Lock**		Selected	Selected
AC-11 (1)	*SESSION LOCK	PATTERN-HIDING DISPLAYS*		Selected	Selected

    ICS Supplemental Guidance: This control assumes a staffed environment where users interact with information system displays. When this assumption does not apply the organization tailors the control appropriately (e.g., the ICS may be physically protected by placement in a locked enclosure). The control may also be tailored for ICS that are not configured with displays, but which have the capability to support displays (e.g., ICS to which a maintenance technician may attach a display). In some cases, session lock for ICS operator workstations/nodes is not advised (e.g., when immediate operator responses are required in emergency situations). Example compensating controls include locating the display in an area with physical access controls that limit access to individuals with permission and need-to-know for the displayed information.

    Control Enhancement: (1) ICS Supplemental Guidance: ICS may employ physical protection to prevent access to a display or to prevent attachment of a display. In situations where the ICS cannot conceal displayed information, the organization employs nonautomated mechanisms or procedures as compensating controls in accordance with the general tailoring guidance.

AC-12   SESSION TERMINATION

CNTL NO.	CONTROL NAME *Control Enhancement Name*	CONTROL BASELINES		
		LOW	MOD	HIGH
AC-12	**Session Termination**		Selected	Selected

    ICS Supplemental Guidance: Example compensating controls include providing increased auditing measures or limiting remote access privileges to key personnel.

AC-14   PERMITTED ACTIONS WITHOUT IDENTIFICATION OR AUTHENTICATION

CNTL NO.	CONTROL NAME *Control Enhancement Name*	CONTROL BASELINES		
		LOW	MOD	HIGH
AC-14	**Permitted Actions without Identification or Authentication**	Selected	Selected	Selected

    No ICS Supplemental Guidance.

AC-17   REMOTE ACCESS

CNTL NO.	CONTROL NAME *Control Enhancement Name*	CONTROL BASELINES		
		LOW	MOD	HIGH
AC-17	**Remote Access**	Selected	Selected	Selected
AC-17 (1)	*REMOTE ACCESS	AUTOMATED MONITORING / CONTROL*		Selected	Selected
AC-17 (2)	*REMOTE ACCESS	PROTECTION OF CONFIDENTIALITY / INTEGRITY USING ENCRYPTION*		Selected	Selected
AC-17 (3)	*REMOTE ACCESS	MANAGED ACCESS CONTROL POINTS*		Selected	Selected
AC-17 (4)	*REMOTE ACCESS	PRIVILEGED COMMANDS / ACCESS*		Selected	Selected

    ICS Supplemental Guidance: In situations where the ICS cannot implement any or all of the components of this control, the organization employs other mechanisms or procedures as compensating controls in accordance with the general tailoring guidance.

    Control Enhancement: (1) ICS Supplemental Guidance: Example compensating controls include employing nonautomated mechanisms or procedures as compensating controls (e.g., following manual authentication [see IA-2], dial-in remote access may be enabled for a specified period of time or a call may be placed from the ICS site to the authenticated remote entity.

Control Enhancement: (2) ICS Supplemental Guidance: ICS security objectives often rank confidentiality below availability and integrity. The organization explores all possible cryptographic mechanism (e.g., encryption, digital signature, hash function). Each mechanism has a different delay impact. Example compensating controls include providing increased auditing for remote sessions or limiting remote access privileges to key personnel).

Control Enhancement: (3) ICS Supplemental Guidance: Example compensating controls include connection-specific manual authentication of the remote entity.

Control Enhancement: (4) No ICS Supplemental Guidance.

ICS Supplemental Guidance: Example compensating controls include employing nonautomated mechanisms or procedures as compensating controls in accordance with the general tailoring guidance.

AC-18   WIRELESS ACCESS

CNTL NO.	CONTROL NAME *Control Enhancement Name*	CONTROL BASELINES		
		LOW	MOD	HIGH
AC-18	Wireless Access	Selected	Selected	Selected
AC-18 (1)	*WIRELESS ACCESS	AUTHENTICATION AND ENCRYPTION*		Selected	Selected
AC-18 (4)	*WIRELESS ACCESS	RESTRICT CONFIGURATIONS BY USERS*			Selected
AC-18 (5)	*WIRELESS ACCESS	CONFINE WIRELESS COMMUNICATIONS*			Selected

ICS Supplemental Guidance: In situations where the ICS cannot implement any or all of the components of this control, the organization employs other mechanisms or procedures as compensating controls in accordance with the general tailoring guidance.

Control Enhancement: (1) ICS Supplemental Guidance: See AC-17 Control Enhancement: (1) ICS Supplemental Guidance. Example compensating controls include providing increased auditing for wireless access or limiting wireless access privileges to key personnel.

Control Enhancement: (4) (5) No ICS Supplemental Guidance.

AC-19   ACCESS CONTROL FOR MOBILE DEVICES

CNTL NO.	CONTROL NAME *Control Enhancement Name*	CONTROL BASELINES		
		LOW	MOD	HIGH
AC-19	Access Control for Mobile Devices	Selected	Selected	Selected
AC-19 (5)	*ACCESS CONTROL FOR MOBILE DEVICES	FULL DEVICE / CONTAINER-BASED ENCRYPTION*		Selected	Selected

No ICS Supplemental Guidance.

AC-20   USE OF EXTERNAL INFORMATION SYSTEMS

CNTL NO.	CONTROL NAME *Control Enhancement Name*	CONTROL BASELINES		
		LOW	MOD	HIGH
AC-20	Use of External Information Systems	Selected	Selected	Selected
AC-20 (1)	*USE OF EXTERNAL INFORMATION SYSTEMS	LIMITS ON AUTHORIZED USE*		Selected	Selected
AC-20 (2)	*USE OF EXTERNAL INFORMATION SYSTEMS	PORTABLE STORAGE MEDIA*		Selected	Selected

ICS Supplemental Guidance: Organizations refine the definition of "external" to reflect lines of authority and responsibility; granularity of organization entity; and their relationships. An organization may consider a system to be external if that system performs different functions, implements different policies, comes under different managers, or does not provide sufficient visibility into the implementation of security controls to allow the establishment of a satisfactory trust relationship. For example, a process control system and a business data processing system would typically be considered external to each other. Access to an ICS for support by a business partner, such as a vendor or support contractor, is another common example. The definition and trustworthiness of external information systems is reexamined with respect to ICS functions, purposes, technology, and limitations to establish a clear documented technical or business case for use and an acceptance of the risk inherent in the use of an external information system.

Control Enhancement: (1, 2) No ICS Supplemental Guidance.

AC-21   INFORMATION SHARING

CNTL NO.	CONTROL NAME *Control Enhancement Name*	CONTROL BASELINES		
		LOW	MOD	HIGH
AC-21	Collaboration and Information Sharing	Added	Selected	Selected

ICS Supplemental Guidance: The organization should collaborate and share information about potential incidents on a timely basis. The DHS National Cybersecurity & Communications Integration Center (NCCIC), http://www.dhs.gov/about-national-cybersecurity-communications-integration-center serves as a centralized location where operational elements involved in cybersecurity and communications reliance are coordinated and integrated. The Industrial Control Systems Cyber Emergency Response Team (ICS-CERT) http://ics-cert.us-cert.gov/ics-cert/ collaborates with international and private sector Computer Emergency Response Teams (CERTs) to share control systems-related security incidents and mitigation measures. Organizations should consider having both an unclassified and classified information sharing capability.

Rationale for adding AC-21 to low baseline: ICS systems provide essential services and control functions and are often connected to other ICS systems or business systems that can be vectors of attack. It is therefore necessary to provide a uniform defense encompassing all baselines.

AC-22   PUBLICLY ACCESSIBLE CONTENT

CNTL NO.	CONTROL NAME *Control Enhancement Name*	CONTROL BASELINES		
		LOW	MOD	HIGH
AC-22	Publicly Accessible Content	Selected	Selected	Selected

ICS Supplemental Guidance: Generally, public access to ICS systems is not permitted. Selected information may be transferred to a publicly accessible information system, possibly with added controls (e.g., introduction of fuzziness or delay).

AWARENESS AND TRAINING – AT

Supplemental Guidance

Supplemental Guidance for all Controls and Control Enhancements in NIST SP 800-53 Rev. 4, Appendix F, should be used in conjunction with the ICS Supplemental Guidance in this overlay, if any.

AT-1   SECURITY AWARENESS AND TRAINING POLICY AND PROCEDURES

CNTL NO.	CONTROL NAME *Control Enhancement Name*	CONTROL BASELINES		
		LOW	MOD	HIGH
AT-1	**Security Awareness and Training Policy and Procedures**	Selected	Selected	Selected

ICS Supplemental Guidance: The policy specifically addresses the unique properties and requirements of ICS and the relationship to non-ICS systems.

AT-2   SECURITY AWARENESS TRAINING

CNTL NO.	CONTROL NAME *Control Enhancement Name*	CONTROL BASELINES		
		LOW	MOD	HIGH
AT-2	**Security Awareness**	Selected	Selected	Selected
AT-2 (2)	*SECURITY AWARENESS	INSIDER THREAT*		Selected	Selected

ICS Supplemental Guidance: Security awareness training includes initial and periodic review of ICS-specific policies, standard operating procedures, security trends, and vulnerabilities. The ICS security awareness program is consistent with the requirements of the security awareness and training policy established by the organization.

Control Enhancement: (2) No ICS Supplemental Guidance.

AT-3   ROLE-BASED SECURITY TRAINING

CNTL NO.	CONTROL NAME *Control Enhancement Name*	CONTROL BASELINES		
		LOW	MOD	HIGH
AT-3	**Role-Based Security Training**	Selected	Selected	Selected

ICS Supplemental Guidance: Security training includes initial and periodic review of ICS-specific policies, standard operating procedures, security trends, and vulnerabilities. The ICS security training program is consistent with the requirements of the security awareness and training policy established by the organization.

AT-4   SECURITY TRAINING RECORDS

CNTL NO.	CONTROL NAME *Control Enhancement Name*	CONTROL BASELINES		
		LOW	MOD	HIGH
AT-4	**Security Training Records**	Selected	Selected	Selected

No ICS Supplemental Guidance.

AUDITING AND ACCOUNTABILITY – AU

Tailoring Considerations for Audit Family

In general, audit information and audit tools are not present on legacy ICS, but on a separate information system (e.g., the historian). In situations where the ICS cannot support the specific Audit and Accountability requirements of a control, the organization employs compensating controls in accordance with the general tailoring guidance. Examples of compensating controls are given with each control, as appropriate.

Supplemental Guidance

Supplemental Guidance for all Controls and Control Enhancements in NIST SP 800-53 Rev. 4, Appendix F, should be used in conjunction with the ICS Supplemental Guidance in this overlay, if any.

AU-1   AUDIT AND ACCOUNTABILITY POLICY AND PROCEDURES

CNTL NO.	CONTROL NAME *Control Enhancement Name*	CONTROL BASELINES		
		LOW	MOD	HIGH
AU-1	**Audit and Accountability Policy and Procedures**	Selected	Selected	Selected

ICS Supplemental Guidance: The policy specifically addresses the unique properties and requirements of ICS and the relationship to non-ICS systems.

AU-2   AUDIT EVENTS

CNTL NO.	CONTROL NAME *Control Enhancement Name*	CONTROL BASELINES		
		LOW	MOD	HIGH
AU-2	**Auditable Events**	Selected	Selected	Selected
AU-2 (3)	*AUDITABLE EVENTS	REVIEWS AND UPDATES*		Selected	Selected

ICS Supplemental Guidance: The organization may designate ICS events as audit events, requiring that ICS data and/or telemetry be recorded as audit data.

Control Enhancement: (3) No ICS Supplemental Guidance.

AU-3   CONTENT OF AUDIT RECORDS

CNTL NO.	CONTROL NAME *Control Enhancement Name*	CONTROL BASELINES		
		LOW	MOD	HIGH
AU-3	**Content of Audit Records**	Selected	Selected	Selected
AU-3 (1)	*CONTENT OF AUDIT RECORDS	ADDITIONAL AUDIT INFORMATION*		Selected	Selected
AU-3 (2)	*CONTENT OF AUDIT RECORDS	CENTRALIZED MANAGEMENT OF PLANNED AUDIT RECORD CONTENT*			Selected

ICS Supplemental Guidance: Example compensating controls include providing an auditing capability on a separate information system.

Control Enhancement: (1, 2) No ICS Supplemental Guidance.

AU-4   AUDIT STORAGE CAPACITY

CNTL NO.	CONTROL NAME *Control Enhancement Name*	SUPPLEMENTED CONTROL BASELINES		
		LOW	MOD	HIGH
AU-4	**Audit Storage Capacity**	Selected	Selected	Selected
AU-4 (1)	*AUDIT STORAGE CAPACITY	TRANSFER TO ALTERNATE STORAGE*	Added	Added	Added

No ICS Supplemental Guidance.

Control Enhancement: (1) ICS Supplemental Guidance: Legacy ICS are typically configured with remote storage on a separate information system (e.g., the historian accumulates historical operational ICS data and is backed up for storage at a different site). ICS are currently using online backup services and increasingly moving to Cloud based and Virtualized services. Retention of some data (e.g., SCADA telemetry) may be required by regulatory authorities.

Rationale for adding AU-4 (1) to all baselines: Legacy ICS components typically do not have capacity to store or analyze audit data. The retention periods for some data, particularly compliance data, may require large volumes of storage.

AU-5   RESPONSE TO AUDIT PROCESSING FAILURES

CNTL NO.	CONTROL NAME *Control Enhancement Name*	CONTROL BASELINES		
		LOW	MOD	HIGH
AU-5	**Response to Audit Processing Failures**	Selected	Selected	Selected
AU-5 (1)	*RESPONSE TO AUDIT PROCESSING FAILURES	AUDIT STORAGE CAPACITY*			Selected
AU-5 (2)	*RESPONSE TO AUDIT PROCESSING FAILURES	REAL-TIME ALERTS*			Selected

No ICS Supplemental Guidance.

AU-6   AUDIT REVIEW, ANALYSIS, AND REPORTING

CNTL NO.	CONTROL NAME *Control Enhancement Name*	CONTROL BASELINES		
		LOW	MOD	HIGH
AU-6	**Audit Review, Analysis, and Reporting**	Selected	Selected	Selected
AU-6 (1)	*AUDIT REVIEW, ANALYSIS, AND REPORTING	PROCESS INTEGRATION*		Selected	Selected
AU-6 (3)	*AUDIT REVIEW, ANALYSIS, AND REPORTING	CORRELATE AUDIT REPOSITORIES*		Selected	Selected
AU-6 (5)	*AUDIT REVIEW, ANALYSIS, AND REPORTING	INTEGRATION / SCANNING AND MONITORING CAPABILITIES*			Selected
AU-6 (6)	*AUDIT REVIEW, ANALYSIS, AND REPORTING	CORRELATION WITH PHYSICAL MONITORING*			Selected

No ICS Supplemental Guidance.

Control Enhancement: (1) ICS Supplemental Guidance: Example compensating controls include manual mechanisms or procedures.

Control Enhancement: (3, 5, 6) No ICS Supplemental Guidance.

AU-7   AUDIT REDUCTION AND REPORT GENERATION

CNTL NO.	CONTROL NAME *Control Enhancement Name*	CONTROL BASELINES		
		LOW	MOD	HIGH
AU-7	**Audit Reduction and Report Generation**		Selected	Selected
AU-7 (1)	*AUDIT REDUCTION AND REPORT GENERATION	AUTOMATIC PROCESSING*		Selected	Selected

No ICS Supplemental Guidance.

Control Enhancement: (1) No ICS Supplemental Guidance.

AU-8   TIME STAMPS

CNTL NO.	CONTROL NAME *Control Enhancement Name*	CONTROL BASELINES		
		LOW	MOD	HIGH
AU-8	**Time Stamps**	Selected	Selected	Selected
AU-8 (1)	*TIME STAMPS	SYNCHRONIZATION WITH AUTHORITATIVE TIME SOURCE*		Selected	Selected

ICS Supplemental Guidance: Example compensating controls include using a separate information system designated as an authoritative time source.

Control Enhancement: (1) ICS Supplemental Guidance: ICS employ suitable mechanisms (e.g., GPS, IEEE 1588) for time stamps.

AU-9 PROTECTION OF AUDIT INFORMATION

CNTL NO.	CONTROL NAME *Control Enhancement Name*	CONTROL BASELINES		
		LOW	MOD	HIGH
AU-9	**Protection of Audit Information**	Selected	Selected	Selected
AU-9 (2)	*PROTECTION OF AUDIT INFORMATION	AUDIT BACKUP ON SEPARATE PHYSICAL SYSTEMS / COMPONENTS*			Selected
AU-9 (3)	*PROTECTION OF AUDIT INFORMATION	CRYPTOGRAPHIC PROTECTION*			Selected
AU-9 (4)	*PROTECTION OF AUDIT INFORMATION	ACCESS BY SUBSET OF PRIVILEGED USERS*		Selected	Selected

No ICS Supplemental Guidance.

AU-10 NON-REPUDIATION

CNTL NO.	CONTROL NAME *Control Enhancement Name*	CONTROL BASELINES		
		LOW	MOD	HIGH
AU-10	**Non-repudiation**			Selected

ICS Supplemental Guidance: Example compensating controls include providing non-repudiation on a separate information system.

AU-11 AUDIT RECORD RETENTION

CNTL NO.	CONTROL NAME *Control Enhancement Name*	CONTROL BASELINES		
		LOW	MOD	HIGH
AU-11	**Audit Record Retention**	Selected	Selected	Selected

No ICS Supplemental Guidance.

AU-12 AUDIT GENERATION

CNTL NO.	CONTROL NAME *Control Enhancement Name*	CONTROL BASELINES		
		LOW	MOD	HIGH
AU-12	**Audit Generation**	Selected	Selected	Selected
AU-12 (1)	*AUDIT GENERATION	SYSTEM-WIDE / TIME-CORRELATED AUDIT TRAIL*			Selected
AU-12 (3)	*AUDIT GENERATION	CHANGES BY AUTHORIZED INDIVIDUALS*			Selected

No ICS Supplemental Guidance.

Control Enhancement: (1) ICS Supplemental Guidance: Example compensating controls include providing time-correlated audit records on a separate information system.

Control Enhancement: (3) ICS Supplemental Guidance: Example compensating controls include employing nonautomated mechanisms or procedures.

SECURITY ASSESSMENT AND AUTHORIZATION – CA

Tailoring Considerations for Security Assessment and Authorization Family
    In situations where the ICS cannot support the specific Security Assessment and Authorization requirements of a control, the organization employs compensating controls in accordance with the general tailoring guidance. Examples of compensating controls are given with each control, as appropriate.

Supplemental Guidance
    Supplemental Guidance for all Controls and Control Enhancements in NIST SP 800-53 Rev. 4, Appendix F, should be used in conjunction with the ICS Supplemental Guidance in this overlay, if any.

CA-1   SECURITY ASSESSMENT AND AUTHORIZATION POLICY AND PROCEDURES

CNTL NO.	CONTROL NAME *Control Enhancement Name*	CONTROL BASELINES		
		LOW	MOD	HIGH
CA-1	**Security Assessment and Authorization Policy and Procedures**	Selected	Selected	Selected

    ICS Supplemental Guidance: The policy specifically addresses the unique properties and requirements of ICS and the relationship to non-ICS systems.

CA-2   SECURITY ASSESSMENTS

CNTL NO.	CONTROL NAME *Control Enhancement Name*	CONTROL BASELINES		
		LOW	MOD	HIGH
CA-2	**Security Assessments**	Selected	Selected	Selected
CA-2 (1)	*SECURITY ASSESSMENTS	INDEPENDENT ASSESSORS*		Selected	Selected
CA-2 (2)	*SECURITY ASSESSMENTS	TYPES OF ASSESSMENTS*			Selected

    ICS Supplemental Guidance: Assessments are performed and documented by qualified assessors (i.e., experienced in assessing ICS) authorized by the organization. The organization ensures that assessments do not interfere with ICS functions. The individual/group conducting the assessment fully understands the organizational information security policies and procedures, the ICS security policies and procedures, and the specific health, safety, and environmental risks associated with a particular facility and/or process. The organization ensures that the assessment does not affect system operation or result in unintentional system modification. If assessment activities must be performed on the production ICS, it may need to be taken off-line before an assessment can be conducted. If an ICS must be taken off-line to conduct an assessment, the assessment is scheduled to occur during planned ICS outages whenever possible.
    Control Enhancement: (1) No ICS Supplemental Guidance.
    Control Enhancement: (2) ICS Supplemental Guidance: The organization conducts risk analysis to support the selection of assessment target (e.g., the live system, an off-line replica, a simulation).

CA-3   SYSTEM INTERCONNECTIONS

CNTL NO.	CONTROL NAME *Control Enhancement Name*	CONTROL BASELINES		
		LOW	MOD	HIGH
CA-3	**Information System Connections**	Selected	Selected	Selected
CA-3 (5)	*SYSTEM INTERCONNECTIONS	RESTRICTIONS ON EXTERNAL SYSTEM CONNECTIONS*		Selected	Selected

    ICS Supplemental Guidance: Organizations perform risk-benefit analysis to support determination whether an ICS should be connected to other information system(s). The Authorizing Official fully understands the organizational information security policies and procedures; the ICS security policies and procedures; the risks to organizational operations and assets, individuals, other organizations, and the Nation associated with the connection to other information system(s); and the specific health, safety, and environmental risks associated with a particular interconnection. The AO documents risk acceptance in the ICS system security plan.
    Control Enhancement: (5) No ICS Supplemental Guidance.

CA-5   PLAN OF ACTION AND MILESTONES

CNTL NO.	CONTROL NAME *Control Enhancement Name*	CONTROL BASELINES		
		LOW	MOD	HIGH
CA-5	Plan of Action and Milestones	Selected	Selected	Selected

No ICS Supplemental Guidance.

CA-6   SECURITY AUTHORIZATION

CNTL NO.	CONTROL NAME *Control Enhancement Name*	CONTROL BASELINES		
		LOW	MOD	HIGH
CA-6	Security Authorization	Selected	Selected	Selected

No ICS Supplemental Guidance.

CA-7   CONTINUOUS MONITORING

CNTL NO.	CONTROL NAME *Control Enhancement Name*	CONTROL BASELINES		
		LOW	MOD	HIGH
CA-7	Continuous Monitoring	Selected	Selected	Selected
CA-7 (1)	*CONTINUOUS MONITORING	INDEPENDENT ASSESSMENT*		Selected	Selected

ICS Supplemental Guidance: Continuous monitoring programs for ICS are designed, documented, and implemented by qualified personnel (i.e., experienced with ICS) selected by the organization. The organization ensures that continuous monitoring does not interfere with ICS functions. The individual/group designing and conducting the continuous monitoring fully understands the organizational information security policies and procedures, the ICS security policies and procedures, and the specific health, safety, and environmental risks associated with a particular facility and/or process. The organization ensures that continuous monitoring does not affect system operation or result in intentional or unintentional system modification. Example compensating controls include external monitoring.

Control Enhancement: (1) No ICS Supplemental Guidance.

CA-8   PENETRATION TESTING

CNTL NO.	CONTROL NAME *Control Enhancement Name*	CONTROL BASELINES		
		LOW	MOD	HIGH
CA-8	Penetration Testing			Selected

ICS Supplemental Guidance: Penetration testing is used with care on ICS networks to ensure that ICS functions are not adversely impacted by the testing process. In general, ICS are highly sensitive to timing constraints and have limited resources. Example compensating controls include employing a replicated, virtualized, or simulated system to conduct penetration testing. Production ICS may need to be taken off-line before testing can be conducted. If ICS are taken off-line for testing, tests are scheduled to occur during planned ICS outages whenever possible. If penetration testing is performed on non-ICS networks, extra care is taken to ensure that tests do not propagate into the ICS network.

CA-9 INTERNAL SYSTEM CONNECTIONS

CNTL NO.	CONTROL NAME *Control Enhancement Name*	CONTROL BASELINES		
		LOW	MOD	HIGH
CA-9	**Internal System Connections**	Selected	Selected	Selected

ICS Supplemental Guidance: Organizations perform risk-benefit analysis to support determination whether an ICS should be connected to other internal information system(s) and (separate) constituent system components. The Authorizing Official fully understands the organizational information security policies and procedures; the ICS security policies and procedures; the risks to organizational operations and assets, individuals, other organizations, and the Nation associated with the connected to other information system(s) and (separate) constituent system components, whether by authorizing each individual internal connection or authorizing internal connections for a class of components with common characteristics and/or configurations; and the specific health, safety, and environmental risks associated with a particular interconnection. The AO documents risk acceptance in the ICS system security plan.

CONFIGURATION MANAGEMENT – CM

Tailoring Considerations for Configuration Management Family

In situations where the ICS cannot be configured to restrict the use of unnecessary functions or cannot support the use of automated mechanisms to implement configuration management functions, the organization employs nonautomated mechanisms or procedures as compensating controls in accordance with the general tailoring guidance. Examples of compensating controls are given with each control, as appropriate.

Supplemental Guidance

Supplemental Guidance for all Controls and Control Enhancements in NIST SP 800-53 Rev. 4, Appendix F, should be used in conjunction with the ICS Supplemental Guidance in this overlay, if any.

CM-1   CONFIGURATION MANAGEMENT POLICY AND PROCEDURES

CNTL NO.	CONTROL NAME *Control Enhancement Name*	CONTROL BASELINES		
		LOW	MOD	HIGH
CM-1	**Configuration Management Policy and Procedures**	Selected	Selected	Selected

ICS Supplemental Guidance: The policy specifically addresses the unique properties and requirements of ICS and the relationship to non-ICS systems.

CM-2   BASELINE CONFIGURATION

CNTL NO.	CONTROL NAME *Control Enhancement Name*	CONTROL BASELINES		
		LOW	MOD	HIGH
CM-2	**Baseline Configuration**	Selected	Selected	Selected
CM-2 (1)	*BASELINE CONFIGURATION	REVIEWS AND UPDATES*		Selected	Selected
CM-2 (2)	*BASELINE CONFIGURATION	AUTOMATION SUPPORT FOR ACCURACY / CURRENCY*			Selected
CM-2 (3)	*BASELINE CONFIGURATION	RETENTION OF PREVIOUS CONFIGURATIONS*		Selected	Selected
CM-2 (7)	*BASELINE CONFIGURATION	CONFIGURE SYSTEMS, COMPONENTS, OR DEVICES FOR HIGH-RISK AREAS*		Selected	Selected

No ICS Supplemental Guidance.

CM-3   CONFIGURATION CHANGE CONTROL

CNTL NO.	CONTROL NAME *Control Enhancement Name*	CONTROL BASELINES		
		LOW	MOD	HIGH
CM-3	**Configuration Change Control**		Selected	Selected
CM-3 (1)	*CONFIGURATION CHANGE CONTROL	AUTOMATED DOCUMENT / NOTIFICATION / PROHIBITION OF CHANGES*			Selected
CM-3 (2)	*CONFIGURATION CHANGE CONTROL	TEST / VALIDATE / DOCUMENT CHANGES*		Selected	Selected

No ICS Supplemental Guidance.

CM-4   SECURITY IMPACT ANALYSIS

CNTL NO.	CONTROL NAME *Control Enhancement Name*	CONTROL BASELINES		
		LOW	MOD	HIGH
CM-4	**Security Impact Analysis**	Selected	Selected	Selected
CM-4 (1)	*SECURITY IMPACT ANALYSIS	SEPARATE TEST ENVIRONMENTS*			Selected

ICS Supplemental Guidance: The organization considers ICS safety and security interdependencies.
Control Enhancement: (1) No ICS Supplemental Guidance.

CM-5   ACCESS RESTRICTIONS FOR CHANGE

CNTL NO.	CONTROL NAME *Control Enhancement Name*	CONTROL BASELINES		
		LOW	MOD	HIGH
CM-5	**Access Restrictions for Change**		Selected	Selected
CM-5 (1)	*ACCESS RESTRICTIONS FOR CHANGE	AUTOMATED ACCESS ENFORCEMENT / AUDITING*			Selected
CM-5 (2)	*ACCESS RESTRICTIONS FOR CHANGE	AUDIT SYSTEM CHANGES*			Selected
CM-5 (3)	*ACCESS RESTRICTIONS FOR CHANGE	SIGNED COMPONENTS*			Selected

No ICS Supplemental Guidance.

CM-6   CONFIGURATION SETTINGS

CNTL NO.	CONTROL NAME *Control Enhancement Name*	CONTROL BASELINES		
		LOW	MOD	HIGH
CM-6	**Configuration Settings**	Selected	Selected	Selected
CM-6 (1)	*CONFIGURATION SETTINGS	AUTOMATED CENTRAL MANAGEMENT / APPLICATION / VERIFICATION*			Selected
CM-6 (2)	*CONFIGURATION SETTINGS	RESPOND TO UNAUTHORIZED CHANGES*			Selected

No ICS Supplemental Guidance.

CM-7   LEAST FUNCTIONALITY

CNTL NO.	CONTROL NAME *Control Enhancement Name*	CONTROL BASELINES		
		LOW	MOD	HIGH
CM-7	**Least Functionality**	Selected	Selected	Selected
CM-7 (1)	*LEAST FUNCTIONALITY	PERIODIC REVIEW*	Added	Selected	Selected
CM-7 (2)	*LEAST FUNCTIONALITY	PREVENT PROGRAM EXECUTION*		Selected	Selected
CM-7 (4)	*LEAST FUNCTIONALITY	UNAUTHORIZED SOFTWARE*		Removed	
CM-7 (5)	*LEAST FUNCTIONALITY	AUTHORIZED SOFTWARE*		Added	Selected

ICS Supplemental Guidance: Ports, as used in NIST SP 800-53 Rev. 4, are part of the address space in network protocols and are often associated with specific protocols or functions. As such, ports are not relevant to non-routable protocols and devices. When dealing with non-routable and non-addressable protocols and devices, prohibiting or restricting the use of specified functions, protocols, and/or services must be implemented for the (sub)system granularity that is available (e.g., at a low level, interrupts could be disabled; at a high level, set points could be made read-only except for privileged users). Example compensating controls include employing nonautomated mechanisms or procedures.

Control Enhancement: (1, 2, 5) No ICS Supplemental Guidance.

Control Baseline Supplement Rationale: (1) Periodic review and removal of unnecessary and/or nonsecure functions, ports, protocols, and services are added to the LOW baseline because many of the LOW impact ICS components could adversely affect the systems to which they are connected.

(4, 5) Whitelisting (CE 5) is more effective than blacklisting (CE 4). The set of applications that run in ICS is essentially static, making whitelisting practical. ICS-CERT recommends deploying application whitelisting on ICS. Reference: http://ics-cert.us-cert.gov/tips/ICS-TIP-12-146-01B

CM-8   INFORMATION SYSTEM COMPONENT INVENTORY

CNTL NO.	CONTROL NAME *Control Enhancement Name*	CONTROL BASELINES		
		LOW	MOD	HIGH
CM-8	**Information System Component Inventory**	Selected	Selected	Selected
CM-8 (1)	*INFORMATION SYSTEM COMPONENT INVENTORY	UPDATES DURING INSTALLATIONS / REMOVALS*		Selected	Selected
CM-8 (2)	*INFORMATION SYSTEM COMPONENT INVENTORY	AUTOMATED MAINTENANCE*			Selected
CM-8 (3)	*INFORMATION SYSTEM COMPONENT INVENTORY	AUTOMATED UNAUTHORIZED COMPONENT DETECTION*		Selected	Selected

CNTL NO.	CONTROL NAME *Control Enhancement Name*	CONTROL BASELINES		
		LOW	MOD	HIGH
CM-8 (4)	INFORMATION SYSTEM COMPONENT INVENTORY | PROPERTY ACCOUNTABILITY INFORMATION			Selected
CM-8 (5)	INFORMATION SYSTEM COMPONENT INVENTORY | ALL COMPONENTS WITHIN AUTHORIZATION BOUNDARY		Selected	Selected

No ICS Supplemental Guidance.

CM-9   CONFIGURATION MANAGEMENT PLAN

CNTL NO.	CONTROL NAME *Control Enhancement Name*	CONTROL BASELINES		
		LOW	MOD	HIGH
CM-9	Configuration Management Plan		Selected	Selected

No ICS Supplemental Guidance.

CM-10   SOFTWARE USAGE RESTRICTIONS

CNTL NO.	CONTROL NAME *Control Enhancement Name*	CONTROL BASELINES		
		LOW	MOD	HIGH
CM-10	Software Usage Restrictions	Selected	Selected	Selected

No ICS Supplemental Guidance.

CM-11   USER-INSTALLED SOFTWARE

CNTL NO.	CONTROL NAME *Control Enhancement Name*	CONTROL BASELINES		
		LOW	MOD	HIGH
CM-11	User-Installed Software	Selected	Selected	Selected

No ICS Supplemental Guidance.

CONTINGENCY PLANNING - CP

Tailoring Considerations for Contingency Planning Family

ICS systems often contain a physical component at a fixed location. Such components may not be relocated logically. Some replacement components may not be readily available. Continuance of essential missions and business functions with little or no loss of operational continuity may not be possible. In situations where the organization cannot provide necessary essential services, support, or automated mechanisms during contingency operations, the organization provides nonautomated mechanisms or predetermined procedures as compensating controls in accordance with the general tailoring guidance. Examples of compensating controls are given with each control, as appropriate.

Supplemental Guidance

Supplemental Guidance for all Controls and Control Enhancements in NIST SP 800-53 Rev. 4, Appendix F, should be used in conjunction with the ICS Supplemental Guidance in this overlay, if any.

CP-1 CONTINGENCY PLANNING POLICY AND PROCEDURES

CNTL NO.	CONTROL NAME *Control Enhancement Name*	CONTROL BASELINES		
		LOW	MOD	HIGH
CP-1	**Contingency Planning Policy and Procedures**	Selected	Selected	Selected

ICS Supplemental Guidance: The policy specifically addresses the unique properties and requirements of ICS and the relationship to non-ICS systems.

CP-2 CONTINGENCY PLAN

CNTL NO.	CONTROL NAME *Control Enhancement Name*	CONTROL BASELINES		
		LOW	MOD	HIGH
CP-2	**Contingency Plan**	Selected	Selected	Selected
CP-2 (1)	*CONTINGENCY PLAN	COORDINATE WITH RELATED PLANS*		Selected	Selected
CP-2 (2)	*CONTINGENCY PLAN	CAPACITY PLANNING*			Selected
CP-2 (3)	*CONTINGENCY PLAN	RESUME ESSENTIAL MISSIONS / BUSINESS FUNCTIONS*		Selected	Selected
CP-2 (4)	*CONTINGENCY PLAN	RESUME ALL MISSIONS / BUSINESS FUNCTIONS*			Selected
CP-2 (5)	*CONTINGENCY PLAN	CONTINUE ESSENTIAL MISSIONS / BUSINESS FUNCTIONS*			Selected
CP-2 (8)	*CONTINGENCY PLAN	IDENTIFY CRITICAL ASSETS*		Selected	Selected

ICS Supplemental Guidance: The organization defines contingency plans for categories of disruptions or failures. In the event of a loss of processing within the ICS or communication with operational facilities, the ICS executes predetermined procedures (e.g., alert the operator of the failure and then do nothing, alert the operator and then safely shut down the industrial process, alert the operator and then maintain the last operational setting prior to failure).

Control Enhancement: (1) ICS Supplemental Guidance: Organizational elements responsible for related plans may include suppliers such as electric power, fuel, fresh water and wastewater.

Control Enhancement: (2) No ICS Supplemental Guidance.

Control Enhancement: (3, 4) ICS Supplemental Guidance: Plans for the resumption of essential missions and business functions, and for resumption of all missions and business functions take into account the effects of the disruption on the environment of operation. Restoration and resumption plans should include prioritization of efforts. Disruptions may affect the quality and quantity of resources in the environment, such as electric power, fuel, fresh water and wastewater, and the ability of these suppliers to also resume provision of essential mission and business functions. Contingency plans for widespread disruption may involve specialized organizations (e.g., FEMA, emergency services, regulatory authorities). Reference: NFPA 1600: Standard on Disaster/Emergency Management and Business Continuity Programs.

Control Enhancement: (5, 8) No ICS Supplemental Guidance.

CP-3   CONTINGENCY TRAINING

CNTL NO.	CONTROL NAME *Control Enhancement Name*	CONTROL BASELINES		
		LOW	MOD	HIGH
CP-3	**Contingency Training**	Selected	Selected	Selected
CP-3 (1)	*CONTINGENCY TRAINING	SIMULATED EVENTS*			Selected

No ICS Supplemental Guidance.

CP-4   CONTINGENCY PLAN TESTING

CNTL NO.	CONTROL NAME *Control Enhancement Name*	CONTROL BASELINES		
		LOW	MOD	HIGH
CP-4	**Contingency Plan Testing**	Selected	Selected	Selected
CP-4 (1)	*CONTINGENCY PLAN TESTING	COORDINATE WITH RELATED PLANS*		Selected	Selected
CP-4 (2)	*CONTINGENCY PLAN TESTING	ALTERNATE PROCESSING SITE*			Selected

No ICS Supplemental Guidance.

CP-6   ALTERNATE STORAGE SITE

CNTL NO.	CONTROL NAME *Control Enhancement Name*	CONTROL BASELINES		
		LOW	MOD	HIGH
CP-6	**Alternate Storage Site**		Selected	Selected
CP-6 (1)	*ALTERNATE STORAGE SITE	SEPARATION FROM PRIMARY SITE*		Selected	Selected
CP-6 (2)	*ALTERNATE STORAGE SITE	RECOVERY TIME / POINT OBJECTIVES*			Selected
CP-6 (3)	*ALTERNATE STORAGE SITE	ACCESSIBILITY*		Selected	Selected

No ICS Supplemental Guidance.

CP-7   ALTERNATE PROCESSING SITE

CNTL NO.	CONTROL NAME *Control Enhancement Name*	CONTROL BASELINES		
		LOW	MOD	HIGH
CP-7	**Alternate Processing Site**		Selected	Selected
CP-7 (1)	*ALTERNATE PROCESSING SITE	SEPARATION FROM PRIMARY SITE*		Selected	Selected
CP-7 (2)	*ALTERNATE PROCESSING SITE	ACCESSIBILITY*		Selected	Selected
CP-7 (3)	*ALTERNATE PROCESSING SITE	PRIORITY OF SERVICE*		Selected	Selected
CP-7 (4)	*ALTERNATE PROCESSING SITE	CONFIGURATION FOR USE*			Selected

No ICS Supplemental Guidance.

CP-8   TELECOMMUNICATIONS SERVICES

CNTL NO.	CONTROL NAME *Control Enhancement Name*	CONTROL BASELINES		
		LOW	MOD	HIGH
CP-8	**Telecommunications Services**		Selected	Selected
CP-8 (1)	*TELECOMMUNICATIONS SERVICES	PRIORITY OF SERVICE PROVISIONS*		Selected	Selected
CP-8 (2)	*TELECOMMUNICATIONS SERVICES	SINGLE POINTS OF FAILURE*		Selected	Selected
CP-8 (3)	*TELECOMMUNICATIONS SERVICES	SEPARATION OF PRIMARY / ALTERNATE PROVIDERS*			Selected
CP-8 (4)	*TELECOMMUNICATIONS SERVICES	PROVIDER CONTINGENCY PLAN*			Selected

ICS Supplemental Guidance: Quality of service factors for ICS include latency and throughput.

Control Enhancement: (1, 2, 3, 4) No ICS Supplemental Guidance.

CP-9   INFORMATION SYSTEM BACKUP

CNTL NO.	CONTROL NAME *Control Enhancement Name*	CONTROL BASELINES		
		LOW	MOD	HIGH
CP-9	**Information System Backup**	Selected	Selected	Selected
CP-9 (1)	*INFORMATION SYSTEM BACKUP	TESTING FOR RELIABILITY / INTEGRITY*		Selected	Selected
CP-9 (2)	*INFORMATION SYSTEM BACKUP	TEST RESTORATION USING SAMPLING*			Selected
CP-9 (3)	*INFORMATION SYSTEM BACKUP	SEPARATE STORAGE FOR CRITICAL INFORMATION*			Selected
CP-9 (5)	*INFORMATION SYSTEM BACKUP	TRANSFER TO ALTERNATE SITE*			Selected

No ICS Supplemental Guidance.

CP-10   INFORMATION SYSTEM RECOVERY AND RECONSTITUTION

CNTL NO.	CONTROL NAME *Control Enhancement Name*	CONTROL BASELINES		
		LOW	MOD	HIGH
CP-10	**Information System Recovery and Reconstitution**	Selected	Selected	Selected
CP-10 (2)	*INFORMATION SYSTEM RECOVERY AND RECONSTITUTION	TRANSACTION RECOVERY*		Selected	Selected
CP-10 (4)	*INFORMATION SYSTEM RECOVERY AND RECONSTITUTION	RESTORE WITHIN TIME PERIOD*			Selected

ICS Supplemental Guidance: Reconstitution of the ICS includes consideration whether system state variables should be restored to initial values or values before disruption (e.g., are valves restored to full open, full closed, or settings prior to disruption). Restoring system state variables may be disruptive to ongoing physical processes (e.g., valves initially closed may adversely affect system cooling).

Control Enhancement: (2, 4) No ICS Supplemental Guidance.

CP-12   SAFE MODE

CNTL NO.	CONTROL NAME *Control Enhancement Name*	SUPPLEMENTED CONTROL BASELINES		
		LOW	MOD	HIGH
CP-12	**Safe Mode**	Added	Added	Added

ICS Supplemental Guidance: The organization-defined conditions and corresponding restrictions of safe mode of operation may vary among baselines. The same condition(s) may trigger different response depending on the impact level. The conditions may be external to the ICS (e.g., electricity supply brown-out). Related controls: SI-17.

Rationale for adding CP-12 to all baselines: This control provides a framework for the organization to plan their policy and procedures for dealing with conditions beyond their control in the environment of operations. Creating a written record of the decision process for selecting incidents and appropriate response is part of risk management in light of changing environment of operations.

IDENTIFICATION AND AUTHENTICATION - IA

Tailoring Considerations for Identification and Authentication Family

Before implementing controls in the IA family, consider the tradeoffs among security, privacy, latency, performance, and throughput. For example, the organization considers whether latency induced from the use of authentication mechanisms employing cryptographic mechanisms would adversely impact the operational performance of the ICS.

In situations where the ICS cannot support the specific Identification and Authentication requirements of a control, the organization employs compensating controls in accordance with the general tailoring guidance. Examples of compensating controls are given with each control, as appropriate.

Supplemental Guidance

Supplemental Guidance for all Controls and Control Enhancements in NIST SP 800-53 Rev. 4, Appendix F, should be used in conjunction with the ICS Supplemental Guidance in this overlay, if any.

IA-1   IDENTIFICATION AND AUTHENTICATION POLICY AND PROCEDURES

CNTL NO.	CONTROL NAME *Control Enhancement Name*	CONTROL BASELINES		
		LOW	MOD	HIGH
IA-1	**Security Identification and Authentication Policy and Procedures**	Selected	Selected	Selected

ICS Supplemental Guidance: The policy specifically addresses the unique properties and requirements of ICS and the relationship to non-ICS systems.

IA-2   USER IDENTIFICATION AND AUTHENTICATION (ORGANIZATIONAL USERS)

CNTL NO.	CONTROL NAME *Control Enhancement Name*	CONTROL BASELINES		
		LOW	MOD	HIGH
IA-2	**Identification and Authentication (Organizational Users)**	Selected	Selected	Selected
IA-2 (1)	*IDENTIFICATION AND AUTHENTICATION	NETWORK ACCESS TO PRIVILEGED ACCOUNTS*	Selected	Selected	Selected
IA-2 (2)	*IDENTIFICATION AND AUTHENTICATION	NETWORK ACCESS TO NON-PRIVILEGED ACCOUNTS*		Selected	Selected
IA-2 (3)	*IDENTIFICATION AND AUTHENTICATION	LOCAL ACCESS TO PRIVILEGED ACCOUNTS*		Selected	Selected
IA-2 (4)	*IDENTIFICATION AND AUTHENTICATION	LOCAL ACCESS TO NON-PRIVILEGED ACCOUNTS*			Selected
IA-2 (8)	*IDENTIFICATION AND AUTHENTICATION	NETWORK ACCESS TO PRIVILEGED ACCOUNTS - REPLAY RESISTANT*		Selected	Selected
IA-2 (9)	*IDENTIFICATION AND AUTHENTICATION	NETWORK ACCESS TO NON-PRIVILEGED ACCOUNTS - REPLAY RESISTANT*			Selected
IA-2 (11)	*IDENTIFICATION AND AUTHENTICATION	REMOTE ACCESS - SEPARATE DEVICE*		Selected	Selected
IA-2 (12)	*IDENTIFICATION AND AUTHENTICATION	ACCEPTANCE OF PIV CREDENTIALS*	Selected	Selected	Selected

ICS Supplemental Guidance: Where users function as a single group (e.g., control room operators), user identification and authentication may be role-based, group-based, or device-based. For certain ICS, the capability for immediate operator interaction is critical. Local emergency actions for ICS are not hampered by identification or authentication requirements. Access to these systems may be restricted by appropriate physical security controls. Example compensating controls include providing increased physical security, personnel security, and auditing measures. For example, manual voice authentication of remote personnel and local, manual actions may be required in order to establish a remote access. See AC-17 ICS Supplemental Guidance. Local user access to ICS components is enabled only when necessary, approved, and authenticated.

Control Enhancement: (1, 2, 3, 4) ICS Supplemental Guidance: Example compensating controls include implementing physical security measures.

Control Enhancement: (8, 9) ICS Supplemental Guidance: Example compensating controls include provide replay-resistance in an external system.

Control Enhancement: (11) No ICS Supplemental Guidance.

Control Enhancement: (12) ICS Supplemental Guidance: Example compensating controls include implementing support for PIV external to the ICS.

IA-3   DEVICE IDENTIFICATION AND AUTHENTICATION

CNTL NO.	CONTROL NAME *Control Enhancement Name*	SUPPLEMENTED CONTROL BASELINES		
		LOW	MOD	HIGH
IA-3	**Device Identification and Authentication**	Added	Selected	Selected
IA-3 (1)	*DEVICE IDENTIFICATION AND AUTHENTICATION | CRYPTOGRAPHIC BIDIRECTIONAL AUTHENTICATION*		Added	Added
IA-3 (4)	*DEVICE IDENTIFICATION AND AUTHENTICATION | DEVICE ATTESTATION*		Added	Added

ICS Supplemental Guidance: The organization may permit connection of devices, also known as non-person entities (NPE), belonging to and authorized by another organization (e.g., business partners) to their ICS. Especially when these devices are non-local, their identification and authentication can be vital. Organizations may perform risk and impact analysis to determine the required strength of authentication mechanisms. Example compensating controls for devices and protocols which do not provide authentication for remote network connections, include implementing physical security measures.

Control Enhancement: (1, 4) ICS Supplemental Guidance: Configuration management for NPE identification and authentication customarily involves a human surrogate or representative for the NPE. Devices are provided with their identification and authentication credentials based on assertions by the human surrogate. The human surrogate also responds to events and anomalies (e.g., credential expiration). Credentials for software entities (e.g., autonomous processes not associated with a specific person) based on properties of that software (e.g., digital signatures) may change every time the software is changed or patched. Special purpose hardware (e.g., custom integrated circuits and printed-circuit boards) may exhibit similar dependencies. Organization definition of parameters may be different among the impact levels.

Rationale (applies to control and control enhancements): ICS may exchange information with many external systems and devices. Identifying and authenticating the devices introduces situations that do not exist with humans. These controls include assignments that enable the organization to categorize devices by types, models, or other group characteristics. Assignments also enable the organizations to select appropriate controls for local, remote, and network connections.

IA-4   IDENTIFIER MANAGEMENT

CNTL NO.	CONTROL NAME *Control Enhancement Name*	CONTROL BASELINES		
		LOW	MOD	HIGH
IA-4	**Identifier Management**	Selected	Selected	Selected

No ICS Supplemental Guidance.

IA-5   AUTHENTICATOR MANAGEMENT

CNTL NO.	CONTROL NAME *Control Enhancement Name*	CONTROL BASELINES		
		LOW	MOD	HIGH
IA-5	**Authenticator Management**	Selected	Selected	Selected
IA-5 (1)	*AUTHENTICATOR MANAGEMENT	PASSWORD-BASED AUTHENTICATION*	Selected	Selected	Selected
IA-5 (2)	*AUTHENTICATOR MANAGEMENT	PKI-BASED AUTHENTICATION*		Selected	Selected
IA-5 (3)	*AUTHENTICATOR MANAGEMENT	IN PERSON REGISTRATION*		Selected	Selected
IA-5 (11)	*AUTHENTICATOR MANAGEMENT	HARDWARE TOKEN-BASED AUTHENTICATION*	Selected	Selected	Selected

ICS Supplemental Guidance: Example compensating controls include physical access control, encapsulating the ICS to provide authentication external to the ICS.

Control Enhancement: (1, 2, 3, 11) No ICS Supplemental Guidance.

IA-6   AUTHENTICATOR FEEDBACK

CNTL NO.	CONTROL NAME *Control Enhancement Name*	CONTROL BASELINES		
		LOW	MOD	HIGH
IA-6	**Authenticator Feedback**	Selected	Selected	Selected

ICS Supplemental Guidance: This control assumes a visual interface that provides feedback of authentication information during the authentication process. When ICS authentication uses an interface that does not support visual feedback, (e.g., protocol-based authentication) this control may be tailored out.

IA-7   CRYPTOGRAPHIC MODULE AUTHENTICATION

CNTL NO.	CONTROL NAME *Control Enhancement Name*	CONTROL BASELINES		
		LOW	MOD	HIGH
IA-7	**Cryptographic Module Authentication**	Selected	Selected	Selected

No ICS Supplemental Guidance.

IA-8   IDENTIFICATION AND AUTHENTICATION (NON-ORGANIZATIONAL USERS)

CNTL NO.	CONTROL NAME *Control Enhancement Name*	CONTROL BASELINES		
		LOW	MOD	HIGH
IA-8	**Identification and Authentication (Non-Organizational Users)**	Selected	Selected	Selected
IA-8 (1)	*IDENTIFICATION AND AUTHENTICATION (NON-ORGANIZATIONAL USERS)	ACCEPTANCE OF PIV CREDENTIALS FROM OTHER AGENCIES*	Selected	Selected	Selected
IA-8 (2)	*IDENTIFICATION AND AUTHENTICATION (NON-ORGANIZATIONAL USERS)	ACCEPTANCE OF THIRD-PARTY CREDENTIALS*	Selected	Selected	Selected
IA-8 (3)	*IDENTIFICATION AND AUTHENTICATION (NON-ORGANIZATIONAL USERS)	USE OF FICAM-APPROVED PRODUCTS*	Selected	Selected	Selected
IA-8 (4)	*IDENTIFICATION AND AUTHENTICATION (NON-ORGANIZATIONAL USERS)	USE OF FICAM-ISSUED PROFILES*	Selected	Selected	Selected

ICS Supplemental Guidance: The ICS Supplemental Guidance for IA-2, Identification and Authentication (Organizational Users), is applicable for Non- Organizational Users.

Control Enhancement: (1, 2, 3, 4) ICS Supplemental Guidance: Example compensating controls include implementing support external to the ICS and multi-factor authentication.

INCIDENT RESPONSE - IR

Tailoring Considerations for Incident Response Family
    The automated mechanisms used to support the tracking of security incidents are typically not part of, or connected to, the ICS.

Supplemental Guidance
    Supplemental Guidance for all Controls and Control Enhancements in NIST SP 800-53 Rev. 4, Appendix F, should be used in conjunction with the ICS Supplemental Guidance in this overlay, if any.

IR-1   **INCIDENT RESPONSE POLICY AND PROCEDURES**

CNTL NO.	CONTROL NAME *Control Enhancement Name*	CONTROL BASELINES		
		LOW	MOD	HIGH
IR-1	Incident Response Policy and Procedures	Selected	Selected	Selected

    <u>ICS Supplemental Guidance:</u> The policy specifically addresses the unique properties and requirements of ICS and the relationship to non-ICS systems.

IR-2   **INCIDENT RESPONSE TRAINING**

CNTL NO.	CONTROL NAME *Control Enhancement Name*	CONTROL BASELINES		
		LOW	MOD	HIGH
IR-2	Incident Response Training	Selected	Selected	Selected
IR-2 (1)	*INCIDENT RESPONSE TRAINING	SIMULATED EVENTS*			Selected
IR-2 (2)	*INCIDENT RESPONSE TRAINING	AUTOMATED TRAINING ENVIRONMENTS*			Selected

    No ICS Supplemental Guidance.

IR-3   **INCIDENT RESPONSE TESTING**

CNTL NO.	CONTROL NAME *Control Enhancement Name*	CONTROL BASELINES		
		LOW	MOD	HIGH
IR-3	Incident Response Testing		Selected	Selected
IR-3 (2)	*INCIDENT RESPONSE TESTING	COORDINATION WITH RELATED PLANS*		Selected	Selected

    No ICS Supplemental Guidance.

IR-4   **INCIDENT HANDLING**

CNTL NO.	CONTROL NAME *Control Enhancement Name*	CONTROL BASELINES		
		LOW	MOD	HIGH
IR-4	Incident Handling	Selected	Selected	Selected
IR-4 (1)	*INCIDENT HANDLING	AUTOMATED INCIDENT HANDLING PROCESSES*		Selected	Selected
IR-4 (4)	*INCIDENT HANDLING	INFORMATION CORRELATION*			Selected

    No ICS Supplemental Guidance.

IR-5   INCIDENT MONITORING

CNTL NO.	CONTROL NAME *Control Enhancement Name*	CONTROL BASELINES		
		LOW	MOD	HIGH
IR-5	Incident Monitoring	Selected	Selected	Selected
IR-5 (1)	*INCIDENT MONITORING	AUTOMATED TRACKING / DATA COLLECTION / ANALYSIS*			Selected

No ICS Supplemental Guidance.

IR-6   INCIDENT REPORTING

CNTL NO.	CONTROL NAME *Control Enhancement Name*	CONTROL BASELINES		
		LOW	MOD	HIGH
IR-6	Incident Reporting	Selected	Selected	Selected
IR-6 (1)	*INCIDENT REPORTING	AUTOMATED REPORTING*		Selected	Selected

ICS Supplemental Guidance: The organization should report incidents on a timely basis. The DHS National Cybersecurity & Communications Integration Center (NCCIC), http://www.dhs.gov/about-national-cybersecurity-communications-integration-center, serves as a centralized location where operational elements involved in cybersecurity and communications reliance are coordinated and integrated. The Industrial Control Systems Cyber Emergency Response Team (ICS-CERT) http://ics-cert.us-cert.gov/ics-cert/, collaborates with international and private sector Computer Emergency Response Teams (CERTs) to share control systems-related security incidents and mitigation measures.

Control Enhancement: (1) ICS Supplemental Guidance: The automated mechanisms used to support the incident reporting process are not necessarily part of, or connected to, the ICS.

IR-7   INCIDENT RESPONSE ASSISTANCE

CNTL NO.	CONTROL NAME *Control Enhancement Name*	CONTROL BASELINES		
		LOW	MOD	HIGH
IR-7	Incident Response Assistance	Selected	Selected	Selected
IR-7 (1)	*INCIDENT RESPONSE ASSISTANCE	AUTOMATION SUPPORT FOR AVAILABILITY OF INFORMATION / SUPPORT*		Selected	Selected

No ICS Supplemental Guidance.

IR-8   INCIDENT RESPONSE PLAN

CNTL NO.	CONTROL NAME *Control Enhancement Name*	CONTROL BASELINES		
		LOW	MOD	HIGH
IR-8	Incident Response Plan	Selected	Selected	Selected

No ICS Supplemental Guidance.

MAINTENANCE - MA

Tailoring Considerations for Maintenance Family

The automated mechanisms used to schedule, conduct, and document maintenance and repairs are not necessarily part of, or connected to, the ICS.

In situations where the ICS cannot support the specific Maintenance requirements of a control, the organization employs compensating controls in accordance with the general tailoring guidance. Examples of compensating controls are given with each control, as appropriate.

Supplemental Guidance

Supplemental Guidance for all Controls and Control Enhancements in NISTSP 800-53 Rev. 4, Appendix F, should be used in conjunction with the ICS Supplemental Guidance in this overlay, if any.

MA-1   SYSTEM MAINTENANCE POLICY AND PROCEDURES

CNTL NO.	CONTROL NAME *Control Enhancement Name*	CONTROL BASELINES		
		LOW	MOD	HIGH
MA-1	Maintenance Policy and Procedures	Selected	Selected	Selected

ICS Supplemental Guidance: The policy specifically addresses the unique properties and requirements of ICS and the relationship to non-ICS systems.

MA-2   CONTROLLED MAINTENANCE

CNTL NO.	CONTROL NAME *Control Enhancement Name*	CONTROL BASELINES		
		LOW	MOD	HIGH
MA-2	Controlled Maintenance	Selected	Selected	Selected
MA-2 (2)	*CONTROLLED MAINTENANCE	AUTOMATED MAINTENANCE ACTIVITIES*			Selected

No ICS Supplemental Guidance.

MA-3   MAINTENANCE TOOLS

CNTL NO.	CONTROL NAME *Control Enhancement Name*	CONTROL BASELINES		
		LOW	MOD	HIGH
MA-3	Maintenance Tools		Selected	Selected
MA-3 (1)	*MAINTENANCE TOOLS	INSPECT TOOLS*		Selected	Selected
MA-3 (2)	*MAINTENANCE TOOLS	INSPECT MEDIA*		Selected	Selected
MA-3 (3)	*MAINTENANCE TOOLS	PREVENT UNAUTHORIZED REMOVAL*			Selected

No ICS Supplemental Guidance.

MA-4   NONLOCAL MAINTENANCE

CNTL NO.	CONTROL NAME *Control Enhancement Name*	CONTROL BASELINES		
		LOW	MOD	HIGH
MA-4	**Non-Local Maintenance**	Selected	Selected	Selected
MA-4 (2)	*NON-LOCAL MAINTENANCE	DOCUMENT NON-LOCAL MAINTENANCE*		Selected	Selected
MA-4 (3)	*NON-LOCAL MAINTENANCE	COMPARABLE SECURITY / SANITIZATION*			Selected

No ICS Supplemental Guidance.

Control Enhancement: (2) No ICS Supplemental Guidance.

Control Enhancement: (3) <u>ICS Supplemental Guidance:</u> In crisis or emergency situations, the organization may need immediate access to non-local maintenance and diagnostic services in order to restore essential ICS operations or services. Example compensating controls include limiting the extent of the maintenance and diagnostic services to the minimum essential activities, carefully monitoring and auditing the non-local maintenance and diagnostic activities.

MA-5   MAINTENANCE PERSONNEL

CNTL NO.	CONTROL NAME *Control Enhancement Name*	CONTROL BASELINES		
		LOW	MOD	HIGH
MA-5	**Maintenance Personnel**	Selected	Selected	Selected
MA-5 (1)	*MAINTENANCE PERSONNEL	INDIVIDUALS WITHOUT APPROPRIATE ACCESS*			Selected

No ICS Supplemental Guidance.

MA-6   TIMELY MAINTENANCE

CNTL NO.	CONTROL NAME *Control Enhancement Name*	CONTROL BASELINES		
		LOW	MOD	HIGH
MA-6	**Timely Maintenance**		Selected	Selected

No ICS Supplemental Guidance.

MEDIA PROTECTION –MP

Supplemental Guidance
      Supplemental Guidance for all Controls and Control Enhancements in NIST SP 800-53 Rev. 4, Appendix F, should be used in conjunction with the ICS Supplemental Guidance in this overlay, if any.

MP-1   MEDIA PROTECTION POLICY AND PROCEDURES

CNTL NO.	CONTROL NAME Control Enhancement Name	CONTROL BASELINES		
		LOW	MOD	HIGH
MP-1	Media Protection Policy and Procedures	Selected	Selected	Selected

      <u>ICS Supplemental Guidance:</u> The policy specifically addresses the unique properties and requirements of ICS and the relationship to non-ICS systems.

MP-2   MEDIA ACCESS

CNTL NO.	CONTROL NAME Control Enhancement Name	CONTROL BASELINES		
		LOW	MOD	HIGH
MP-2	Media Access	Selected	Selected	Selected

      No ICS Supplemental Guidance.

MP-3   MEDIA MARKING

CNTL NO.	CONTROL NAME Control Enhancement Name	CONTROL BASELINES		
		LOW	MOD	HIGH
MP-3	Media Marking		Selected	Selected

      No ICS Supplemental Guidance.

MP-4   MEDIA STORAGE

CNTL NO.	CONTROL NAME Control Enhancement Name	CONTROL BASELINES		
		LOW	MOD	HIGH
MP-4	Media Storage		Selected	Selected

      No ICS Supplemental Guidance.

MP-5   MEDIA TRANSPORT

CNTL NO.	CONTROL NAME Control Enhancement Name	CONTROL BASELINES		
		LOW	MOD	HIGH
MP-5	Media Transport		Selected	Selected
MP-5 (4)	MEDIA TRANSPORT | CRYPTOGRAPHIC PROTECTION		Selected	Selected

      No ICS Supplemental Guidance.

MP-6   MEDIA SANITIZATION

CNTL NO.	CONTROL NAME *Control Enhancement Name*	CONTROL BASELINES		
		LOW	MOD	HIGH
MP-6	**Media Sanitization**	Selected	Selected	Selected
MP-6 (1)	*MEDIA SANITIZATION	TRACKING / DOCUMENTING / VERIFYING*			Selected
MP-6 (2)	*MEDIA SANITIZATION	EQUIPMENT TESTING*			Selected
MP-6 (3)	*MEDIA SANITIZATION	NON-DESTRUCTIVE TECHNIQUES*			Selected

No ICS Supplemental Guidance.

MP-7   MEDIA USE

CNTL NO.	CONTROL NAME *Control Enhancement Name*	CONTROL BASELINES		
		LOW	MOD	HIGH
MP-7	**Media Use**	Selected	Selected	Selected
MP-7 (1)	*MEDIA USE	ORGANIZATIONAL RESTRICTIONS*		Selected	Selected

No ICS Supplemental Guidance.

PHYSICAL AND ENVIRONMENTAL PROTECTION – PE

Supplemental Guidance

Supplemental Guidance for all Controls and Control Enhancements in NIST SP 800-53 Rev. 4, Appendix F, should be used in conjunction with the ICS Supplemental Guidance in this overlay, if any.

PE-1   **PHYSICAL AND ENVIRONMENTAL PROTECTION POLICY AND PROCEDURES**

CNTL NO.	CONTROL NAME *Control Enhancement Name*	CONTROL BASELINES		
		LOW	MOD	HIGH
PE-1	Physical and Environmental Protection Policy and Procedures	Selected	Selected	Selected

ICS Supplemental Guidance: The policy specifically addresses the unique properties and requirements of ICS and the relationship to non-ICS systems. The ICS components can be distributed over a large facility footprint or geographic area and can be an entry point into the entire organizational network ICS. Regulatory controls may also apply.

PE-2   **PHYSICAL ACCESS AUTHORIZATIONS**

CNTL NO.	CONTROL NAME *Control Enhancement Name*	CONTROL BASELINES		
		LOW	MOD	HIGH
PE-2	Physical Access Authorizations	Selected	Selected	Selected

No ICS Supplemental Guidance.

PE-3   **PHYSICAL ACCESS CONTROL**

CNTL NO.	CONTROL NAME *Control Enhancement Name*	CONTROL BASELINES		
		LOW	MOD	HIGH
PE-3	Physical Access Control	Selected	Selected	Selected
PE-3 (1)	*PHYSICAL ACCESS CONTROL	INFORMATION SYSTEM ACCESS*			Selected

ICS Supplemental Guidance: The organization considers ICS safety and security interdependencies. The organization considers access requirements in emergency situations. During an emergency-related event, the organization may restrict access to ICS facilities and assets to authorized individuals only. ICS are often constructed of devices that either do not have or cannot use comprehensive access control capabilities due to time-restrictive safety constraints. Physical access controls and defense-in-depth measures are used by the organization when necessary and possible to supplement ICS security when electronic mechanisms are unable to fulfill the security requirements of the organization's security plan. Primary nodes, distribution closets, and mechanical/electrical rooms should be locked and require key or electronic access control and incorporate intrusion detection sensors.

Control Enhancement: (1) No ICS Supplemental Guidance.

PE-4   **ACCESS CONTROL FOR TRANSMISSION MEDIUM**

CNTL NO.	CONTROL NAME *Control Enhancement Name*	CONTROL BASELINES		
		LOW	MOD	HIGH
PE-4	Access Control for Transmission Medium		Selected	Selected

No ICS Supplemental Guidance.

PE-5   ACCESS CONTROL FOR OUTPUT DEVICES

CNTL NO.	CONTROL NAME *Control Enhancement Name*	CONTROL BASELINES		
		LOW	MOD	HIGH
PE-5	**Access Control for Output Devices**		Selected	Selected

No ICS Supplemental Guidance.

PE-6   MONITORING PHYSICAL ACCESS

CNTL NO.	CONTROL NAME *Control Enhancement Name*	SUPPLEMENTED CONTROL BASELINES		
		LOW	MOD	HIGH
PE-6	**Monitoring Physical Access**	Selected	Selected	Selected
PE-6 (1)	*MONITORING PHYSICAL ACCESS	INTRUSION ALARMS / SURVEILLANCE EQUIPMENT*		Selected	Selected
PE-6 (4)	*MONITORING PHYSICAL ACCESS	MONITORING PHYSICAL ACCESS TO INFORMATION SYSTEMS*		Added	Selected

ICS Supplemental Guidance: Physical access controls and defense-in-depth measures are used as compensating controls by the organization when necessary and possible to supplement ICS security when electronic mechanisms are unable to monitor, detect and alarm when an ICS has been accessed. These compensating controls are in addition to the PE-6 controls (e.g., employing PE-3(4) Lockable Casings and/or PE-3(5) Tamper Protection).

Control Enhancement: (1) No ICS Supplemental Guidance.

Control Enhancement: (4) ICS Supplemental Guidance: The locations of ICS components (e.g., field devices, remote terminal units) can include various remote locations (e.g., substations, pumping stations).

Rationale (adding CE 4 to MODERATE baseline): Many of the ICS components are in remote geographical and dispersed locations with little capability to monitor all ICS components. Other components may be in ceilings, floors, or distribution closets with minimal physical barriers to detect, delay or deny access to the devices and no electronic surveillance or guard forces response capability.

PE-8   VISITOR ACCESS RECORDS

CNTL NO.	CONTROL NAME *Control Enhancement Name*	CONTROL BASELINES		
		LOW	MOD	HIGH
PE-8	**Visitor Access Records**	Selected	Selected	Selected
PE-8 (1)	*VISITOR ACCESS RECORDS	AUTOMATED RECORDS MAINTENANCE / REVIEW*			Selected

No ICS Supplemental Guidance.

PE-9   POWER EQUIPMENT AND CABLING

CNTL NO.	CONTROL NAME *Control Enhancement Name*	SUPPLEMENTED CONTROL BASELINES		
		LOW	MOD	HIGH
PE-9	**Power Equipment and Cabling**		Selected	Selected
PE-9 (1)	*POWER EQUIPMENT AND CABLING	REDUNDANT CABLING*		Added	Added

No ICS Supplemental Guidance.

Control Enhancement: (1) No ICS Supplemental Guidance.

Rationale (for adding (1)): Continuity of ICS control and operation requires redundant power cabling.

PE-10　EMERGENCY SHUTOFF

CNTL NO.	CONTROL NAME *Control Enhancement Name*	CONTROL BASELINES		
		LOW	MOD	HIGH
PE-10	Emergency Shutoff		Selected	Selected

ICS Supplemental Guidance: It may not be possible or advisable to shutoff power to some ICS. Example compensating controls include fail in known state and emergency procedures.

PE-11　EMERGENCY POWER

CNTL NO.	CONTROL NAME *Control Enhancement Name*	SUPPLEMENTED CONTROL BASELINES		
		LOW	MOD	HIGH
PE-11	Emergency Power	Added	Selected	Selected
PE-11 (1)	EMERGENCY POWER | LONG-TERM ALTERNATE POWER SUPPLY - MINIMAL OPERATIONAL CAPABILITY	Added	Added	Selected
PE-11 (2)	EMERGENCY POWER | LONG-TERM ALTERNATE POWER SUPPLY - SELF-CONTAINED			Added

ICS Supplemental Guidance: Emergency power production, transmission and distribution systems are a type of ICS that are required to meet extremely high performance specifications. The systems are governed by international, national, state and local building codes, must be tested on a continual basis, and must be repaired and placed back into operations within a short period of time. Traditionally, emergency power has been provided by generators for short to mid-term power (typically for fire and life safety systems, some IT load, and evacuation transport) and UPS battery packs in distribution closets and within work areas to allow some level of business continuity and for the orderly shutdown of non-essential IT and facility systems. Traditional emergency power systems typically are off-line until a loss of power occurs and are typically on a separate network and control system specific to the facility they support. New methods of energy generation and storage (e.g., solar voltaic, geothermal, flywheel, microgrid, distributed energy) that have a real-time demand and storage connection to local utilities or cross connected to multiple facilities should be carefully analyzed to ensure that the power can meet the load and signal quality without disruption of mission essential functions.

Control Enhancement: (1) No ICS Supplemental Guidance.

Rationale for adding control to baseline: ICS may support critical activities which will be needed for safety and reliability even in the absence of reliable power from the public grid.

PE-12　EMERGENCY LIGHTING

CNTL NO.	CONTROL NAME *Control Enhancement Name*	CONTROL BASELINES		
		LOW	MOD	HIGH
PE-12	Emergency Lighting	Selected	Selected	Selected

No ICS Supplemental Guidance.

PE-13   FIRE PROTECTION

CNTL NO.	CONTROL NAME *Control Enhancement Name*	CONTROL BASELINES		
		LOW	MOD	HIGH
PE-13	**Fire Protection**	Selected	Selected	Selected
PE-13 (1)	*FIRE PROTECTION | DETECTION DEVICES / SYSTEMS*			Selected
PE-13 (2)	*FIRE PROTECTION | SUPPRESSION DEVICES / SYSTEMS*			Selected
PE-13 (3)	*FIRE PROTECTION | AUTOMATIC FIRE SUPPRESSION*		Selected	Selected

ICS Supplemental Guidance: Fire suppression mechanisms should take the ICS environment into account (e.g., water sprinkler systems could be hazardous in specific environments).

Control Enhancement: (1, 2, 3) No ICS Supplemental Guidance.

PE-14   TEMPERATURE AND HUMIDITY CONTROLS

CNTL NO.	CONTROL NAME *Control Enhancement Name*	CONTROL BASELINES		
		LOW	MOD	HIGH
PE-14	**Temperature and Humidity Controls**	Selected	Selected	Selected

ICS Supplemental Guidance: Temperature and humidity controls are typically components of other ICS systems such as the HVAC, process, or lighting systems, or can be a standalone and unique ICS system. ICS can operate in extreme environments and both interior and exterior locations. For a specific ICS, the temperature and humidity design and operational parameters dictate the performance specifications. As ICS and IS become interconnected and the network provides connectivity across the hybrid domain, power circuits, distribution closets, routers and switches that support fire protection and life safety systems must be maintained at the proper temperature and humidity.

PE-15   WATER DAMAGE PROTECTION

CNTL NO.	CONTROL NAME *Control Enhancement Name*	CONTROL BASELINES		
		LOW	MOD	HIGH
PE-15	**Water Damage Protection**	Selected	Selected	Selected
PE-15 (1)	*WATER DAMAGE PROTECTION | AUTOMATION SUPPORT*			Selected

ICS Supplemental Guidance: Water damage protection and use of shutoff and isolation valves is both a procedural action, and also a specific type of ICS. ICS that are used in the manufacturing, hydropower, transportation/navigation, water and wastewater industries rely on the movement of water and are specifically designed to manage the quantity/flow and pressure of water. As ICS and IS become interconnected and the network provides connectivity across the hybrid domain, power circuits, distribution closets, routers and switches that support fire protection and life safety systems should ensure that water will not disable the system (e.g. a fire that activates the sprinkler system does not spray onto the fire control servers, router, switches and short out the alarms, egress systems, emergency lighting, and suppression systems).

Control Enhancement: (1) No ICS Supplemental Guidance.

PE-16   DELIVERY AND REMOVAL

CNTL NO.	CONTROL NAME *Control Enhancement Name*	CONTROL BASELINES		
		LOW	MOD	HIGH
PE-16	**Delivery and Removal**	Selected	Selected	Selected

No ICS Supplemental Guidance.

PE-17   ALTERNATE WORK SITE

CNTL NO.	CONTROL NAME *Control Enhancement Name*	CONTROL BASELINES		
		LOW	MOD	HIGH
PE-17	Alternate Work Site		Selected	Selected

No ICS Supplemental Guidance.

PE-18   LOCATION OF INFORMATION SYSTEM COMPONENTS

CNTL NO.	CONTROL NAME *Control Enhancement Name*	CONTROL BASELINES		
		LOW	MOD	HIGH
PE-18	Location of Information System Components			Selected

No ICS Supplemental Guidance.

PLANNING – PL

Supplemental Guidance

Supplemental Guidance for all Controls and Control Enhancements in NIST SP 800-53 Rev. 4, Appendix F, should be used in conjunction with the ICS Supplemental Guidance in this overlay, if any.

PL-1   SECURITY PLANNING POLICY AND PROCEDURES

CNTL NO.	CONTROL NAME *Control Enhancement Name*	CONTROL BASELINES		
		LOW	MOD	HIGH
PL-1	**Security Planning Policy and Procedures**	Selected	Selected	Selected

ICS Supplemental Guidance: The policy specifically addresses the unique properties and requirements of ICS and the relationship to non-ICS systems.

PL-2   SYSTEM SECURITY PLAN

CNTL NO.	CONTROL NAME *Control Enhancement Name*	SUPPLEMENTED CONTROL BASELINES		
		LOW	MOD	HIGH
PL-2	**System Security Plan**	Selected	Selected	Selected
PL-2 (3)	*SYSTEM SECURITY PLAN	PLAN / COORDINATE WITH OTHER ORGANIZATIONAL ENTITIES*	Added	Selected	Selected

No ICS Supplemental Guidance.

Control Enhancement: (3) No ICS Supplemental Guidance.

Rationale for adding PL-2 (3) to low baseline: When systems are highly inter-connected, coordinated planning is essential. A low impact system could adversely affect a higher impact system.

PL-4   RULES OF BEHAVIOR

CNTL NO.	CONTROL NAME *Control Enhancement Name*	CONTROL BASELINES		
		LOW	MOD	HIGH
PL-4	**Rules of Behavior**	Selected	Selected	Selected
PL-4 (1)	*RULES OF BEHAVIOR	SOCIAL MEDIA AND NETWORKING RESTRICTIONS*		Selected	Selected

No ICS Supplemental Guidance.

PL-7   SECURITY CONCEPT OF OPERATIONS (CONOPS)

CNTL NO.	CONTROL NAME *Control Enhancement Name*	SUPPLEMENTED CONTROL BASELINES		
		LOW	MOD	HIGH
PL-7	**Security Concept of Operations**		Added	Added

No ICS Supplemental Guidance.

Rationale for adding PL-7 to moderate and high baselines: ICS are complex systems. Organizations typically employ a CONOPS to help define a system and share that understanding with personnel involved with that system and other systems with which it interacts. A CONOPS often helps identify information protection requirements.

PL-8   INFORMATION SECURITY ARCHITECTURE

CNTL NO.	CONTROL NAME *Control Enhancement Name*	CONTROL BASELINES		
		LOW	MOD	HIGH
PL-8	**Information Security Architecture**		Selected	Selected

No ICS Supplemental Guidance.

PERSONNEL SECURITY – PS

Supplemental Guidance

　　　Supplemental Guidance for all Controls and Control Enhancements in NIST SP 800-53 Rev. 4, Appendix F, should be used in conjunction with the ICS Supplemental Guidance in this overlay, if any.

PS-1　　PERSONNEL SECURITY POLICY AND PROCEDURES

CNTL NO.	CONTROL NAME *Control Enhancement Name*	CONTROL BASELINES		
		LOW	MOD	HIGH
PS-1	Personnel Security Policy and Procedures	Selected	Selected	Selected

　　　ICS Supplemental Guidance: The policy specifically addresses the unique properties and requirements of ICS and the relationship to non-ICS systems.

PS-2　　POSITION RISK DESIGNATION

CNTL NO.	CONTROL NAME *Control Enhancement Name*	CONTROL BASELINES		
		LOW	MOD	HIGH
PS-2	Position Risk Designation	Selected	Selected	Selected

　　　No ICS Supplemental Guidance.

PS-3　　PERSONNEL SCREENING

CNTL NO.	CONTROL NAME *Control Enhancement Name*	CONTROL BASELINES		
		LOW	MOD	HIGH
PS-3	Personnel Screening	Selected	Selected	Selected

　　　No ICS Supplemental Guidance.

PS-4　　PERSONNEL TERMINATION

CNTL NO.	CONTROL NAME *Control Enhancement Name*	CONTROL BASELINES		
		LOW	MOD	HIGH
PS-4	Personnel Termination	Selected	Selected	Selected
PS-4 (2)	*PERSONNEL TERMINATION	AUTOMATED NOTIFICATION*			Selected

　　　No ICS Supplemental Guidance.

PS-5　　PERSONNEL TRANSFER

CNTL NO.	CONTROL NAME *Control Enhancement Name*	CONTROL BASELINES		
		LOW	MOD	HIGH
PS-5	Personnel Transfer	Selected	Selected	Selected

　　　No ICS Supplemental Guidance.

PS-6   ACCESS AGREEMENTS

CNTL NO.	CONTROL NAME *Control Enhancement Name*	CONTROL BASELINES		
		LOW	MOD	HIGH
PS-6	Access Agreements	Selected	Selected	Selected

No ICS Supplemental Guidance.

PS-7   THIRD-PARTY PERSONNEL SECURITY

CNTL NO.	CONTROL NAME *Control Enhancement Name*	CONTROL BASELINES		
		LOW	MOD	HIGH
PS-7	Third-Party Personnel Security	Selected	Selected	Selected

No ICS Supplemental Guidance.

PS-8   PERSONNEL SANCTIONS

CNTL NO.	CONTROL NAME *Control Enhancement Name*	CONTROL BASELINES		
		LOW	MOD	HIGH
PS-8	Personnel Sanctions	Selected	Selected	Selected

No ICS Supplemental Guidance.

RISK ASSESSMENT – RA

Supplemental Guidance

Supplemental Guidance for all Controls and Control Enhancements in NIST SP 800-53 Rev. 4, Appendix F, should be used in conjunction with the ICS Supplemental Guidance in this overlay, if any.

RA-1   RISK ASSESSMENT POLICY AND PROCEDURES

CNTL NO.	CONTROL NAME *Control Enhancement Name*	CONTROL BASELINES		
		LOW	MOD	HIGH
RA-1	Risk Assessment Policy and Procedures	Selected	Selected	Selected

ICS Supplemental Guidance: The policy specifically addresses the unique properties and requirements of ICS and the relationship to non-ICS systems.

RA-2   SECURITY CATEGORIZATION

CNTL NO.	CONTROL NAME *Control Enhancement Name*	CONTROL BASELINES		
		LOW	MOD	HIGH
RA-2	Security Categorization	Selected	Selected	Selected

No ICS Supplemental Guidance.

RA-3   RISK ASSESSMENT

CNTL NO.	CONTROL NAME *Control Enhancement Name*	CONTROL BASELINES		
		LOW	MOD	HIGH
RA-3	Risk Assessment	Selected	Selected	Selected

No ICS Supplemental Guidance.

RA-5   VULNERABILITY SCANNING

CNTL NO.	CONTROL NAME *Control Enhancement Name*	CONTROL BASELINES		
		LOW	MOD	HIGH
RA-5	Vulnerability Scanning	Selected	Selected	Selected
RA-5 (1)	*VULNERABILITY SCANNING	UPDATE TOOL CAPABILITY*		Selected	Selected
RA-5 (2)	*VULNERABILITY SCANNING	UPDATE BY FREQUENCY / PRIOR TO NEW SCAN / WHEN IDENTIFIED*		Selected	Selected
RA-5 (4)	*VULNERABILITY SCANNING	DISCOVERABLE INFORMATION*			Selected
RA-5 (5)	*VULNERABILITY SCANNING	PRIVILEGED ACCESS*		Selected	Selected

ICS Supplemental Guidance: Active vulnerability scanning, which introduces network traffic, is used with care on ICS systems to ensure that ICS functions are not adversely impacted by the scanning process. The organization makes a risk-based determination whether to employ active scanning. Passive monitoring /sniffing may be used as part of a compensating control. Example compensating controls include providing a replicated, virtualized, or simulated system to conduct scanning. Production ICS may need to be taken off-line before scanning can be conducted. If ICS are taken off-line for scanning, scans are scheduled to occur during planned ICS outages whenever possible. If vulnerability scanning tools are used on non-ICS networks, extra care is taken to ensure that they do not scan the ICS network. Network scanning is not applicable to non-addressable communications. Vulnerability examination may be performed using other mechanisms than scanning to identify the objects being examined. Host-based vulnerability examination is an example compensating control.

Control Enhancement: (1, 2, 4, 5) No ICS Supplemental Guidance.

SYSTEM AND SERVICES ACQUISITION – SA

Tailoring Considerations for System and Services Acquisition Family
In situations where the ICS cannot support the specific System and Services Acquisition requirements of a control, the organization employs compensating controls in accordance with the general tailoring guidance. Examples of compensating controls are given with each control, as appropriate.

Supplemental Guidance
Supplemental Guidance for all Controls and Control Enhancements in NIST SP 800-53 Rev. 4, Appendix F, should be used in conjunction with the ICS Supplemental Guidance in this overlay, if any.

SA-1   SYSTEM AND SERVICES ACQUISITION POLICY AND PROCEDURES

CNTL NO.	CONTROL NAME *Control Enhancement Name*	CONTROL BASELINES		
		LOW	MOD	HIGH
SA-1	System and Services Acquisition Policy and Procedures	Selected	Selected	Selected

ICS Supplemental Guidance: The policy specifically addresses the unique properties and requirements of ICS and the relationship to non-ICS systems.

SA-2   ALLOCATION OF RESOURCES

CNTL NO.	CONTROL NAME *Control Enhancement Name*	CONTROL BASELINES		
		LOW	MOD	HIGH
SA-2	Allocation of Resources	Selected	Selected	Selected

No ICS Supplemental Guidance.

SA-3   SYSTEM DEVELOPMENT LIFE CYCLE

CNTL NO.	CONTROL NAME *Control Enhancement Name*	CONTROL BASELINES		
		LOW	MOD	HIGH
SA-3	System Development Life Cycle	Selected	Selected	Selected

No ICS Supplemental Guidance.

SA-4   ACQUISITION PROCESS

CNTL NO.	CONTROL NAME *Control Enhancement Name*	CONTROL BASELINES		
		LOW	MOD	HIGH
SA-4	Acquisition Process	Selected	Selected	Selected
SA-4 (1)	*ACQUISITION PROCESS	FUNCTIONAL PROPERTIES OF SECURITY CONTROLS*		Selected	Selected
SA-4 (2)	*ACQUISITION PROCESS	DESIGN / IMPLEMENTATION INFORMATION FOR SECURITY CONTROLS*		Selected	Selected
SA-4 (9)	*ACQUISITION PROCESS	FUNCTIONS / PORTS / PROTOCOLS / SERVICES IN USE*		Selected	Selected
SA-4 (10)	*ACQUISITION PROCESS	USE OF APPROVED PIV PRODUCTS*	Selected	Selected	Selected

ICS Supplemental Guidance: Since ICS security has historically focused on physical protection and isolation, vendors and developers may be unfamiliar with cybersecurity. Organizations should anticipate a need to engage with ICS suppliers to raise awareness of cybersecurity needs. The SCADA/Control Systems Procurement Project provides example cybersecurity procurement language for ICS. References: Web: https://ics-cert.us-cert.gov/sites/default/files/documents/Procurement_Language_Rev4_100809.pdf

Control Enhancements: (1, 2, 9) ICS Supplemental Guidance: Developers may not have access to required information.

Control Enhancement: (10) ICS Supplemental Guidance: Example compensating controls include employing external products on the FIPS 201-approved products list for Personal Identity Verification (PIV) capability in conjunction with ICS products.

SA-5 INFORMATION SYSTEM DOCUMENTATION

CNTL NO.	CONTROL NAME *Control Enhancement Name*	CONTROL BASELINES		
		LOW	MOD	HIGH
SA-5	Information System Documentation	Selected	Selected	Selected

No ICS Supplemental Guidance.

SA-8 SECURITY ENGINEERING PRINCIPLES

CNTL NO.	CONTROL NAME *Control Enhancement Name*	CONTROL BASELINES		
		LOW	MOD	HIGH
SA-8	Security Engineering Principles		Selected	Selected

No ICS Supplemental Guidance.

SA-9 EXTERNAL INFORMATION SYSTEM SERVICES

CNTL NO.	CONTROL NAME *Control Enhancement Name*	CONTROL BASELINES		
		LOW	MOD	HIGH
SA-9	External Information System Services	Selected	Selected	Selected
SA-9 (2)	*EXTERNAL INFORMATION SYSTEMS	IDENTIFICATION OF FUNCTIONS / PORTS / PROTOCOLS / SERVICES*		Selected	Selected

No ICS Supplemental Guidance.

SA-10 DEVELOPER CONFIGURATION MANAGEMENT

CNTL NO.	CONTROL NAME *Control Enhancement Name*	CONTROL BASELINES		
		LOW	MOD	HIGH
SA-10	Developer Configuration Management		Selected	Selected

No ICS Supplemental Guidance.

SA-11 DEVELOPER SECURITY TESTING AND EVALUATION

CNTL NO.	CONTROL NAME *Control Enhancement Name*	CONTROL BASELINES		
		LOW	MOD	HIGH
SA-11	Developer Security Testing and Evaluation		Selected	Selected

No ICS Supplemental Guidance.

SA-12 SUPPLY CHAIN PROTECTION

CNTL NO.	CONTROL NAME *Control Enhancement Name*	CONTROL BASELINES		
		LOW	MOD	HIGH
SA-12	Supply Chain Protection			Selected

No ICS Supplemental Guidance.

SA-15   DEVELOPMENT PROCESS, STANDARDS, AND TOOLS

CNTL NO.	CONTROL NAME *Control Enhancement Name*	CONTROL BASELINES		
		LOW	MOD	HIGH
SA-15	Development Process, Standards, and Tools			Selected

No ICS Supplemental Guidance.

SA-16   DEVELOPER-PROVIDED TRAINING

CNTL NO.	CONTROL NAME *Control Enhancement Name*	CONTROL BASELINES		
		LOW	MOD	HIGH
SA-16	Developer-Provided Training			Selected

No ICS Supplemental Guidance.

SA-17   DEVELOPER SECURITY ARCHITECTURE AND DESIGN

CNTL NO.	CONTROL NAME *Control Enhancement Name*	CONTROL BASELINES		
		LOW	MOD	HIGH
SA-17	Developer Security Architecture and Design			Selected

No ICS Supplemental Guidance.

SYSTEM AND COMMUNICATIONS PROTECTION - SC

Tailoring Considerations for System and Communications Protection Family

The use of cryptography is determined after careful consideration of the security needs and the potential ramifications on system performance. For example, the organization considers whether latency induced from the use of cryptography would adversely impact the operational performance of the ICS. While the legacy devices commonly found within ICS often lack direct support of cryptographic functions, compensating controls (e.g., encapsulations) may be used to meet the intent of the control.

In situations where the ICS cannot support the specific System and Communications Protection requirements of a control, the organization employs compensating controls in accordance with the general tailoring guidance. Examples of compensating controls are given with each control, as appropriate.

Supplemental Guidance

Supplemental Guidance for all Controls and Control Enhancements in NIST SP 800-53 Rev. 4, Appendix F, should be used in conjunction with the ICS Supplemental Guidance in this overlay, if any.

SC-1   SYSTEM AND COMMUNICATIONS PROTECTION POLICY AND PROCEDURES

CNTL NO.	CONTROL NAME *Control Enhancement Name*	CONTROL BASELINES		
		LOW	MOD	HIGH
SC-1	System and Communications Protection Policy and Procedures	Selected	Selected	Selected

ICS Supplemental Guidance: The policy specifically addresses the unique properties and requirements of ICS and the relationship to non-ICS systems.

SC-2   APPLICATION PARTITIONING

CNTL NO.	CONTROL NAME *Control Enhancement Name*	CONTROL BASELINES		
		LOW	MOD	HIGH
SC-2	Application Partitioning		Selected	Selected

ICS Supplemental Guidance: Systems used to manage the ICS should be separate from the operational ICS components. Example compensating controls include providing increased auditing measures.

SC-3   SECURITY FUNCTION ISOLATION

CNTL NO.	CONTROL NAME *Control Enhancement Name*	CONTROL BASELINES		
		LOW	MOD	HIGH
SC-3	Security Function Isolation			Selected

ICS Supplemental Guidance: Example compensating controls include providing increased auditing measures, limiting network connectivity, architectural allocation.

SC-4   INFORMATION IN SHARED RESOURCES

CNTL NO.	CONTROL NAME *Control Enhancement Name*	CONTROL BASELINES		
		LOW	MOD	HIGH
SC-4	Information in Shared Resources		Selected	Selected

ICS Supplemental Guidance: Example compensating controls include architecting the use of the ICS to prevent sharing system resources.

SC-5   DENIAL OF SERVICE PROTECTION

CNTL NO.	CONTROL NAME *Control Enhancement Name*	CONTROL BASELINES		
		LOW	MOD	HIGH
SC-5	**Denial of Service Protection**	Selected	Selected	Selected

ICS Supplemental Guidance: Example compensating controls include ensuring a loss of communication results in the ICS operating in nominal or safe mode. Risk-based analysis informs the establishment of policy and procedure.

SC-7   BOUNDARY PROTECTION

CNTL NO.	CONTROL NAME *Control Enhancement Name*	SUPPLEMENTED CONTROL BASELINES		
		LOW	MOD	HIGH
SC-7	**Boundary Protection**	Selected	Selected	Selected
SC-7 (3)	*BOUNDARY PROTECTION	ACCESS POINTS*		Selected	Selected
SC-7 (4)	*BOUNDARY PROTECTION	EXTERNAL TELECOMMUNICATIONS SERVICES*		Selected	Selected
SC-7 (5)	*BOUNDARY PROTECTION	DENY BY DEFAULT / ALLOW BY EXCEPTION*		Selected	Selected
SC-7 (7)	*BOUNDARY PROTECTION	PREVENT SPLIT TUNNELING FOR REMOTE DEVICES*		Selected	Selected
SC-7 (8)	*BOUNDARY PROTECTION	ROUTE TRAFFIC TO AUTHENTICATED PROXY SERVERS*			Selected
SC-7 (18)	*BOUNDARY PROTECTION	FAIL SECURE*		Added	**Selected**
SC-7 (21)	*BOUNDARY PROTECTION	ISOLATION OF INFORMATION SYSTEM COMPONENTS*			Selected

No ICS Supplemental Guidance.

Control Enhancement: (3, 4, 5, 7, 8, 21) No ICS Supplemental Guidance.

Control Enhancement: (18) ICS Supplemental Guidance: The organization selects an appropriate failure mode (e.g., permit or block all communications).

Rationale for adding SC-7 (18) to Moderate Baseline: As part of the architecture and design of the ICS, the organization selects an appropriate failure mode in accordance with the function performed by the ICS and the operational environment. The ability to choose the failure mode for the physical part of the ICS differentiates the ICS from other IT systems. This choice may be a significant influence in mitigating the impact of a failure.

SC-8   TRANSMISSION CONFIDENTIALITY AND INTEGRITY

CNTL NO.	CONTROL NAME *Control Enhancement Name*	CONTROL BASELINES		
		LOW	MOD	HIGH
SC-8	**Transmission Confidentiality and Integrity**		Selected	Selected
SC-8 (1)	**transmission confidentiality and integrity	cryptographic or alternate physical protection**		Selected	Selected

No ICS Supplemental Guidance.

Control Enhancement: (1) ICS Supplemental Guidance: The organization explores all possible cryptographic integrity mechanisms (e.g., digital signature, hash function). Each mechanism has a different delay impact.

SC-10   NETWORK DISCONNECT

CNTL NO.	CONTROL NAME *Control Enhancement Name*	CONTROL BASELINES		
		LOW	MOD	HIGH
SC-10	**Network Disconnect**		Selected	Selected

ICS Supplemental Guidance: Example compensating controls include providing increased auditing measures or limiting remote access privileges to key personnel.

SC-12   CRYPTOGRAPHIC KEY ESTABLISHMENT AND MANAGEMENT

CNTL NO.	CONTROL NAME *Control Enhancement Name*	CONTROL BASELINES		
		LOW	MOD	HIGH
SC-12	**Cryptographic Key Establishment and Management**	Selected	Selected	Selected
SC-12 (1)	*CRYPTOGRAPHIC KEY ESTABLISHMENT AND MANAGEMENT | AVAILABILITY*			Selected

> ICS Supplemental Guidance: The use of cryptographic key management in ICS is intended to support internal nonpublic use.
>
> Control Enhancement: (1) No ICS Supplemental Guidance.

SC-13   CRYPTOGRAPHIC PROTECTION

CNTL NO.	CONTROL NAME *Control Enhancement Name*	CONTROL BASELINES		
		LOW	MOD	HIGH
SC-13	**Cryptographic Protection**	Selected	Selected	Selected

> No ICS Supplemental Guidance.

SC-15   COLLABORATIVE COMPUTING DEVICES

CNTL NO.	CONTROL NAME *Control Enhancement Name*	CONTROL BASELINES		
		LOW	MOD	HIGH
SC-15	**Collaborative Computing Devices**	Selected	Selected	Selected

> No ICS Supplemental Guidance.

SC-17   PUBLIC KEY INFRASTRUCTURE CERTIFICATES

CNTL NO.	CONTROL NAME *Control Enhancement Name*	CONTROL BASELINES		
		LOW	MOD	HIGH
SC-17	**Public Key Infrastructure Certificates**		Selected	Selected

> No ICS Supplemental Guidance.

SC-18   MOBILE CODE

CNTL NO.	CONTROL NAME *Control Enhancement Name*	CONTROL BASELINES		
		LOW	MOD	HIGH
SC-18	**Mobile Code**		Selected	Selected

> No ICS Supplemental Guidance.

SC-19   VOICE OVER INTERNET PROTOCOL

CNTL NO.	CONTROL NAME *Control Enhancement Name*	CONTROL BASELINES		
		LOW	MOD	HIGH
SC-19	**Voice Over Internet Protocol**		Selected	Selected

> ICS Supplemental Guidance: The use of VoIP technologies is determined after careful consideration and after verification that it does not adversely impact the operational performance of the ICS.

SC-20   SECURE NAME / ADDRESS RESOLUTION SERVICE (AUTHORITATIVE SOURCE)

CNTL NO.	CONTROL NAME *Control Enhancement Name*	CONTROL BASELINES		
		LOW	MOD	HIGH
SC-20	Secure Name /Address Resolution Service (Authoritative Source)	Selected	Selected	Selected

ICS Supplemental Guidance: The use of secure name/address resolution services is determined after careful consideration and after verification that it does not adversely impact the operation of the ICS.

SC-21   SECURE NAME / ADDRESS RESOLUTION SERVICE (RECURSIVE OR CACHING RESOLVER)

CNTL NO.	CONTROL NAME *Control Enhancement Name*	CONTROL BASELINES		
		LOW	MOD	HIGH
SC-21	Secure Name /Address Resolution Service (Recursive or Caching Resolver)	Selected	Selected	Selected

ICS Supplemental Guidance: The use of secure name/address resolution services is determined after careful consideration and after verification that it does not adversely impact the operation of the ICS.

SC-22   ARCHITECTURE AND PROVISIONING FOR NAME / ADDRESS RESOLUTION SERVICE

CNTL NO.	CONTROL NAME *Control Enhancement Name*	CONTROL BASELINES		
		LOW	MOD	HIGH
SC-22	Architecture and Provisioning for Name/Address Resolution Service	Selected	Selected	Selected

ICS Supplemental Guidance: The use of secure name/address resolution services is determined after careful consideration and after verification that it does not adversely impact the operational performance of the ICS.

SC-23   SESSION AUTHENTICITY

CNTL NO.	CONTROL NAME *Control Enhancement Name*	CONTROL BASELINES		
		LOW	MOD	HIGH
SC-23	Session Authenticity		Selected	Selected

ICS Supplemental Guidance: Example compensating controls include auditing measures.

SC-24   FAIL IN KNOWN STATE

CNTL NO.	CONTROL NAME *Control Enhancement Name*	SUPPLEMENTED CONTROL BASELINES		
		LOW	MOD	HIGH
SC-24	Fail in Known State		Added	Selected

ICS Supplemental Guidance: The organization selects an appropriate failure state. Preserving ICS state information includes consistency among ICS state variables and the physical state which the ICS represents (e.g., whether valves are open or closed, communication permitted or blocked, continue operations).

Rationale for adding SC-24 to moderate baseline: As part of the architecture and design of the ICS, the organization selects an appropriate failure state of an ICS in accordance with the function performed by the ICS and the operational environment. The ability to choose the failure mode for the physical part of the ICS differentiates the ICS from other IT systems. This choice may be a significant influence in mitigating the impact of a failure, since it may be disruptive to ongoing physical processes (e.g., valves failing in closed position may adversely affect system cooling).

SC-28   PROTECTION OF INFORMATION AT REST

CNTL NO.	CONTROL NAME *Control Enhancement Name*	CONTROL BASELINES		
		LOW	MOD	HIGH
SC-28	**Protection of Information at Rest**		Selected	Selected

ICS Supplemental Guidance: The use of cryptographic mechanisms is determined after careful consideration and after verification that it does not adversely impact the operational performance of the ICS.

SC-39   PROCESS ISOLATION

CNTL NO.	CONTROL NAME *Control Enhancement Name*	CONTROL BASELINES		
		LOW	MOD	HIGH
SC-39	**Process Isolation**	Selected	Selected	Selected

ICS Supplemental Guidance: Example compensating controls include partition processes to separate platforms.

SC-41   PORT AND I/O DEVICE ACCESS

CNTL NO.	CONTROL NAME *Control Enhancement Name*	SUPPLEMENTED CONTROL BASELINES		
		LOW	MOD	HIGH
SC-41	**Port and I/O Device Access**	Added	Added	Added

No ICS Supplemental Guidance.

Rationale for adding SC-24 to all baselines: The function of ICS can be readily determined in advance, making it easier to identify ports and I/O devices that are unnecessary. Disabling or removing ports reinforces air-gap policy.

SYSTEM AND INFORMATION INTEGRITY - SI

Tailoring Considerations for System and Information Integrity Family
　　In situations where the ICS cannot support the specific System and Information Integrity requirements of a control, the organization employs compensating controls in accordance with the general tailoring guidance. Examples of compensating controls are given with each control, as appropriate.

Supplemental Guidance
　　Supplemental Guidance for all Controls and Control Enhancements in NIST SP 800-53 Rev. 4, Appendix F, should be used in conjunction with the ICS Supplemental Guidance in this overlay, if any.

SI-1　　SYSTEM AND INFORMATION INTEGRITY POLICY AND PROCEDURES

CNTL NO.	CONTROL NAME *Control Enhancement Name*	CONTROL BASELINES		
		LOW	MOD	HIGH
SI-1	**System and Information Integrity Policy and Procedures**	Selected	Selected	Selected

　　ICS Supplemental Guidance: The policy specifically addresses the unique properties and requirements of ICS and the relationship to non-ICS systems.

SI-2　　FLAW REMEDIATION

CNTL NO.	CONTROL NAME *Control Enhancement Name*	CONTROL BASELINES		
		LOW	MOD	HIGH
SI-2	**Flaw Remediation**	Selected	Selected	Selected
SI-2 (1)	*FLAW REMEDIATION	CENTRAL MANAGEMENT*			Selected
SI-2 (2)	*FLAW REMEDIATION	AUTOMATED FLAW REMEDIATION STATUS*		Selected	Selected

　　ICS Supplemental Guidance: Flaw Remediation is complicated since many ICS employ operating systems and other software that is not current, is no longer being maintained by the vendors, and is not resistant to current threats. ICS operators are often dependent on product vendors to validate the operability of a patch and also sometimes to perform the installation. Often flaws cannot be remediated based on circumstances outside of the ICS operator's control (e.g., lack of a vendor patch). Sometime the organization has no choice but to accept additional risk. In these situations, compensating controls should be implemented (e.g., limit the exposure of the vulnerable system). Other compensating controls that do not decrease the residual risk but increase the ability to respond may be desirable (e.g., provide a timely response in case of an incident; devise a plan to ensure the ICS can identify the exploitation of the flaw). Testing flaw remediation in an ICS may require more resources than the organization can commit.
　　Control Enhancement: (1) No ICS Supplemental Guidance.
　　Control Enhancement: (2) ICS Supplemental Guidance: In situations where the ICS cannot support the use of automated mechanisms to conduct and report on the status of flaw remediation, the organization employs nonautomated mechanisms or procedures which incorporate methods to apply, track, and verify mitigation efforts as compensating controls in accordance with the general tailoring guidance.

SI-3　　MALICIOUS CODE PROTECTION

CNTL NO.	CONTROL NAME *Control Enhancement Name*	CONTROL BASELINES		
		LOW	MOD	HIGH
SI-3	**Malicious Code Protection**	Selected	Selected	Selected
SI-3 (1)	*MALICIOUS CODE PROTECTION	CENTRAL MANAGEMENT*		Selected	Selected
SI-3 (2)	*MALICIOUS CODE PROTECTION	AUTOMATIC UPDATES*		Selected	Selected

　　ICS Supplemental Guidance: The use and deployment of malicious code protection is determined after careful consideration and after verification that it does not adversely impact the operation of the ICS. Malicious code protection tools should be configured to minimize their potential impact on the ICS (e.g., employ notification rather than quarantine). Example compensating controls include increased traffic monitoring and auditing.

Control Enhancement: (1) ICS Supplemental Guidance: The organization implements central management of malicious code protection with consideration of the impact on operation of the ICS. Example compensating controls include increased auditing.

Control Enhancement: (2) ICS Supplemental Guidance: The organization implements automatic updates of malicious code protection with consideration of the impact on operation of the ICS. In situations where the ICS cannot support the use of automatic update of malicious code protection, the organization employs nonautomated procedures as compensating controls in accordance with the general tailoring guidance.

SI-4   INFORMATION SYSTEM MONITORING

CNTL NO.	CONTROL NAME *Control Enhancement Name*	CONTROL BASELINES		
		LOW	MOD	HIGH
SI-4	**Information System Monitoring**	Selected	Selected	Selected
SI-4 (2)	*INFORMATION SYSTEM MONITORING | AUTOMATED TOOLS FOR REAL-TIME ANALYSIS*		Selected	Selected
SI-4 (4)	*INFORMATION SYSTEM MONITORING | INBOUND AND OUTBOUND COMMUNICATIONS TRAFFIC*		Selected	Selected
SI-4 (5)	*INFORMATION SYSTEM MONITORING | SYSTEM-GENERATED ALERTS*		Selected	Selected

ICS Supplemental Guidance: The organization ensures that the use of monitoring tools and techniques does not adversely impact the operational performance of the ICS. Example compensating controls include deploying sufficient network monitoring.

Control Enhancement: (2) ICS Supplemental Guidance: In situations where the ICS cannot support the use of automated tools to support near-real-time analysis of events, the organization employs compensating controls (e.g., providing an auditing capability on a separate system, nonautomated mechanisms or procedures) in accordance with the general tailoring guidance.

Control Enhancement: (4) ICS Supplemental Guidance: In situations where the ICS cannot monitor inbound and outbound communications traffic, the organization employs compensating controls include providing a monitoring capability on a separate information system.

Control Enhancement: (5) ICS Supplemental Guidance: Example compensating controls include manual methods of generating alerts.

SI-5   SECURITY ALERTS, ADVISORIES, AND DIRECTIVES

CNTL NO.	CONTROL NAME *Control Enhancement Name*	CONTROL BASELINES		
		LOW	MOD	HIGH
SI-5	**Security Alerts, Advisories, and Directives**	Selected	Selected	Selected
SI-5 (1)	*SECURITY ALERTS, ADVISORIES, AND DIRECTIVES | AUTOMATED ALERTS AND ADVISORIES*			Selected

ICS Supplemental Guidance: The DHS Industrial Control Systems Cyber Emergency Response Team (ICS-CERT) generates security alerts and advisories relative to ICS http://ics-cert.us-cert.gov/ .

Control Enhancement: (1) No ICS Supplemental Guidance.

SI-6   SECURITY FUNCTIONALITY VERIFICATION

CNTL NO.	CONTROL NAME *Control Enhancement Name*	CONTROL BASELINES		
		LOW	MOD	HIGH
SI-6	**Security Function Verification**			Selected

ICS Supplemental Guidance: The shutting down and restarting of the ICS may not always be feasible upon the identification of an anomaly; these actions should be scheduled according to ICS operational requirements.

SI-7　SOFTWARE AND INFORMATION INTEGRITY

CNTL NO.	CONTROL NAME *Control Enhancement Name*	CONTROL BASELINES		
		LOW	MOD	HIGH
SI-7	**Software, Firmware, and Information Integrity**		Selected	Selected
SI-7 (1)	*SOFTWARE, FIRMWARE, AND INFORMATION INTEGRITY	INTEGRITY CHECKS*		Selected	Selected
SI-7 (2)	*SOFTWARE, FIRMWARE, AND INFORMATION INTEGRITY	AUTOMATED NOTIFICATIONS OF INTEGRITY VIOLATIONS*			Selected
SI-7 (5)	*SOFTWARE, FIRMWARE, AND INFORMATION INTEGRITY	AUTOMATED RESPONSE TO INTEGRITY VIOLATIONS*			Selected
SI-7 (7)	*SOFTWARE, FIRMWARE, AND INFORMATION INTEGRITY	INTEGRATION OF DETECTION AND RESPONSE*		Selected	Selected
SI-7 (14)	*SOFTWARE, FIRMWARE, AND INFORMATION INTEGRITY	BINARY OR MACHINE EXECUTABLE CODE*			Selected

ICS Supplemental Guidance: The organization determines whether the use of integrity verification applications would adversely impact the operation of the ICS and employs compensating controls (e.g., manual integrity verifications that do not affect performance.

Control Enhancements: (1) ICS Supplemental Guidance: The organization ensures that the use of integrity verification applications does not adversely impact the operational performance of the ICS.

Control Enhancement: (2) ICS Supplemental Guidance: In situations where the organization cannot employ automated tools that provide notification of integrity discrepancies, the organization employs nonautomated mechanisms or procedures. Example compensating controls include performing scheduled manual inspections for integrity violations.

Control Enhancement: (5) ICS Supplemental Guidance: The shutting down and restarting of the ICS may not always be feasible upon the identification of an anomaly; these actions should be scheduled according to ICS operational requirements.

Control Enhancement: (7) ICS Supplemental Guidance: In situations where the ICS cannot detect unauthorized security-relevant changes, the organization employs compensating controls (e.g., manual procedures) in accordance with the general tailoring guidance.

Control Enhancement: (14) No ICS Supplemental Guidance.

SI-8　SPAM PROTECTION

CNTL NO.	CONTROL NAME *Control Enhancement Name*	SUPPLEMENTED CONTROL BASELINES		
		LOW	MOD	HIGH
SI-8	**Spam Protection**		Selected	Selected
SI-8 (1)	*SPAM PROTECTION	CENTRAL MANAGEMENT OF PROTECTION MECHANISMS*		Selected	Selected
SI-8 (2)	*SPAM PROTECTION	AUTOMATIC UPDATES*		Selected	Selected

ICS Supplemental Guidance: ICS spam protection may be implemented by removing spam transport mechanisms, functions and services (e.g., electronic mail, Internet access) from the ICS. If any spam transport mechanisms, functions and services are present in the ICS, spam protection in ICS takes into account operational characteristics of ICS that differ from general purpose information systems, (e.g., unusual traffic flow that may be misinterpreted and detected as spam. Example compensating controls include whitelist mail transfer agents (MTA), digitally signed messages, acceptable sources, and acceptable message types.

Control Enhancement: (1) ICS Supplemental Guidance: Example compensating controls include employing local mechanisms or procedures.

Control Enhancement: (2) No ICS Supplemental Guidance.

SI-10   INFORMATION INPUT VALIDATION

CNTL NO.	CONTROL NAME *Control Enhancement Name*	CONTROL BASELINES		
		LOW	MOD	HIGH
SI-10	Information Input Validation		Selected	Selected

No ICS Supplemental Guidance.

SI-11   ERROR HANDLING

CNTL NO.	CONTROL NAME *Control Enhancement Name*	CONTROL BASELINES		
		LOW	MOD	HIGH
SI-11	Error Handling		Selected	Selected

No ICS Supplemental Guidance.

SI-12   INFORMATION HANDLING AND RETENTION

CNTL NO.	CONTROL NAME *Control Enhancement Name*	CONTROL BASELINES		
		LOW	MOD	HIGH
SI-12	Information Handling and Retention	Selected	Selected	Selected

No ICS Supplemental Guidance.

SI-13   PREDICTABLE FAILURE PREVENTION

CNTL NO.	CONTROL NAME *Control Enhancement Name*	SUPPLEMENTED CONTROL BASELINES		
		LOW	MOD	HIGH
SI-13	Predictable Failure Prevention			Added

ICS Supplemental Guidance: Failures in ICS can be stochastic or deterministic. Stochastic failures can be analyzed using probability theory, while analysis of deterministic failures is based on non-random properties of the system. Known ICS failure modes and causes are considered. The calculation and use of statistical descriptors, such as Mean Time To Failure (MTTF), should incorporate additional analysis to determine how those failures manifest within the cyber and physical domains. Knowledge of these possible manifestations may be necessary to detect whether a failure has occurred within the ICS, as failures of the information systems may not be easily identifiable. Emergent properties, which may arise both within the information systems and physical processes, can potentially cause system failures should be incorporated into the analysis. For example, cumulative effects of resource exhaustion (e.g., memory leakage) or errors (e.g., rounding and truncation) can occur when ICS processes execute for unexpectedly long periods. Deterministic failures (e.g., integer counter overflow), once identified, are preventable.

Often substitute components may not be available or may not be sufficient to protect against faults occurring before predicted failure. Non-automated mechanisms or physical safeguards should be in place in order to protect against these failures.

In addition to information concerning newly discovered vulnerabilities (i.e., latent flaws) potentially affecting the system/applications that are discovered by forensic studies, new vulnerabilities may be identified by organizations with responsibility for disseminating vulnerability information (e.g., ICS-CERT) based upon an analysis of a similar pattern of incidents reported to them or vulnerabilities reported by other researchers.

Related controls: IR-5, IR-6, RA-5, SI-2, SI-5, SI-11.

Rationale for adding control to baseline: ICS are designed and built with certain boundary conditions, design parameters, and assumptions about their environment and mode of operation. ICS may run much longer than conventional systems, allowing latent flaws to become effective that are not manifest in other environments. For example, integer overflow might never occur in systems that are re-initialized more frequently than the occurrence of the overflow. Experience and forensic studies of anomalies and incidents in ICS can lead to identification of emergent properties that were previously unknown, unexpected, or unanticipated. Preventative and restorative actions (e.g., re-starting the system or application) are prudent but may not be acceptable for operational reasons in ICS.

SI-16   MEMORY PROTECTION

CNTL NO.	CONTROL NAME *Control Enhancement Name*	CONTROL BASELINES		
		LOW	MOD	HIGH
SI-16	Memory Protection		Selected	Selected

No ICS Supplemental Guidance.

SI-17   FAIL-SAFE PROCEDURES

CNTL NO.	CONTROL NAME *Control Enhancement Name*	SUPPLEMENTED CONTROL BASELINES		
		LOW	MOD	HIGH
SI-17	Fail-Safe Procedures	Added	Added	Added

ICS Supplemental Guidance: The selected failure conditions and corresponding procedures may vary among baselines. The same failure event may trigger different response depending on the impact level. Mechanical and analog system can be used to provide mechanisms to ensure fail-safe procedures. Fail-safe states should incorporate potential impacts to human safety, physical systems, and the environment. Related controls: CP-6.

Rationale for adding SI-17 to all baselines: This control provides a structure for the organization to identify their policy and procedures for dealing with failures and other incidents. Creating a written record of the decision process for selecting incidents and appropriate response is part of risk management in light of changing environment of operations.

ORGANIZATION-WIDE INFORMATION SECURITY PROGRAM MANAGEMENT CONTROLS - PM

Characteristics of Organization-Wide Information Security Program Management Control Family

Organization-Wide Information Security Program Management Controls are deployed organization-wide supporting the information security program. They are not associated with security control baselines and are independent of any system impact level.

Supplemental Guidance

Supplemental Guidance for all Controls and Control Enhancements in NIST SP 800-53 Rev. 4, Appendix F, should be used in conjunction with the ICS Supplemental Guidance in this overlay, if any.

PM-1   INFORMATION SECURITY PROGRAM PLAN

CNTL NO.	CONTROL NAME *Control Enhancement Name*
PM-1	Information Security Program Plan Policy and Procedures

ICS Supplemental Guidance: The policy specifically addresses the unique properties and requirements of ICS, the relationship to non-ICS systems, and the relationship to other programs concerned with operational characteristics of ICS (e.g., safety, efficiency, reliability, resilience).

PM-2   SENIOR INFORMATION SECURITY OFFICER

CNTL NO.	CONTROL NAME *Control Enhancement Name*
PM-2	Senior Information Security Officer

No ICS Supplemental Guidance.

PM-3   INFORMATION SECURITY RESOURCES

CNTL NO.	CONTROL NAME *Control Enhancement Name*
PM-3	Information Security Resources

ICS Supplemental Guidance: Capital planning and investment decisions address all of the relevant technologies and all phases of the life cycle and needs to be informed by ICS experts as well as other subject matter experts (e.g., information security). Marshaling interdisciplinary working teams to advise capital planning and investment decisions can help tradeoff and balance among conflicting equities, objectives, and responsibilities such as capability, adaptability, resilience, safety, security, usability, and efficiency.

PM-4   PLAN OF ACTION AND MILESTONES PROCESS

CNTL NO.	CONTROL NAME *Control Enhancement Name*
PM-4	Plan of Action and Milestones Process

ICS Supplemental Guidance: The plan of action and milestones includes both computational and physical ICS components. Records of observed shortcomings and appropriate remedial action may be maintained in a single document or in multiple coordinated documents (e.g., future engineering plans).

PM-5　INFORMATION SYSTEM INVENTORY

CNTL NO.	CONTROL NAME *Control Enhancement Name*
PM-5	Information System Inventory

No ICS Supplemental Guidance.

PM-6　INFORMATION SECURITY MEASURES OF PERFORMANCE

CNTL NO.	CONTROL NAME *Control Enhancement Name*
PM-6	Information Security Measures of Performance

No ICS Supplemental Guidance.

PM-7　ENTERPRISE ARCHITECTURE

CNTL NO.	CONTROL NAME *Control Enhancement Name*
PM-7	Enterprise Architecture

No ICS Supplemental Guidance.

PM-8　CRITICAL INFRASTRUCTURE PLAN

CNTL NO.	CONTROL NAME *Control Enhancement Name*
PM-8	Critical Infrastructure Plan

No ICS Supplemental Guidance.
References: Executive Order 13636– Improving Critical Infrastructure Cybersecurity, February 12, 2013

PM-9　RISK MANAGEMENT STRATEGY

CNTL NO.	CONTROL NAME *Control Enhancement Name*
PM-9	Risk Management Strategy

ICS Supplemental Guidance: Risk management of ICS is considered along with other organizational risks affecting mission/business success from an organization-wide perspective. Organization-wide risk management strategy includes sector-specific guidance as appropriate.

PM-10　SECURITY AUTHORIZATION PROCESS

CNTL NO.	CONTROL NAME *Control Enhancement Name*
PM-10	Security Authorization Process

ICS Supplemental Guidance: The authorization to operate processes for ICS involves multiple disciplines that have existing approval and risk management process (e.g., physical security, safety). Organization-wide risk management requires harmonization among these disciplines.

PM-11 MISSION/BUSINESS PROCESS DEFINITION

CNTL NO.	CONTROL NAME *Control Enhancement Name*
PM-11	Mission/Business Process Definition

ICS Supplemental Guidance: Mission/business processes refinement requires protection of physical assets from damage originating in the cyber domain. These needs are derived from the mission/business needs defined by the organization, the mission/business processes selected to meet the stated needs, and the organizational risk management strategy.

PM-12 INSIDER THREAT PROGRAM

CNTL NO.	CONTROL NAME *Control Enhancement Name*
PM-12	Insider Threat Program

No ICS Supplemental Guidance.

PM-13 INFORMATION SECURITY WORKFORCE

CNTL NO.	CONTROL NAME *Control Enhancement Name*
PM-13	Information Security Workforce

ICS Supplemental Guidance: All aspects of information security workforce development and improvement programs include knowledge and skill levels in both computational and physical ICS components.

PM-14 TESTING, TRAINING, AND MONITORING

CNTL NO.	CONTROL NAME *Control Enhancement Name*
PM-14	Testing, Training, and Monitoring

No ICS Supplemental Guidance.

PM-15 CONTACTS WITH SECURITY GROUPS AND ASSOCIATIONS

CNTL NO.	CONTROL NAME *Control Enhancement Name*
PM-15	Contacts with Security Groups and Associations

No ICS Supplemental Guidance.

PM-16 THREAT AWARENESS PROGRAM

CNTL NO.	CONTROL NAME *Control Enhancement Name*
PM-16	Threat Awareness Program

ICS Supplemental Guidance: The organization should collaborate and share information about potential incidents on a timely basis. The DHS National Cybersecurity & Communications Integration Center (NCCIC), http://www.dhs.gov/about-national-cybersecurity-communications-integration-center serves as a centralized location where operational elements involved in cybersecurity and communications reliance are coordinated and integrated. The Industrial Control Systems Cyber Emergency Response Team (ICS-CERT) http://ics-cert.us-cert.gov/ics-cert/ collaborates with international and private sector Computer Emergency Response Teams (CERTs) to share control systems-related security incidents and mitigation measures. Organizations should consider having both an unclassified and classified information sharing capability.

Made in the USA
Middletown, DE
14 August 2023

36691268R00139